T0197007

A CENTURY OF
MEMORIES

A CENTURY OF
MEMORIES

Triggered by Email

PEGGY BERGLAND

I wish to thank the many friends and relatives who contributed to my story by sending me emails or wrote notes that added to the story. Thank you, OZ, Melody, Joy, Elaine, and even the unknown authors whose work helped me to refresh my memory.

A CENTURY OF MEMORIES
TRIGGERED BY EMAIL

iUniverse books may be ordered through booksellers or by contacting:

iUniverse
1663 Liberty Drive
Bloomington, IN 47403
www.iuniverse.com
1-800-Authors (1-800-288-4677)

ISBN: 978-1-5320-4723-7 (sc)
ISBN: 978-1-5320-4724-4 (e)

Library of Congress Control Number: 2018904902

Print information available on the last page.

iUniverse rev. date: 04/24/2018

Included are many stories, verses,
and traveling experiences
throughout my nearly One Hundred
Years of living in Idaho,
Washington, Southern California, Oregon, and Arizona

═══════════════════════════════════════

I hope you enjoy reading this book as much
as I enjoyed writing it in my nineties

═══════════════════════════════════════

I dedicate this book to the memories of
my husband of 60 years:
Thomas O. Bergland, 1920—2001
My daughter Janice E. Bergland Luna, 1951—1982

My five still living children:
Thomas L. Bergland and wife, Karen
Judith E. Bergland Marqullan
Jacqueline M. Bergland Bates
David K. Bergland and wife, Sue
Lawrence K. Bergland and wife, Robin

And my eleven grandchildren:
Michael, Steven, Amanda, Laura,
Jennifer, Jessica, Wally III,
Shannon, Cody, Alex, and Kyle. and
eight great grandchildren.

Special thanks to my daughter-in-law and best friend,
Karen Bergland, who put up with me
while I spent hours typing
on the computer, making this narrative possible.

INTRODUCTION

If there are older people in your family, I suggest you question them about their life when they were younger. You will lose out on different life experiences if you don't find the information while they are still living. Don't wait and be sorry later. I say this from experience. My maternal grandparents could have told me many things from the 1800's if I had known to ask them of their experiences, and if I had listened. They had experience with the Indians. I do not think they were afraid of them or I would have heard stories.

My grandmother made friends with everyone. Hunters would bring their ducks to her to dress when they hunted in the nearby area. From the pictures I have seen there must have been good duck hunting in the area. She had dozens of ducks hung on the wall of their house near Upham. North Dakota. They homesteaded in North Dakota before it was a state. I understand my grandfather built a hotel in Upham, North Dakota, but I do not know of any way to find out about it. There was supposed to be dishes from that hotel with the name Enger on them. If they exist, I would at least love to see one of them. Now it is only a rumor. Who is left to tell me about it? It's too late now and I regret it.

Go ahead, ask questions, and get those older relatives of yours to tell you about when they were young. Maybe it will be in short sessions, but listen well. Help them to jog their memory by you telling them some story. Use some kind of a recorder so you can go back and write it down later. As you listen to what is recorded or written down, it will help you to trigger questions to help them along. Just do it.

I have had many requests to write down my experiences *but it was a request from my daughters that really prompted me to go ahead with it.* My children, but especially my daughters, have been after me for years to write down my experiences and put it in a book. *It was after I got the following request, in writing, more than two years ago that I decided in earnest to go ahead with this book. I hope you enjoy it. I have outlived most of the people I have written about as well as those I have heard from.*

"Mom, this is history!!! I hope you have kept all your "Peggy's comments" you have added to these emails because this is what you have personally seen in your lifetime! Please keep these journals because it may be another book. We did not know how much you remember in the history lessons, this is invaluable, and you have not told us about these things before. Also, Dad had so much history that we didn't even scratch the surface, and your young life in Benewah with him. How you met Dad, life without electricity and running water, outhouses, and on and on is something we want to learn about. We didn't know a lot and would like to hear more. So, please remember to keep these things in writing for us so we can learn these things."

This book will contain many things that I remember from my ninety-five years of living on this planet. As I receive emails from the long list of people with whom I correspond, they remind me of something that has occurred to me or that I do remember something about. It is not in any kind of chronological order so please bear with me if I skip all over as to the age I mention at the time I am writing some of this material. I think of it over a period of months or years, then rearrange it to hopefully make it more clear or of more interest. Among stories and verses will be some of the items I have written over the years, some of it published in the news letter written by me and for the local mobile home park community where I lived at the time.

There could be much more but there is not enough room to tell everything in one book. As time goes on I will undoubtedly remember a lot more than I have written here. That will have to wait for another time.

I have published one novel called *"Who Cares Who Milks the Cow"*. That book is not in any way biographical of me. I did use a few experiences like the coming of electricity and the telephone as a basis for what I wrote. It is pure fiction and is not about any barnyard animals, especially cows. That book was fiction. This one is not fiction, but is as I remember what has happened and as true as I can remember along with what other relatives and friends have helped me along my memory lane.

In this book I will write everything as I remember and recall from my memory that the emails have reminded me of. Some of the stories and verses I wrote during the years will be copied here. I am learning that our minds really do store an immense amount of what we have experienced over the years. Putting it down on paper also takes quite a while— after all, look how long it took to put it into our minds. As I write this it will not be in any chronological order, so please bear with me.

As I write this, I am past ninety years of age. I will mention many different ages in different stories, so please bear with me about how old I say I am at different times. In 2017 I am 95 years of age.

A LITTLE ABOUT ME

I tried for a long time to get a birth certificate in Washington without success. I finally tried Idaho before having to get affidavits from others who knew of my birth. I had always thought I was born in a house located between Palouse, Washington and Potlatch, Idaho. Someone had pointed out a house we had lived in that was located on the State line near Palouse. Since the family lived around the Palouse area in the 20's, I assumed I was born in that house. I knew I had been born at home and my parents and grandparents had lived in Palouse so it made sense to me that that house was the one in which I was born. Before giving up I tried Idaho and hit the jackpot. When I received my birth certificate from Idaho I wondered why it read that I was born east of Viola, Idaho with a doctor from Palouse, Washington. I learned much later from Irene Enger that she remembered the house we lived in was located across the road from Grandpa and Grandma Horine and that Aunt Olga had a baby there. Thanks to Irene my long time puzzle was solved. This shows how valuable the memories of others can be to help fill in the gaps in our lives, even some eighty or more years later. At the time I was born more than 95 percent of all births took place at home. By 1937 ninety five percent of babies were born in a hospital. This was quite a reverse in birthing places.

I married Thomas Bergland (1920—2001) soon after graduating from North Central High School in January, 1941. My husband and I lived in Spokane and vicinity for several years, moved to Idaho for several more years, then back to Spokane in 1951 until 1959 when we moved to California. My high school, North Central, had a good commercial course, which I had made my major. The courses were bookkeeping, shorthand, and other office practice studies. To further my education I took a college course in accounting after we moved to California. I worked at several different jobs there. I definitely used my high school education. In fact it was twenty years after I graduated before I went to work outside my home. That North Central High education served me well. I went to work using my commercial education without having a refresher course and believe it or not, I made it OK.

In 1974 we relocated to Portland, Oregon. I became a tax preparer for several years in Portland. I moved back to California after my husband died from a fatal fall in June of 2001. Now retired, I live with my oldest son, Tom, and daughter-in-law, Karen, in Spokane. They bought a home in Yuma to use for the wintertime. It will be Spokane in the summer time and winters in Yuma, Arizona from now on.

MY YOUNGER DAYS

This starts with what I remember as an eighteen month old child. Then it goes forward to my memory of my grandparents' house burning down just about the time I turned two years old in the summer of 1924.

Most of my earliest years were spent in that area called Flanagan Creek, located six miles east of Viola in Idaho. That is where my paternal grandparents had a small farm. We were in the process of constantly moving around the country, so spending time off and on with my Idaho grandparents was the only stability I had until I was about twelve years old. In the years following the age of twelve we were living near my Mother's parents in Spokane, Washington.

Some things seem to trigger memories better than others. When I open my email, many of the items can jog my memory about things that I had experienced in the past. This covers almost a century as I turned 95 a few months ago. As I would read my email, I was inspired to write any memory that came up in my mind and add my two cents worth. Some is funny, some otherwise, and hopefully none of it is boring.

Let me describe my earliest memory. I had been in my grandparents' house in the morning before we left for town. It was the winter before their house burned down. I definitely remember going from there to town by a horse drawn sleigh. The horses had bells that jingled as they trotted. I know I was only about eighteen months of age because there was deep snow on the ground and my grandparents' house burned down right after I was two years old in May the following spring of 1924. They put a heated brick at our feet to help keep us warm during the ride. For some reason it seems to me that we were going to town (Viola) to catch a train. I do remember riding in a train a couple of times but I don't know where to or anything more about it. Possibly we may have gone to North Dakota to visit my mother's parents. I have seen a picture taken of me when I was standing on a car by my grandmother. I have been told that my grandmother had seen me looking down the hole of a cistern and grabbed me away from it. If I had fallen in I would not have survived as it was very deep and there was not equipment to rescue anyone in those days. This was before Grandma Enger moved to Spokane. I do not know how old I was when the picture was taken, although it was not in the winter time and I was very evidently not very old, but somewhere around the age of two. My grandmother would not have had a car, and there is no one to ask about whose car it was. There was no information on the picture. That information would have been valuable to me now.

People seem to think babies do not know what is going on around them, but I know they do because I remember very clearly about the ride in the sleigh and the house burning down. I was in that house when the fire started. Grandma was baking sugar cookies at the time. I always remember how good her sugar cookies were. Evidently someone must have smelled the odor of something burning (not the cookies), and went up the stairs to the second floor to investigate. I can remember following someone up the stairs and seeing the red hot chimney (I was always curious). It was a chimney fire that had started the house on fire. The next thing I remember was watching from a distance while furniture was being thrown out a window, trying to save whatever they could. There are pictures somewhere in the family that someone took of me sitting on a blanket near the building my grandparents moved into after the fire. That must be where I was put for safekeeping while the house was burning. I do not have that picture, but I have seen it and recognized the building I was sitting by. The burned house was never replaced. Only the cement foundation was left. We kids used that foundation as a place to play, that is, until the stinging nettles took over. Playing in the creek is what I remember best.

After the house burned, they moved into one of the outbuildings which consisted of one long narrow room turned into a kitchen and living room and two bedrooms, one down, one up stairs. There was no bathroom. Of course there was an outhouse. Only about 14 percent of the homes in the United States had a bathtub. We used the same tub we washed clothes in to take a bath. Another large room was used as a bedroom. A second bedroom was in the attic. I remember the bedroom was always kept dark. My grandmother seemed to have severe headaches which I believe must have been migraine headaches. That is probably the reason for the dark bedroom. She used many bottles of Bromo-Seltzer. We kids used those pretty blue Bromo bottles to play with as toys. I also remember a coffee grinder used as a toy. That coffee grinder would be considered an antique today.

This farm was in rural Idaho, located by Flanagan Creek, about six miles from the small town of Viola, Idaho. There were no telephones to be able to call neighbors for help at that time. Only about 8 percent of the homes in the United States had telephones. With no phones or electricity to pump water the closest water was in the creek, at least 400 feet from the house, so no water was available to fight the fire. The creek was too far away to carry water in buckets to put out a fire. Water was carried from the creek for all uses. There never had been water inside the house. It was impossible to save the house.

My grandparents were never able to rebuild, probably because grandpa was ill, and the depression years also came on around 1929. Grandpa died in 1931 from cancer. I remember he had been sick for quite a while. I doubt that they had any insurance on the house. I do not know what year Grandma and Uncle Morris sold the farm and moved to the Benewah area, where uncle Ray Horine lived, so they could be near other family connections. Later they moved from the Benewah Valley to Plummer, Idaho, where they had more modern conveniences. They lived there until after Grandma passed away.

A lot of the time in rural areas a house was built with stovepipe to get rid of the smoke and did not have masonry chimneys. (There is no one left any more to ask if that was the case.) I am only guessing that the house may have been nearly new, as my grandparents had just sold their property over near Palouse, Washington and moved to this location, known as Flanagan Creek. The structure that they moved into, after the fire, had a garage attached leads me to believe the burned house was a new one. I remember there was a pit dug into that garage that they used to keep milk cool as there was no refrigeration of any kind available to them. I don't remember of ever seeing a car parked in that garage. In fact, I don't remember of their having a car at all in those early years. My father had a car but don't remember my grandparents having one. I remember having to push the car when stuck in mud in spring thaws. The roads were dirt, not pavement and muddy in winter or rainy weather. In summer the dirt was very deep and when disturbed it would fly all over making the air dusty. Paved highways were still scarce in those days, but were being built regularly. It was after 1920 that the government started building highways in ernest, when they wanted highways leading to the national parks.

My grandparents were farmers and had relocated from North Dakota to the farming country around Palouse, Washington and from there to the area around Flanagan Creek in Idaho. The location had a beautiful year-around creek where we could play in the water. In the summertime, the water was about twelve inches deep, twelve feet wide, and crystal clear. Us kids would catch frogs, try to catch "skippers:" (bugs that skipped on top of the water) and were kept entertained by whatever that creek had to offer. Believe me, it was never boring. In the spring, the water got very high and we had to stay far away from that creek. It was deep and swift from the runoff of winter snow melting in the hills around. I don't remember of it ever overflowing, only that it was very very deep.

The next summer after the house fire we may have gone to North Dakota to visit my mother's parents. I have seen a picture taken of me when I was standing on a car, probably a Model T, by my grandmother. I have been told that my grandmother had seen me looking down the hole of a cistern and grabbed me away from it. If I had fallen in I would not have survived as it was very deep and there was no equipment to rescue anyone in those days. This was before Grandma moved to Spokane. I do not know how old I was when the picture was taken, although it was not in the winter time and I was very evidently not very old, but somewhere around the age of two. My grandmother would not have had a car, so whose car it was, there is no one to ask. There was no information on the picture. That information would have been valuable to me now. What year was the picture taken. I do not remember the occasion so the information is lost and I recall what I have been told in the past is my only clue.

WE LOCATED THE FARM

Two or three years ago my cousin, Elaine Smith, and I located the site of where the farm buildings had been. (In Flanagan Creek) Now the formerly dirt road is paved up to the crossroads by the property. The crossroad was now named Davis. It took a while to find the farm, as I was about twelve years old the last time I had seen the property and everything had changed. It was hard to find the location. In many places the scenery was changed due to trees growing where there had been no trees, or trees gone where some had been when I was there. Now there are many new homes on Flanagan Creek Road up to and past Davis. There was no street named Davis when I was young. It was the creek which had supplied water for the home and the animals, along with the crossroad, that finally helped me recognize the farm location. That lovely creek had not changed and was as I remember it from eighty-or more years ago.

Every one of the buildings was gone and all we could see was a herd of cattle grazing where the buildings had been. The new barn they had built when I was there as a young child was nowhere to be seen, not a remnant of any kind. No wonder I had trouble locating everything. Of course none of their former neighbors would still be living to help me locate anything so I had to figure it out from my memory of the cross road and the creek, which was so vivid in my mind. We inquired of a few people in the neighborhood, but no one had been around at the time my grandparents lived there and there was no one left to remember anything. The house was never rebuilt, maybe because Grandpa was ill. Grandpa died in 1931 of cancer.

I remember he had been sick for quite a while. I doubt that they had any insurance on the house. They moved into one of the other outbuildings and used it for the rest of the years they lived in that area.

I do not know what year Grandma and Uncle Morris Horine sold the farm and moved to the Benewah Valley area, where uncle Ray Horine lived. They probably moved to the Benewah because of family connections. From the Benewah Valley they moved to Plummer, Idaho, where they lived until after Grandma passed away.

Update: May 14, 2016. On this date my son, Tom, drove me past the Flanagan Creek farm and by now there was a new barn built in the same location where I remember the old one had been. Still no house, but an old trailer house was parked there. I am assuming someone may have been in the process of building a new home there. We also drove around the loop road where I had never been before, except as far as the first building. I had thought it would end up returning to the Flanagan Creek road, but we probably made a wrong turn someplace and were surprised to end up in Potlatch. Everything was changed everywhere.

Lighting in those days of 1920's to early 1930's in rural areas consisted of kerosene lamps and occasionally a candle. There were times when kerosene was scarce because of lack of money to purchase more. Then they used rags twisted together into a kind of rope like wick and placing it into a plate of some kind of grease such as lard. Sometimes they would stick the wick into a bottle. I even saw them take a rag and tie it around a button and setting that in some grease.

This method of having light was crude but it gave light like a night light does now with electricity. It was better than nothing. Kerosene was purchased at a gas station for their lanterns.

The first gas stations were in Pittsburg, Pennsylvania in 1913. Before that gas and kerosene was purchased in hardware stores, or on the sidewalk. By 1924 they were more plentiful and were Service Stations where you could get service, like car repairs and flat tires repaired, not just gas as it is today.

The main road to what was called Flanagan Creek, was formerly only dirt that was very muddy when the weather was wet, and inches deep with dust in dry weather. The road is now paved from Viola down to the corner of Davis where the paving abruptly ends. The rest is still a dirt road. The corner is now posted with a sign with the name Davis on it. I do know there was no sign at the time my grandparents lived there. That corner is where my grandparents' property started. The crossroad did not have a name during my grandparents' time, or none that I ever knew of. I discovered it on a post a couple of years ago at the same time I located the property. I do remember there was a man who lived up that crossroad and I believe his name may have been Davis. It makes sense if someone by the name of Davis lived up that road and it was named after him. It would give it identity. The road now named Davis is a loop road but we did not drive up that road on that day. I remember only the fact it came back to the main road called Flanagan Creek Road. I do remember there was a road that went on to Potlatch from Flanagan Creek. I was about six when I had been staying with my aunt Celia Pool, who lived between Flanagan Creek and Potlatch. It was on that road I had tried to run away from them, only to have a neighbor keep me at their place after I stopped in to inquire which branch to take at a fork in the road. They kept me there until my uncle came to get me. I was trying to return to my grandparents farm.

My grandparents weathered the Depression quite well because they had cows, chickens, pigs, and a huge garden. They had very little cash but the cream and eggs paid for their property taxes and by careful management were able to get along quite well. The price of eggs was pretty high at 50 cents a dozen. Coffee was 30 cents a pound.

A blacksmith shop was located on the property. They had work horses and a couple of mules, raised hay for the cattle, sold eggs and cream, raised a huge garden, and in the fall there were turkeys to sell for the holiday trade. I remember one year they had about an acre of potatoes that were planted. When the potatoes were harvested they tasted very sweet. It seems they used some kind of fertilizer on them that caused them to taste as if they had sugar on them. I tasted, but don't remember eating any of those potatoes, and don't know what they did with them. They certainly were not like Yams or Sweet potatoes. They probably ended up feeding them to the pigs. What started out to be a paying crop ended up a disaster and undoubtedly was a nasty pinch to the pocketbook.

They had a huge flock of chickens of a variety called White Leghorns, which included a number of big roosters. Since I loved to watch Grandpa milk the cows, I went out to the barn one time and we were approached by several huge white roosters. Grandpa told me "*if they ever attack you*

*pick up a stick and hit them". He should not have said that
to me.* I just could not, and did not, wait for Grandpa to
finish milking the cows. I left the barn and I went back out
and found myself a stick about six feet long. That stick was
so long I could hardly manage it (I was only five). I chased
those roosters until I got one with that stick. They tell me I
ran into the house calling, "I made him sit up! I made him
sit up!" That rooster must have been leaning on his legs
when I hit it and gave the appearance of sitting up. Well,
it was one way to get a chicken dinner. I don't remember
if they punished me for my deed or not, but those roosters
had not attacked me and I never heard if they ever attacked
anyone else either. I didn't give them a chance. The dinner
was delicious.

ANOTHER ROOSTER

A lot of people don't know that a rooster can do a lot of
damage with their spurs and it can happen very quickly and
unexpectedly. I found that out about three years ago when
visiting a friend in southern Idaho. I was just standing
looking at their beautiful big red rooster, watching him, but
minding my own business. Then, whammo! He suddenly
jumped at me and put a big gash in my leg with his spur. All
I had been doing was standing near the bird and he attacked
without warning. The friends said that wasn't allowed and
they took that rooster to another friend who had a bunch of
hens and gave it to her. They were afraid it might attack
others when visiting. I felt bad because that red rooster
was a pet. Maybe the animal was now happier because my
friends had no other chickens and maybe the bird had been
lonesome. They never replaced him. I told them they didn't
need to get rid of the bird, but they felt his attack on me was

not to be put up with. The people they gave the bird to had a fenced-in pen for him. I did learn later that a coyote did the poor thing in, along with a hen or two. The coyote must have been in need of a meal. Nobody even suggested a chicken dinner for us either, for which I am glad. This incident did remind me of the rooster I had made "sit up" when I was five years old.

MOONSHINE SOLD

By 1929, when the Depression started, people became fortunate to be able to have enough money for food. In the next ten years, there were a great number of homeless people in the cities who were begging for food. They would knock on your door and offer to work for a meal. They did not shirk on the amount of work they did either. We also did not have to worry about them stealing from us when they worked for food. There probably were thefts but not by the people who asked for food and worked for it.

During the 1930's decade, a number of families resorted to moon-shining in small amounts in order to feed their families. My father did not make the whiskey himself, but he evidently sold a gallon or two after someone else made it. Of course, the local police were always on the lookout for stills, which were quite numerous in any rural region. I believe those making moonshine were always on the lookout for the appearance of authorities. Some neighbors may have been arrested. If they didn't make the moonshine they sold it or delivered it for their neighbor or relative. Everyone was afraid of being caught. This could be the reason why Glen Horine (my father)(1894-1968) always seemed to be paranoid about the police looking for him and why he frequently moved the family around the country—seeming to move late into the night when this occurred. I know he didn't make the stuff, but he did deliver two or three gallon jugs one time. The one delivering the whiskey was also arrested if caught. I remember going with my father one time when he delivered and sold a couple gallons. It was never big business, just a small amount occasionally. He went out to the big farming area to farmers who wanted the alcohol. It could not be purchased in stores as these were prohibition years along with the depression times. That is the reason it was taken to the farmers. The price for a gallon of whiskey was $3.00 if I remember right. Not a very big money maker, but $3.00 bought a lot of groceries in those days. For several years everything went on with our family getting up in the middle of the night every few weeks or months with no other warning that we were moving. It didn't make room for a stable family life. It became stable when my mother left with us kids in 1933.

THE ONLY CLUE WE HAVE
FROM OUR PAST

See the following story written by my father's sister, Ruby Ruth Horine Peters, in 1981. It is about family moving to Idaho and Washington. Her story is the only clue we have about the past lives of our families and why so many families left their North Dakota farms and moved to the area around Palouse, Washington. We do not know why they chose Palouse as their destination. Oh, why didn't we think to ask those questions while someone was living who could answer our questions. It never dawned on us that we would be interested in that information some day. So far as any of us know now, that information is gone forever. All we can do now is surmise. Too bad, too bad. Unless we can locate someone else who has a written record or someone's diary, the information is forever lost to us. I have updated some changes from the years that have passed as most are now deceased.

This story was written by my aunt, Ruth Horine Peters, (1897--1990) who had lived in Farmington. I was visiting her in the summer of 1938, when Helen and Walt decided to take a trip to Benewah to visit our uncle, Ray Horine, and family. This is the time and occasion and place where I met Tom Bergland who became my husband a few years later. The next time I saw Tom Bergland was two years later when he called me to ask if I wanted to go with him to a dance being held at the Benewah schoolhouse. This schoolhouse is the one that became used as a community center when it was no longer used for a school. Any of the children living in the area are now bussed into St. Maries for both grade and high school.

My cousin, Elaine Peters Stotsenberg Smith, supplied me with a copy in better condition than the one I had of the following story from my father's sister. It tells us of our families and their move from the Midwest to Washington. It is information we would not have had without it. It is also an example of the importance of getting information from our ancestors while they are still living and can supply it for us. Most of those written about are now no longer living or are in their late 80's and mid 90's. Time marches on.

MY MEMORIESOF WARD COUNTY, GASMAN TOWNSHIP, NORTH DAKOTA 1905 TO 1919

(*Updates by Peggy Horine Bergland—marked by an* and enclosed with parentheses, mostly dates of death)

"My parents, John Mark Horine (1863-1931) and Jennie Elizabeth Fyfe Horine (1869-1948) emigrated to northern Minnesota from Newell, Pocahontas County, Iowa. They traveled with two covered wagons and the family arrived in Park Rapids, Minnesota in the fall of 1902. I was four years old. My father, John Mark, or "Mark" as he was known worked in the woods until the fall of 1904. The lure of homestead land in North Dakota was the reason for our next move.

Our family consisted of four boys and two girls. The three oldest were boys. Earl Eugene, Raymond Richmond (1892), and George Glen (*1894-1968). Next was my sister, Celia Celesta, and me, Ruby Ruth. The youngest was my brother, Morris Mark. In the fall of 1904 my father, Mark Horine, with his two oldest sons, Earl, then sixteen, and Ray twelve, took a team and wagon and headed west toward North Dakota.

In Ward County, near Sawyer, they found work. Dad was plowing and breaking new land with a steam engine for some people by the name of Colburn. Earl got a job at the Colburn's too. Ray found work at the Charlie Stafford ranch herding cattle. When they were not working, they were looking for a homestead. They found what they were looking for in Ward County, about eighteen miles south of Minot. They found one hundred sixty acres of land in what was later to become Gasman Township. Dad and the boys built a ten by twelve homestead shack and lived there the first winter. The following spring, dad sent for the rest of the family to join him and the boys.

I was seven years old and I remember very well, mother, with Glen, Celia, Morris, and me waiting at the depot for the train that would take us to Minot, North Dakota. Glen was about nine and was very impatient. He wanted to get on every train that arrived at the station. Finally our train came and we were on our way to our new home. We arrived in Minot in the evening of that day in May 1905. Dad was at the station with a team and wagon to meet us. They bedded us kids down in the bottom of the wagon box and we drove the eighteen miles to the homestead that night. We finally arrived and they somehow got us all bedded down for the rest of the night in that little one room shack. Early the next morning we kids were anxious to explore our new homeland. We ran to the top of the hill behind the house to see as far as we could see. I didn't notice when the others turned back toward the house. When I realized I was alone, I started to run, but in the opposite direction. I was lost. That vast expanse of barren territory terrified me. All those childish fears ran through my head. Where would I sleep tonight? Then I heard my brothers calling me, setting me right again.

That summer, dad put up a tent for the boys to sleep in while he built a two-story addition to the house. Later he added a lean-to which became our kitchen. Those five rooms were our home all the time we lived there. Dad built a big hip roof barn for the livestock and hay.

My father used oxen to break the new land. I can remember when dad needed another ox, which he didn't have, he used one of our cows to help pull the plow. Later he did get some horses. The horses available then were either broncos from the prairies of Montana, which had to be broken to the harness, or old worn-out horses shipped in from Iowa.

Dad tried raising grains but had better luck raising potatoes. He somehow got hold of an old corn planter and made a special two row potato planter from it. Celia and I were his planters. We sat on the back of it and dropped the potatoes in the planter for him. He raised really good crops of potatoes. One year he sold a carload of potatoes to the Gurney Seed Company of Yankton, South Dakota. Dad was never bothered with potato bugs and he told that to the Gurney buyer. The next year, Gurney came out with a "Bugless Seed Potatoes."

I remember the first car I ever saw. I think it was a 1910 Maxwell. The hardware man from Minot, Martin Jacobsen, came out to see dad about something. Dad was in the field with Celia and me planting potatoes. Mr. Jacobsen took Celia and me for a short ride in that little red car. What a thrill that was.

About 1907, the community built a one-room schoolhouse and held school four months in the fall and three months in the spring. That lasted about three years when that schoolhouse was moved to within a mile from our home. They held a nine month term after that, and I finished the eighth grade there. I loved school and had good teachers. My favorites were the Bevins, Gladys and Guy Bevins. There was a little incident that happened to Glen at that school and he could never live it down.

Some neighbors' cattle were passing through the school yard. Glen went to drive them away. A two year old heifer turned on him and got him down. He grabbed her by the horns with his legs around her neck and his back on the ground. He hung there. He begged us girls to reach into his pocket to get his knife, which was a little single blade pocket knife. He wanted to cut the cows' throat. He hung that way until the teacher could get on her horse and, with a board for a weapon, she gave the heifer a few spats and the battle was over.

Those were happy times, in spite of the hardships. There were several families in the area with from four to twelve children of all ages. There were house parties and long walks of five or six miles, all of us together in the moonlight. In the winter there were house dances and in the summer when the big barns were empty of hay, there were barn dances. In our crowd there were several musicians. There were fiddlers, piano, organ, and accordion players, and square dance callers. My brother, Ray, and I played the fiddle, but the Larson boys, Cole and Thorval were the best fiddlers. Celia and I both corded on the piano. Everyone took part and we had fun.

Winters were long and cold, but when spring did come it was so welcome that we soon forgot how cold and miserable it had been. When the grass did come, it was beautiful and green. With spring would come the wild flowers and the return of the wild ducks and prairie chickens. We had lots of sloughs and the ducks were plentiful in the lake by our house. I used to take dad's twelve gage, double barrel shotgun, and pot-shoot ducks with both barrels at once. It would kick me over, but by the time I would get back up, I would have three or four ducks for dinner.

I liked horseback riding too. It was always bareback and sometimes it wasn't any too pleasant. Morris began to grow up and I was still kid enough to play. He and I used to break some of the calves to drive when they got about six months old.

In the fall of 1915 I took a job with another girl, cooking in a cookhouse, for a threshing crew, for two dollars a day. That lasted twenty-five days. I took twelve dollars of those earnings and bought my first violin from Sears Roebuck. I traded violins with my brother Ray a few times but I ended up with the one I originally got from Sears and I still have that one, sixty-six years later.

In the fall of 1916, my father had a stroke, which left him unable to do much farming. By 1918 most of the family had grown, married, and gone out on their own. That fall, my parents left the homestead and went to Palouse, Washington. They bought a farm, built a big house and remodeled a big barn. They were there only a short time and sold it again.

(*That is the place that had been pointed out to me, where I assumed I had been born. I found out later when I got my Idaho birth certificate that I was born east of Viola.)

They bought another place, just across the Washington, Idaho State line, between Moscow and Potlatch, Idaho. *(*Flanagan Creek, out of Viola, Idaho)* They lived there until my father died in 1931 at the age of 67 years. Mother, Jennie Horine, lived with her youngest son, Morris, in Plumber, Idaho, until her death in 1948. She was 79 years old.

My brother, Earl Eugene Horine, (1888-1973) was the first to leave home. He married in Iowa to Ruth Nellist, who died in Spokane, Washington in 1946. They had four children, Marvel Horine Borrink (*Oct 2, 1913) Wilbur (Bill) Eugene Horine (*Aug. 15, 1915-Nov. 26, 2014) who both lived in Iowa. Donald Arthur Horine (*Aug. 21, 1919-Oct 21, 2015), Arizona, and Lois Elizabeth Horine Johnson (*March 8, 1922 Lois says she is still kicking in 2016—Lois furnished the birthdates of her siblings for me) lives in Michigan. Earl married a second time to Jose Bosch, and they retired in Island City, Oregon, where they lived the remainder of their lives.

Raymond Richmond Horine(1892-1975) married Mabel Hillestad in Minot, North Dakota in 1919. They came to Palouse soon after their marriage. They lived at Benewah and moved to St. Maries, Idaho (*so their daughters could go to high school). After Ray's death, his widow lived in Spokane, Washington with her daughter Betty, until her death in 1980. There were four children in this family. Arthur LeRoy and LaVerne Horine and their sister Betty Horine Swafford all live in Spokane. Vera May Horine Icard lives in Las Vegas, Nevada (Note:* In this year of 2015 Vera Mae lives in Montana. Both LeRoy Horine and wife, Anita, and LaVerne Horine and wife, Alene, are deceased.)

"George Glen Horine (*1894-1968) married Olga Enger (*1901-1994) in Minot, North Dakota in 1919. They moved to Palouse, Washington that same year. There were four children born to this family. (Note*—actually there were five, see note later). Peggy Horine Bergland lives in Portland. Dorothy Horine Schlagel lives in Tacoma, Washington. Albert Horine Bradley lives in Medford, Oregon. and Donald Douglas Horine, in Spokane, Washington. Olga

Enger Horine, married a second time—in 1945 to Arthur Ball (1900-1968). She became widowed from Arthur Ball in 1968, lives in Spokane.

Celia Celesta Horine (1895-1934) married Arthur Fisher in Minot, North Dakota in 1916. Arthur Fisher was killed in a car accident just before their first child, a daughter, was born. That daughter, Artha Fisher Bennett lives in Farmington, Washington. Celia remarried in Palouse, Washington in 1919 to Guy Pool. They had four children. Marlin "Bill" Pool, died in Corydon, Indiana in 1977. Chester Pool lives in California, Cecil Pool lives in Spokane, and Jean Pool Edmonds lives in Post Falls, Idaho. Guy Pool died in Spokane. Celia (1895-1934) died in Moscow, Idaho after the birth of her last child.

Ruby Ruth Horine (*1897--1990) married Guy Peters in Minot, North Dakota in 1916. Guy Peters family also homesteaded just seven miles south and west of the Horine homestead. Guy and Ruth farmed in Foster and Eddy Counties of North Dakota. We lived in Farmington, Washington (1933) and Rosalia, Washington. We are now retired and live in the Spokane Valley, at Greenacres, Washington. In this year of 1981, we will have been married for 65 years. Both Guy and I are the last surviving members of our immediate families. There are four children in this family. Irene Peters Enger, lives in Gig Harbor, Washington, Helen Peters Miller (*May 16, 1919-November 5, 2015), lives in Deer Park, Washington, Walter Peters lives in Salem, Oregon and Ruth Elaine Peters Stotsenberg Smith lives in Port Orchard, Washington.

Morris Mark Horine (*1901-1970) married Patricia Mitchell. Morris died in Caldwell, Idaho. His widow lives in Olympia,

Washington. They had one adopted daughter, Gloria Horine Briggs, who lived in Lancaster, California. *(NOTE: Gloria now lives near Roseburg, Oregon. Both Morris and Patsy Horine are buried in a cemetery near Chehalis, Washington. Patsy lived the last few years of her life in a nursing home in Lacey, Washington.)*

Mark and Jennie Horine had sixty-eight grandchildren. Most of them are grown and now have families of their own.

Back to the story of Ruth Horine Peters: "I, Ruby "Ruth" Horine Peters, am the only survivor of the original Horine family that lived on the old homestead in Gasman Township, Ward County, North Dakota. I am 83 years and my husband, Guy Peters is 87 years old. We shall celebrate our 65th wedding anniversary this year of 1981. We both enjoy better than average good health. Keep our own home and garden. Still go fishing and do some traveling. In 1977, we visited North Dakota and saw the old Horine homestead. We were surprised to see the little one room schoolhouse had been moved onto the farm. Otherwise, it was much the same as we remembered it.

Information contained in the story includes the following:

www.glorecords.blm.gov Search land patent

John Mark Horine Section 10 Township 152 Range 83 Ward County NE – SW
Ray Horine Section 17 Township 152 Range 83
Abram Sovine Peters homestead Section 5 Township 15 Range 81 Ward County

NOTES

That information was in 1981 and this is where family members lived at the time.

Ruby Ruth Horine Peters passed away April 9, 1990, in Bremerton, Washington. Guy Archie Peters, passed away March 9, 1983, in Spokane, Washington. Both are buried in Farmington, Washington.

Questions Elaine would like to have asked her mother: "When you and Morris broke the calves to drive, did you use a cart? The reason I ask is, when Walt was young, mother made him a little cart to drive behind his pony. Walt used to say, "I sat right back there with my nose in the exhaust." Mom was handy to make fun things. She made me stilts when I was a kid. I walked all over Farmington on my stilts. I made stilts for my grandchildren too, but they never learned to walk on them."

Why did Grandma and Grandpa pick Palouse in 1919? I think some of their North Dakota homestead friends went to Palouse too, but who went there first? Was it the Horine's or other families? If anyone knows the answers to my questions please tell me. This is why we should always question our elders in order to learn about our ancestry before it is too late. We would like to know the answers now.

Note—The above story, was written by my aunt, Ruth Peters. (1898--1990). I would not have known about our family members without her story. I have added dates to the story to update it the best I could find—marked with a *and parentheses. Both Morris Horine and his wife, Patsy, are buried in a cemetery near Chehalis, Washington. I have some very good memories of Patsy Horine from when I was a child. She was so very good to me whenever I was at the farm. When I found out that she was in a nursing home in Lacey, Washington I used to visit her every time I went to Tacoma to visit my mother, Olga Ball. I will always remember her (Patsy) giving me a cup and letting me take it to the supply of thick cream and telling me I could drink all the cream I wanted as long as I did not waste it. I got my fill of cream, and quit drinking it before I got sick. What a treat that was for me. I still like cream, but I was satisfied and never craved it again.

This answered the questions I had wondered about for years—why they moved to the Palouse, Washington area from North Dakota. I still don't know what year Uncle Morris, Patsy, and Grandma left the farm in Flanagan Creek and moved to the Benewah area and then to Plummer. As everyone was becoming older, I assume the farm got to be a bit too much to care for any more.

Sad news: (2015) I just received word that Bill Horine passed away at the age of 99. Artha Bennett made it to the age of 97. Both passed away in the spring of 2015. Helen Peters Miller and Donald Arthur Horine both passed away in October 2015, after each reached 97 years of age. There were two Donald Horine's, Donald A. Horine was the son of Earl Horine and Donald D.(1931-1996). the son of Glen Horine.

Further updates—Peggy Horine Bergland was married to Thomas Oliver Bergland (March 9, 1920-June 21, 2001)

Peggy Bergland now lives in Spokane, Washington with her son, Tom. Dorothy Horine Schlagel Hokanson (*May 27, 1924-2009) was married to Lester Schlagel. After Lester died, Dorothy married a second time to Harry Hokanson and lived in Tacoma the rest of her life. Albert Horine Bradley (1927-1986) lived in Post Falls, Idaho. Albert changed his name to Bradley when he found that people seemed to find it hard to pronounce his name while he was in business. Olga Enger Horine, married a second time—to Arthur Ball, in 1945. She became widowed from Arthur Ball in 1968.

NOTE:*I have updated this paragraph as of February 2015. (Albert died in Alaska in 1986 under mysterious circumstances. When he died a woman declared he had no relatives, that she was his *only* relative— but she was a complete stranger to Al's family. She had him cremated. In fact he had a wife, four children, two sisters, a brother, his mother, uncles, aunts, and many cousins all living at the time. All this leads the family to believe that he may have died under suspicious circumstances.)

POEM BREAK

Aunt Ruth also wrote a poem one time after visiting Bert and Irene at their home in Gig Harbor. (On Purdy Lagoon)

Their cat had a batch of kittens that needed a good home. Bert had offered one to Guy and Ruth. When they got home in Spokane there was a kitten in their vehicle. This poem is the result of their surprise:

THE CAT AND THE DIRTY RAT

Bert Enger, You're a dirty rat
To send us home with that darn cat!
I saw you smiling when we drove out,
But couldn't guess what it was all about.
When we got home and heard that "meow"
I could only think—I'll get even somehow!
But when we let him out to scratch and dirty,
He took off like a shot, headed for Purdy.

So if he shows up some night quite late
You'll know he crossed the whole darn state.
If we couldn't laugh and joke a little
Life would hardly be worth living.
Though I didn't ask for that darn cat
I'm going to be a little forgiving.
But—your safety depends on you—no more cats!

MORE POEM BREAKS

I wrote the following verse after realizing how often people seemed to gather in the kitchen when they visited. This may also be why so many kitchens were sometimes the largest room in the house in the old farmsteads, and maybe there was no, what we, today, call the "living room" or "family room". The kitchen is the most friendly room in the house. The kitchen draws people like a magnet.

COME SIT IN MY KITCHEN

Come sit in my kitchen, share it with me
While I fix your dinner so we can visit you see.

It brings pleasant memories of my childhood past
As I remember the good times
and kitchen friendships that last.
I hope it leaves you memories like a beautiful song
So come sit in my kitchen where I believe you belong.
It's a gesture of friendship we will always share
Do come sit in my kitchen, I want you there.

MY FIRST ONE ROOM SCHOOLHOUSE

When I visited the Flanagan Creek area a couple of years ago I looked for the schoolhouse I attended in the first grade. It was a one room schoolhouse with up to eight grades for one teacher to teach. My first grade teacher's name was Miss Anderson. I really loved her and remember her to this day. I think there were fifteen students. I do not believe the building is around there any more. At least I could not find it. I hope to visit that area again some day and will inquire of nearby residents to see if anyone there knows anything about what has happened to the old schoolhouse. I hope the building has been preserved like the one in Benewah has been. Of course there have been very many changes over the past 90 years. Some old buildings may have been preserved and others eliminated.

In case you are wondering about a teacher having eight grades to teach in a one room schoolhouse, I really believe it was a great advantage to the students. Those of us in the lower grades could hear the teacher teaching the upper grades and we learned from that, way ahead of those having only one grade in a room. While there usually were not students in all eight grades at one time, the teacher had to know how to teach each grade. Kids don't have to be very old to pick up what they hear from what is being taught the other children. I also believe the higher grades would listen to the teacher with the lower grades and if they had trouble with reading or anything else they did not have to be sent back a grade, but picked up what they may have missed earlier. A great system it seems.

I also remember in learning to read I had a great deal of trouble with the words "*the*" and "*that*" and also "*and*". I don't remember why, but for some reason those three words still linger in my mind as being troublesome for me.

Today the teacher is apt to have thirty students to teach, all thirty in one grade, all thirty in one room. This makes for a different situation than in a one room schoolhouse.

We had instructions at home that if we needed a spanking at school we also got one when we got home. I said spanking and not beating (there *is a big difference—a spanking is a swat on the buttocks*). I don't remember any student getting spanked. Parents made kids behave in those days, at least better than they do now. Also, if a child got some kind of punishment at school, the parent did not rush to school and accost the teacher for doing what the parent should have done. I am sure there were some mischievous children then, but not as destructive or vicious as they are at times now. The world has changed, and actions seem more severe now.

We walked to school, carrying our lunch in a bucket. Our parents had purchased either syrup or lard in those buckets. The lard buckets were usually nicely decorated by the manufacturer. The syrup buckets originally held Karo syrup and were usually plain with a wire handle to hold onto. Nothing went to waste in those days. People used lard extensively in their cooking. It was used for frying potatoes, onions, makng gravy, pies, and many other items. If a person butchered a pig, the fat was rendered and used for cooking. Flour sacks had very pretty prints and made nice dresses or shirts for us kids. Many times the flour sack prints were made into what were hung on the windows as attractive curtains.

Our lunch was made with bread baked at home. If one of the other kids had bakery bread they would trade with someone who had sandwiches made from home baked bread. To each what the other one had was either a treat or at least a change. A lot of the sandwiches were peanut butter and honey or homemade jam. Each kind of bread was a treat to the other so trading went on extensively between the kids, either because of the bread or the filling that was different. I never heard of any kid fighting over lunch, it was a mutual trade-off that we looked forward to each day. The grass always looked greener on the other side of the bucket.

1924 TEACHER CONTRACT INFORMATION

I do have a document (an actual contract signed by a teacher) from 1924. I got my information from both the contract and from a later reunion of the former students. The teacher got twenty dollars a month, also had to do janitorial work and many other chores for those twenty dollars a month. Can you imagine anyone teaching for that kind of salary today? They had to be a very good teacher then if they wanted to keep their job. They don't do janitorial jobs today and they are paid a lot more for less physical work. *Today the teacher has up to 30 kids in one grade* and that is not easy to handle.

The kids do not always behave and that adds to the job. To be a teacher now requires dedication to the job to handle it. The teacher is also required to have more education and many more subjects are required that were never thought of before.

There were a few chores required of the teacher as well as some of the students. These one room schoolhouses were located in rural areas, requiring the teachers to do janitorial work not required of city schools. There was no one else available to do some of the work. This was in the 1920's. The contract required that "the teacher shall be held responsible for the care of all school property entrusted to them, shall exercise watchful care over the conduct and habits of the pupils while under their jurisdiction. Shall maintain strict order and discipline in their schools at all times". Any neglect of this requirement shall be considered good cause for dismissal. Corporal punishment may be resorted to when it becomes necessary to the preservation of proper discipline. No cruel or unusual punishment shall be inflicted: and no teacher shall administer punishment on or about the head of any pupil. (*I believe the teacher was allowed corporal punishment those days.)*

"The use of tobacco in any form or place by a teacher is discountenanced and the use of alcoholic stimulants in any form or place as a beverage is prohibited. The use of tobacco or any other narcotic on the school premises by a teacher shall work a forfeiture of his certificate." *In other words—do not smoke and do not drink anywhere.*

Teachers were required to be at their respective schoolrooms at least thirty minutes before the time of opening of school in the morning and fifteen minutes before the opening of school in the afternoon. Teachers were really restricted in many ways.

THE SCHOOL WEST OF SPOKANE & THE REUNION

Further information is from a reunion of the former students of the school described above. It is the school my husband, Tom Bergland, went to after coming to the States from Canada. I do not know what year the neighborhood got together to build this school, but it was probably around 1923 before the 1924 time dated on the teachers contract I have in my possession. Times and requirements have changed greatly since then. Most of these one room schoolhouses are no longer in use, or very rarely if at all. Children are bussed to larger schools, sometimes a very long distance.

Parents got together to form a school district so their children could go to school. One parent dug a well so they would have water. The state was asked to form a district and build a school but the state refused. The parents took up a collection and bought property, built a school, bought materials, textbooks, supplies, as well as the teachers' salary. After everything was completed and the school was operating the state accepted the responsibility for the school but made no reimbursement to the parents for their contributions.

Each year there were four lucrative contracts let. The main contract was for wood. Many cords of fir or tamarack, had to be cut, split, and piled in the woodshed. The difficulty in procuring it was due to the distance for this kind of wood. I do not know if these contracts were before or after the state took over from the parents.

The second contract was for the cleaning of the boys and girls privies. The school north of Spokane was the type which had drawers directly under the seats. These drawers had to be removed from behind, cleaned, and lined. Eighth grade boys or a school board member was usually given this job. I cannot imagine a student doing this job, but maybe it was no worse than cleaning a barn after the cows were milked or cleaning the horse stalls. All it was was fecal matter from either source, one no worse than the other.

The third contract was for cleaning the school well before the fall term. Two eighth grade boys were the ones who sought after the job as it was a daring thing to go down into the long dark, hole on a ladder. They would clean and wash down the walls before climbing back out. The water was pumped by hand and bailed with a bucket until most of the water was out, then they would go down and do what had to be done below. They had to remove the silt, roots, dead rodents, and garter snakes. The side walls then were plastered with cement where rodents, snakes, etc. might enter the well.

The fourth contract was the janitorial contract which was usually handled by a 7th or 8th grade boy. This job was let out on a monthly basis and entailed washing the blackboard, which went all the way across the front, spreading the red sawdust compound on the floor and sweeping it, dusting the desks and furniture, and making sure all the ink wells were filled.

When punishment was required, the mental punishment was usually considered the worst. This was doing jobs that needed to be done, but the one in the contract was the one who received the money while the student in trouble did the work. The jobs were raking the yard, hauling in all of the wood for the next day, splitting kindling, washing down the inside walls of the restrooms and washing windows. "The idea of doing someone else's job and receiving no pay, was more than we could take."

"The large wood furnace in the corner of the room used wood that we brought in before we had recess in the morning. It was required before we could go out to play so it was always kept full."

SOME INFORMATION FROM 1915

The speed limit was 10 miles per hour in the cities. Twenty-five miles per hour was considered excessive. Some roads today have a speed limit of 80 miles per hour and when you are on them you might be passed up like you were standing still. What a difference a century makes. Twenty-five miles an hour was scary, probably felt very dangerous.

Many adults could not read or write. Only 10 percent of all Americans had graduated from high school. The average wage in America in 1910 was 22 cents per hour. Remember the school teacher's wage was all of $20.00 a month in 1924. In 1950 we had never heard of Pampers so we made cloth diapers and washed them out when they were soiled. Back in those old days of 1950 we didn't know what a computer was. Now messages can be sent all over the world in a matter of seconds and typewriters are antiques. There have been an enormous number of changes in my lifetime. It is impossible to imagine what it may be like in another 100 years.

I used my computer to check out the figures I used in this story to make sure they were accurate. There were many adults who had never learned to read or write, probably because they had to help support their family or had even lived so far from the school that it was considered unimportant under the circumstances. Today there is no excuse for not attending school and it is required by law to attend. Children are bussed if the distance is far from the school.

It is impossible to imagine what it may be like in another 100 years,

LAS VEGAS

The population of Las Vegas, Nevada was only 1500 until 1920. By 1950 it had bloomed up to 2000. In 1946 we drove through Las Vegas and it was only a "wide spot in the road". There were none of the big casinos then. We stopped at a gas station and they did have a slot machine. Tom handed me a quarter to put in it. I lost that quarter and wouldn't waste another quarter in the darn machine. Look at Las Vegas now.

THE FARM AT FLANAGAN CREEK
vs. BENEWAH

All of us kids had a wonderful time playing in Flanagan Creek in the summer. It was our own private "swimming pool." I do believe I would enjoy having that creek today.

The water was crystal clear and quite cold. The creek was about six feet wide and a foot deep in the summer, but very deep and very swift and dangerous in the spring when the snow melted in the surrounding hills. We were kept away from it then.

The following information applied to both Flanagan and Benewah Creeks, quite a number of years apart, but under the same living conditions. Both homes had a nearby creek close to the house but no indoor plumbing. My early childhood was by Flanagan Creek and the later times were by Benewah Creek. While Benewah Creek was a nice clear creek, it was not conducive to playing in it as Flanagan Creek had been. Benewah Creek was not as wide and the forrest came right up to the creek, whereas Flanagan Creek was more in the open, maybe because the timber had been cleared away and it was in more of a valley. Both had crystal clear water and were year around creeks. Benewah Creek was a bit smaller than Flanagan Creek, but still substantial.

Water was carried into the house from the creek, and dirty or used water was also carried out. There was no inside toilet. We had an "outhouse" to use as a toilet. It usually stunk and we used a catalog—either from Sears or Wards for toilet paper. In the winter time it was very cold to go out to that little "house" behind the house, but that is the reason we also used a "chamber pot" at night. It was a way of life most people don't even know about these days. I doubt they could even survive for long if they were suddenly thrown into living conditions of seventy or eighty years ago.

Try living with no telephones, no electricity, no water in the house, no bathrooms in the house, no paved roads, carry your water in from a creek, and then the dirty water back out again. As there was no large bathtub in your house, you took a bath in the washtub that you used to wash clothes in. The water was carried into the house, lifted into a boiler on the stove to heat. Carried the hot water to where you wanted to use the water, then carried it out again when you were through with it—after you used that precious water to scrub your floors of course.

I have a wash tub and a scrub board in my shed if anyone would like to see it. I will even let you try it out if you'd like (I won't let you bathe in it though). Bring on your laundry. Since I have already done my share of scrubbing on the washboard, I'll let you do yours on your own. I'll even furnish you some water from a faucet so you won't have to carry the water in. Fun, Fun, Fun. This was also the same routine for bath water. Try taking a bath all scrunched up in a small tub. You did the best you could. You made that water count. Carrying that water was a lot of work so you did not waste it.

When the water was used to bathe in you used some of it to scrub the floor, then you carried it outside to empty it. You did not waste water that you had to carry, and bath water was good enough to scrub the floor. The water used to rinse the clothes after they were washed was especially good for scrubbing the floor.

During World War 2—1941-1946—things were not only rationed but very hard to get. We survived. It was hard, but it also didn't kill us. When we got the electric line in, Tom dug a well and piped water into the house. One of the first things I got when we got electricity was an electric cook stove and an electric washing machine.

Now I can talk about the "Good Old Days" that actually were not so good, even if we didn't let it bother us at the time. For some reason the whole family survived it. Now I have a telephone, television, indoor plumbing, with a real bathtub, shower, and toilet, running water *and the bills to pay for it all!* What more could I ask for?

Today's men and women have not been conditioned to living in that manner. Being so many years away from that kind of living, they would not know what to do and would end up lost and confused. They might not even be able to physically stand up to the task. It was physically hard work to survive. This was on a rural farm, not in the city. If you were fortunate you would have a gasoline powered washing machine with an engine that could be balky and might not want to start. Otherwise you had to wash clothes on a scrub board. I used that scrub board many times when I could not get my gasoline engine to start. I had to do it as I had diapers to wash. In the winter I hung the diapers out on the clothes line to freeze dry, and then took them inside to dry the rest of the dampness out of them. Hanging wet clothes outside when the weather was freezing made for very cold hands, but you did it because your baby needed a change of diapers. That was before the invention of disposable diapers and drying machines. In order to save some work I would tear squares of old rags and use them to line the diapers. If the diaper was soiled, the rag would be disposed of, but the ones only wet were washed and re-used. No need for that with today's disposable diaper. You washed and re-used the squares because you would run out of material if you didn't.

Life was always a case of 'make due with what you have on hand or do without entirely.'

It was usually the women, who did these chores as the men were out tending to the animals and the farming, which was also very hard work, so the women had to do it. To say the least, everyone was very tired at night and no one would lie awake trying to get to sleep. It didn't kill us, so we survived in spite of how hard it might have been. My husband was working fifteen to twenty hours a day hauling logs, poles, grain, or lumber up to Spokane and to Moses Lake from where we lived in Idaho. Living conditions were tough for both of us but we survived.

The great depression was from 1929 to approximately 1941. Yes, at that time the prices of everything seem so very low to us today, but wages were also extremely low then in comparison to this day. If you were paid a dollar a day, you really had it made. That was for a day, not an hour. Those were really the *"GOOD OLD DAYS"* before that, but not financially. The bombing of Pearl Harbor started World War 2 for us and it changed the world as we knew it before. Women went to work and have never returned to being "just a housewife." Instead of caring for their own children, they hired baby-sitters to care for the children and now it is common for others to raise the children. This has upset the balance of family life to the detriment of the family. Nothing has been the same since.

The one improvement I have noticed is that more men help out with housework and caring for the children now that their wife is working. Before, you seldom heard of a man doing something like changing a diaper, or cleaning up after the children, or anything else they considered "women's work." Of course, one reason for that was because the men usually also had to do a lot of backbreaking work so it was not practical for them to work inside the home. That is not the usual way of things today, since the wife is working outside the home now and she needs help.

Divorce is much more common now. Couples are not as committed to staying together through the thick and thin of a marriage as they used to be. Long time marriages are getting rare, which is too bad because it also affects the children when parents separate. People don't seem to have the stamina to find a way to get along. They don't use their brains to figure out that they need to be kind to each other. If they did they would not be so quick to head for the divorce courts. A lot of people, both men and women, don't realize that taking up with someone not their mate is an act of treachery that leads to the end of a marriage which seems to be common today. Too bad, really too bad.

I GRADUATED
FROM HIGH SCHOOL

I graduated from North Central High School in Spokane in January of 1941 in a class of over three hundred. I don't remember how I got into the mid-year class because when I started first grade it was in the fall after I had turned six the previous May. I was always an A grade student so it was not because I failed any grade, but probably it was because of moving around and missing half a year. In those days you could start first grade in January if you were six years of age by then. I believe it was about that time in 1941 the schools discontinued the January entrance policy. Now they have to be six before September. They did not have Kindergarten for young children until many years later.

It was soon after I graduated from high school, that Tom Bergland and I were married. We lived in Spokane for about a year. He had several various jobs until he went to work in a mine in Metaline Falls where he worked for about a year. Since working underground was not a very rewarding job, when he had a chance to transfer to a job in Idaho, working outdoors, he jumped at the opportunity.

My marriage to Tom Bergland (1920-2001) lasted sixty years and three weeks and only ended when he fell one morning and his injuries ended his life. Sure, we had our differences, but we faced them and went on with our lives and did not run away from them. Yes, I really do miss Tom, but life goes on.

OLGA ENGER HORINE BALL (1901-1994)

MOTHER LEFT WITH US IN 1933

In 1932 my mother got sick and I remember her being loaded onto a bed and put in the back of a truck and taken to a hospital in Potlatch, Idaho. I was ten, Dorothy was eight, Albert was five and Donald was only a year old. Between Uncle Morris, Patsy, and Grandma we were taken care of during that time. Mom had surgery and was in the hospital for only a few days when my father went to the hospital and took Mom out, very much against the doctor's orders. We were all loaded up in a truck and were on the move again, this time, near to where my mother's sister, Mabel Collier, lived. I do remember we spent the winter of 1932 in Vancouver, Washington. My Aunt Mabel (Mom's sister) who lived in nearby Camas, Washington said Mom was full of infection and should have been in the hospital longer. It was a wonder she didn't die. There was no penicillin in those days. There was no need for us to go to Vancouver, nor anywhere else, as we were always welcome at the farm. Mom was sick and should not have been moved.

I do know my father was very mentally abusive to her, as I was old enough to remember. He also was jealous without any reason to be. If she even said "hello" to a neighbor he accused her of wrongdoing. I also remember Mom took us kids to our uncles' house to ask for food at least one time. I believe we walked to their house, a distance of about two miles carrying my brother who could not walk yet as he was about a year old. It also seems in my memory that there was a dozen eggs in the house and my father ate all of them. I also saw him kill our horse at that time when the horse refused to do or could not do something he wanted it to do. It is a bad memory I have of that poor horse. This was the summer of 1928. I was six years old.

While my dad was mentally abusive to Mom I don't recall his ever hitting her. There are many ways to abuse people other than physically. Years later I did see them struggle over something when he came to see us, but other than that the abuse seemed to only be mental. At least one time I remember a woman brought in to assist my mother after she had the surgery and things were going on that should not have been, especially visible to us kids. Mom had very good reason to leave my dad.

I do not remember him being an alcoholic as I do not believe there was ever much alcohol around and I never did see him drunk.. My mother did not drink. In fact she got very irate at me one time when I took her to the Worlds Fair in Spokane and ordered a Margarita for her. She did not know what a Margarita was until she got it served. Boy was she ever mad at me. My father was a very handsome man. He could make friends with people but for some reason he evidently felt no responsibility to support his family, and it was not because of the depression and lack of jobs, it was his lack of care or something. My father died in 1968 and I do not have very nice memories of him.

By the time I was eleven years old, I had never spent a full semester in any school until my mother got fed up with our living conditions. This had gone on until my mother finally divorced my father in 1933. When she left him, *we left with only the clothes on our backs, literally.* Years later she told me she would not have left him if he had seen that the children were provided for. I know he did not treat her very well. While I believe many divorces are entered into without merit, it was the best thing she could have done for all four of us kids. It was not until she left him that our lives became stable. My youngest brother, Donald, was two years old at that time. I remember the bad odor of gas from the apartment we lived in there in Vancouver in winter of 1932 and 1933. Who could not remember that awful smelling odor. The cooking stove was operated by inserting coins in a gas meter. The building was an older one and the odor was very unpleasant and I can almost still smell those awful odors. That apartment was located close to the bridge that crossed the Columbia River. It was also fairly close to the railroad station. My mother would sometimes take us down to the river to watch the ships when they came in. In 1933 there was a showing of the ship called *"Old Ironsides"*. I do not remember anything about the ship, but the name of it did stick with me. It seemed to me at the time that it was quite large, but it does stick in my memory that it was docked close to the banks of the Columbia River. I don't remember if we went aboard. I do remember that it seemed to be black and long. The ship was a museum piece as a historic reminder.

THE SNOW WAS DEEP THAT WINTER

The snow that winter of 1932 was quite deep, probably 18 or more inches deep, as I remember. It was above my knees and I was about eleven years old. The snow was all melted by the time we left Vancouver. When we left Vancouver, we boarded a train in the city, and went on the SP&S railway to Spokane. We had no baggage of any kind, only the clothes we were wearing. I do not know who paid our train fare.

(I lived across the river in North Portland for twenty-eight years, from 1974 until 2001, and the snow was never as deep in all those years as it was the winter of 1932. I think it got about six inches deep in two different years during that time we lived in Portland.)

When we got to Spokane we moved into the two front rooms of Grandma Enger's house at 1402 West Buckeye in Spokane. I was eleven, my sister, Dorothy, was nine, my oldest brother, Albert, was six and the youngest brother, Donald, was two years of age. In 1933 Mom sued for divorce from my father. Her lawyer asked her to put on a better dress than she was wearing for her appearance in court. She told him she had it on—a housedress, the only dress she had. At this time there was very little help for women and children who were destitute. She did housework to pay the lawyer.

Later, the government was starting up a program called (ADC) "Aid for Dependent Children". This was a tremendous help when we received this. I believe Mom got $30.00 a month for four children. When I became sixteen it was cut in half. They expected me to go to work. I couldn't even get a baby sitting job for twenty-five cents for an entire evening and for that twenty-five cents was expected to also clean the house. Mom went to the Welfare office and told them to put us in an orphanage so we would have food and shelter. The bluff worked and they restored the amount to the original grant of $30 and I was able to stay in school. Even men couldn't get a job those days. Many men tried to join the military to get work, but were turned down because too many men volunteered. I remember a friend of my uncle's trying to join the Army while in Spokane and he was told there were no vacancies. That was around 1933. That was changed in 1941 with the bombing of Pearl Harbor.

We lived in those two front rooms until my mother could earn enough money to rent a house. She found one for five dollars a month, a lot of money in 1933, especially when she was only paid twenty-five cents an hour. She borrowed a stove and beds from a friend, and moved into that house. I remember the name of the street was Madison. I don't remember how long we lived at that location. From the house on Madison we moved into a small house at 820 West Chelan. My mother bought it from Grandpa Enger, who had taken the house in trade on the house he built on Buckeye Avenue. The house on Chelan was a one bedroom house.

A friend helped us out by adding a very small dining room and one bedroom, also small. The enclosed back porch was handy to house a washing machine. The one bathroom joined the little kitchen. Even though the house was quite small, it was a home of our own and we didn't have to move any more. Mom paid Grandpa the sum of twelve dollars a month until it was paid for. She lived there until she married Arthur Ball in 1945. By the time mom married Arthur Ball all of us kids were gone except my youngest brother Donald.

To support four children, my mother worked doing housework in homes or hotels or wherever she could get work. The pay was twenty-five cents an hour. Many times she held down two jobs. She would do housework at one job in the morning and maybe go to a hotel and work in the kitchen in the afternoon. After my mother left with us kids, my father did not contribute to help support us four kids even once that I can remember. See about what happened on my fifteenth birthday when I tell about it later.

One time Mom was working across the alley from the house we lived in on Madison Avenue and she could see through our kitchen window. Donald was less than three years old and the woman would not let Mom bring Donald to work with her so she had to leave him alone until I got home from school. That was a terrible situation. It eventually had its repercussions too. Fortunately he was alone for less than two hours, until I got home from school, but that was too long. It was work those two hours or all of us would go hungry. No one knows how terrible that must have been for our mother. She could see in the kitchen window and Mom would call Donald on the phone so she could run home if anything went wrong. A terrible way to have to live, but she managed somehow for short periods of time. Fortunately the place she was working was across the alley from our house and Mom could see through the window enough to see that my little brother was OK. She had also instructed him how to use the telephone and she would call him and check on him that way. When the rest of us kids were home from school we did the baby sitting. Welfare was *NOT* available at that time. Welfare in the form of Aid for Dependent Children (ADC) came much later. My father did not contribute anything to help us financially. (I have a story to tell later about money he had and kept for himself).

From the sixth grade on I went to school just as the children of most normal families do; only changing schools as I advanced to a higher grade. I think the reason I survived staying in school and never failing was because I loved to go to school. My sister and I would wash our dresses at night and iron them in the morning to wear to school. In seventh grade we were taught sewing and I made my own dresses after that. Sure it was hard, but I look back and it didn't hurt me physically in any manner.

I think the kids of today are truly missing out on things that really did prepare us for living. What about sewing for girls, and shop for the boys? Those lessons are needed today as well as they were then. In my opinion the wrong studies were dropped. Those studies helped the kids learn things that prepared them for life. Now everything is electronic. Too bad! Too bad! Drop the electronics and now what would be left. No one is prepared today for living in such a primitive way. They would not be able to exist.

Mom took me with her one time when she went to work at a hotel and I was allowed to have all the ice cream I wanted to eat, a special treat for me. We went by city bus to any place we needed to go or we walked. We never did have a car. By this time my brothers were both in school.

By 1942 all three of us older kids had moved away on our own. By this time we were in World War 2 and Mom had a job at Kaiser's Aluminum Plant. By 1945 Mom met, fell in love with, and married Arthur Ball, who became the grandfather my children really loved, and his love for them was all anyone could ever ask for. It was not until he died in August 1968 from a heart attack that the children learned he was not their biological grandfather. That was something we never even thought of as he was really their grandfather right from the beginning. We were all very fortunate to have had him.

Sometime in 1946 Mom and Art had sold the house on Chelan and purchased a large old house in Spokane Valley, at 7305 East Fairview, which they remodeled into a duplex. There were five lots included with the house. This gave them plenty of space for the wonderful gardens they grew and which they shared with everyone. The ground was very rocky but it produced bountiful crops. There seemed to be nothing but pebbles, but a great garden it grew. They lived in that house until Art died and until Mom got to the point that she needed care.

All of my father's relatives remained lifetime friends with my mother after she divorced my father. When she remarried ten years later, they also welcomed her husband, Arthur Ball, who became grandfather to her grandchildren. He loved all the grandchildren and they loved him. No one ever even thought to say anything to the children that he was not their biological grandfather so they were shocked to find that out after he died. It had been so natural for Arthur Ball to be their grandfather that no one even thought anything about any biological connections. He really was their grandfather, and a very good one. They mourned his passing away very greatly and speak fondly of him to this day. Grandfather Arthur Ball was with the grandchildren from 1945 until his death in 1968. The children were still barely babies at the time Mom and Art were married. They were three months, one and a half years, and three years of age in 1945. The other three children were born later so they all grew up together. A person sure doesn't have to have biological connections to be a good parent or Grandparent. We were all very fortunate to have had Arthur Ball for the time we did.

In the summer of 1968 my two sons, David and Larry, went up to Spokane to spend the summer with Tom and Karen. We had lived in California for nine years by this time. While in Spokane, Art spent much time with the boys. David had just turned twelve, and Larry was nine at the time. Art had a boat and one day took the boys over to Lake Pend Oreille in Idaho for an outing so they could fish and enjoy the day. This is quite a large lake and they were way out from shore when suddenly Art asked David if he could get the boat back to shore if he (Art) could not. Of course David said he could (at 12?). He didn't catch on that something was wrong. Art got the boat to shore and the boys unloaded the boat. There was a resort right where the boat was moored. If he'd have only gotten help right there instead of thinking only of two kids who would have been all right. The sheriff or anyone at the resort could have seen that they would get home.

Art was only thinking of the kids not himself. He was a wonderful grandfather, who was dearly loved.

He started back and kept asking David if he could drive the car back to Spokane if he couldn't. They made it to Spokane and when Art got to the door Mom could see he wasn't well, and got him into bed. Just then a friend happened to call and when Mom answered she told the friend that Art was very sick and she didn't know what to do. The friend just told her to tell the phone operator that she needed an ambulance, which she did. The ambulance took Art and Mom to Sacred Heart Hospital. There was no such thing as 911 at that time and you had to depend on the telephone operator to advise you and to connect you to whatever organization you needed. The operator ordered an ambulance and Mom went to the hospital with Art in the ambulance.

About midnight David called us in California because he was worried that he hadn't heard anything. We knew instantly that something serious was wrong and decided I had better fly up to Spokane immediately. We suspected a heart attack. As we hung up we got a call from another relative that it was a heart attack and the doctors had tried desperately to save him, but he did not survive. I called an airline and there was one plane leaving Los Angeles in one hour. Being we lived 70 miles from LA we figured we could not make that plane even by breaking all speed limits at that time of night and it was best to just wait until morning.

I got the earliest morning flight I could get and arrived in Spokane. I ended up being the one who had to make the funeral arrangements. There were no other relatives in Spokane that I could call on. Everyone was gone, this being vacation time. That was very stressful as I no longer knew my way around Spokane and any of the friends I remembered were away for the summer. I stumbled through everything the best I knew how to do. I didn't know until much later that Pall Bearers were supposed to be personal friends and called on some organization to do the honor, people who did not know him or any of the family personally. As I said, I did not know the difference at the time. I did find someone I knew who could give the funeral discourse and he really did a nice job.

I stayed in Spokane for a couple of weeks and helped my mother get several things taken care of before returning to California with the two boys. Because my mother wanted to get rid of the boat and all Art's camping gear I helped her sell it. It didn't take long as there were a lot of people up from California who were looking for camping gear and other than the boat bought all she had. There was also a car that she wanted to sell, as there were two cars available, so I bought the 1940 Ford from her. She wanted to keep the other car so my sister could drive it whenever she came over to Spokane to stay with Mom. I ended up driving that old Ford car down to California with the two boys and Mom. We started out from Spokane and spent the first night in Tacoma and left there early in the morning. Just south of Portland, I stopped in a rest stop to take a nap and was awakened by a Highway Patrolman, who questioned me—I had dealer plates on the car and I explained to him my brother was a dealer and I was taking the car to California. I explained that it had belonged to Art and he had died. He let me go and I had no trouble from the police on the rest of the way home. Mom stayed with me for about two weeks before flying back to Spokane.

I REMEMBER GRANDMA BALL

As told by Grandson Tommy Bergland

She once told me about when she was a young child. Her duties were to gather Buffalo and cow chips for fire fuel. The Buffalo had been exterminated many years before that. The reason for gathering these chips was one of survival. Her parents had emigrated from Norway to the North Dakota plains. They homesteaded in this treeless area and crop failures meant that you could not afford the expensive coal or wood that had to be imported into the area. At that time there were no government backup programs.

Grandma always made a big fuss about her grandchildren. She liked to cook and eat. Her favorites included Lefsa and Lutefisk and "dairy products"—which really meant cream. She liked creamed vegetables and added butter whenever she could. Most of us liked the Lefsa but I am glad she enjoyed her lutefisk as I really didn't. I noticed she liked to stick to her home. Traveling more than one day away from home was out of the question. The only exception was an occasional minimum stay at close relatives. The reverse was OK. Anyone visiting her house was welcome to stay as long as they could.

She liked to work hard and long—a lot more than was necessary. It was probably due to hard times of growing up under conditions in North Dakota, the Depression and having to raise four kids alone. Also, many people get pleasure and satisfaction out of hard work. Examples of this are Grandpa Art and Grandma raising a garden each year that was ample for themselves and several other people.

There are probably many overlooked and forgotten memories that cannot be brought to mind right now.

Note: My son, Tom, wrote the above for me to add to my memorial for my mother after she had died. I made a little booklet to keep stories people sent to me about her. This was one.

IN 1943 WE MOVED TO BENEWAH
AND THEN CAME RATIONING

In 1943 we had moved from Ione, Washington to Benewah, Idaho, a community south of Spokane. We had lived in Ione for about a year while Tom worked in the mines at Metaline Falls. Benewah is located between St. Maries, Idaho and Tekoa, Washington. We lived there for eight years. This community had no telephones or electricity available. The following story is during the time we first moved there. More will come later.

During World War 2 we had rationing, which we had never had before. We were not notified in advance that everything would suddenly, overnight, not be available. On Saturday you could buy anything you wanted. On Sunday you could not buy gas for your car, nor most everything else we took for granted. Besides gasoline there was no meat, shoes, sugar, or tires for your car. Rationing stamps were issued. You had to have those stamps to buy almost everything. We ended up trading the stamps we didn't need for what we did need. I needed stamps to buy sugar to can fruit with, so I traded meat stamps to others who needed meat. I didn't need more shoes, so traded those stamps for something I did need. That was the way we got by.

Cars were no longer manufactured because of the war, so no new cars were available until years after the war was declared over. Even a used car was hard to get and you really had to negotiate to get one. The OPA was instituted. That was the *Office of Price Administration* which regulated what you could sell your goods for. This OPA could be notified if you thought someone was gouging you on the price of what you were buying. You could be fined triple of the selling price if you asked too much. Because of the price freeze on everything if you wanted a car, or if you could even find one to buy, you had to get around the OPA. If you bought a car you also had to buy something else at quite a price, like someone's goat, or their dog. Of course you didn't want the goat or the dog so you never picked it up, but you got the car. The seller got the price he really wanted for the car. Used cars became a premium item because they were not readily available.

I had a nearly new electric washing machine which I advertised to sell when we moved to Idaho and had no electricity to run it with. When that ad ran in the newspaper I got swamped with calls, even some long distance calls begging me for that machine. The first call was from someone owning an apartment complex and telling me how badly that machine was needed and how many people it would help, so I promised it to him. I felt bad when a lady called and said she had newborn twins and really needed a washer, but I had already promised it to the man with the small apartment house. A few months later I got a letter from the OPA saying the man who had purchased the machine wanted triple damages for the machine. I was very very upset about that and wrote to the OPA that I would gladly give the man his money back, that I had sold the machine at a very low price, much less than it was worth, and I would keep it until I got electricity. I never heard anything more from the OPA. Fifty dollars for a washing machine that was only a few months old was not only a reasonable price but a bargain. This was especially so when you considered that they were not available new at any price and extremely rare to find a used one that was less than a year old. Rationing finally ended in 1946. In Idaho, with no electricity, that washing machine was useless to me, but I also needed a washing machine. Tom found an old square tub Maytag washer that could be used with a gas motor. I was glad to get it. There were many times I could not get that motor started and ended up scrubbing diapers on a washboard. The motor was just like those on a lawn mower and gave the same kind of trouble you might have with the lawn mower engine. Tom paid a lot more for that gasoline powered machine than we sold the electric machine for and we were glad to get it. No, we did not complain to the OPA about the price. Everything considered, what we paid for that gas powered machine was not too much. I was fortunate someone had one that could be purchased, one not needing electricity.

My husband and I lived in Benewah for the eight years he was involved in the logging and lumber hauling business. Benewah is still listed on some maps. At one time there was a post office and a sawmill that employed quite a large number of local residents. The post office was long gone when we moved to Benewah. There is no longer any sign of that thriving community as I knew it. The area where the sawmill was located has been cleaned up so there is no evidence whatever that there had ever been a mill there. The pond that had been created on the creek is not visible any more. There is no evidence that there had ever been a pond of any sort at all. Only the one room schoolhouse building is left. Although it is no longer used as a school the building has now been turned into a community center. The children are now bussed into St. Maries to attend school, a distance of about eighteen miles. Any children living in both Benewah and in Alder Creek are sent into St. Maries by bus, a long ride for them.

There are very few houses left on the Benewah road itself. Most of the new housing is up in the Alder Creek area where there have been many nice houses built. All of this is the opposite of when we lived there. The house we lived in burned down several years ago and the only sign left is the light pole still standing nearby. It is even hard to see the creek we enjoyed. Bushes have grown up around the creek and the area where the house had been. Trees were filling up the field that had been clear before.

My son and two oldest daughters started school in Benewah in that one room schoolhouse which is now used only as a community center. This is the very same school I attended for a short time in the first grade. While I started school in the Idaho community called Flanagan I also attended school for a few months in the Benewah schoolhouse. Wonder why I spent first grade in two schools? My father was a very unstable man and he moved us around a lot, sometimes without any notice of any kind except to suddenly announce that we were moving.

As an adult I attended many dances and parties held in that one room Benewah school. Even as a schoolhouse, it was used for the benefit of the entire community from its very beginning. Any kind of a gathering was at that school, whether it was a picnic or a dance. Life centered around that building, so it was natural to make it into a community center when it was no longer used as a schoolhouse.

While living in Benewah, I wrote the local community news for two newspapers, one in St. Maries, Idaho and the other in Tekoa, Washington. Benewah is between the two cities. I remember one incident I wrote about. A prominent neighbor had a birthday and turned thirty-five. Of course I ended up writing about his age in my news column. Whoowee!!. He did not like that at all. I learned quickly that some men are just as private about their age as women are. Never did that again. Also I do remember what I was thinking at the time. My own thoughts were "Gee, he sure is getting old". I was about twenty myself then so thirty five must have seemed to be very ancient. You know what I think now? To me someone who is twice thirty five and is now at seventy years of age is still pretty young. Whatever happened to thirty-five being old? Time sure does something to change our minds. As I write this in the year 2014, I am ninety-two and I am still not OLD!!

Our family lived in the Benewah community from 1943 to 1951. It was while we lived in Benewah that my three daughters were born in Tekoa. There was no hospital in Tekoa, Washington so the doctor used the home of Mrs. Billups as a Maternity home for childbirth. Dr. Abegglen delivered a lot of babies in that home, with Mrs. Billups as his nurse. Many Benewah babies were born in Tekoa. Both Dr. Abegglen and Mrs. Billups are now deceased.

WE MOVED BACK TO SPOKANE

DECEMBER 1951

It was in the fall of 1951 that we traded some acreage we owned in the Alder Creek area for a large house in Spokane. We sold our truck and Benewah home, and then my husband moved our family back to Spokane in December. After about a year Tom went into business with my brother, Albert, buying and selling used cars. Tom managed the used car lot for several years, buying and selling cars. At times we would go over to Montana and buy a few cars and drive them back to Spokane to sell. After a few years, Tom bought out my brother and operated the business with Leroy, his own brother. Leroy found it kept him away from his family too much to be in Spokane so he went back to Benewah. Tom stayed in the used car business until we moved south to California in 1959 after selling our house.

During the first four years of the eight years we lived in Spokane we lived in that large home. While we lived in that first house located in the north part of Spokane, we welcomed our second son. One day someone knocked on our door and asked us if we wanted to sell our house. We sold that first house and then we bought a new home out in Spokane Valley. In 1955 we bought that new house for $14,000. It was made of colored sandstone bricks, a beautiful 3 bedroom home with a full basement, attached garage, on a large lot with paved streets. The year was 1955. We lived in the Spokane Valley for four more years, during which we added another son to our family group. Our older kids were starting into high school.

IN 1959 WE MOVED TO CALIFORNIA

By the time we had spent eight years in Spokane some family members convinced us it would be a good move to relocate to a warmer climate, which we did. It was in 1959 that the economy went into a slump so we decided it was a good time to close the car lot and start for Riverside, California. Toms' parents also were getting along in years and had needed a warmer climate so they had moved to be with their son in California. Tom's parents were needing assistance a lot of the time by then. They had been with one son for a few years, but the son's wife had become ill and he needed some help with their parents at times. We sold our Spokane Valley house, some of our possessions, bought an older truck and loaded it with the furniture we hadn't sold among which was our piano. That is when someone came back and decided they would buy our piano after all. By that time it was already loaded on the truck. We then told them they were too late. The piano was not going to be unloaded. It went with us to California.

Everything was in place and we were ready, so off we went, headed for California, camping along the way..

The first day out we found the truck was overloaded and by the time we got to Pasco the truck was overheating. We ended up buying a trailer and changed some items from the truck over to the trailer to lighten the load. I was driving the car and had never driven on any long distance trip before nor had I ever pulled a trailer before. That was some experience. I didn't do too badly until people started cutting in between me and that truck. I needed to keep the truck in sight as I would have been lost if we got separated. This was before the days of cell phones, so there would have been no way to contact each other. One time I had to speed up to pass a car that had squeezed in front of me. When I got in front of that car I cut them too short, not realizing I had to leave much more room to maneuver the car and trailer. That was scary as it could have caused an accident. I was more careful after that happened.

We used our camping equipment on the journey from Spokane, almost all the way to Riverside, California. The first night we stayed in a park along the Columbia River at Pasco. When we arrived in California we pulled over into a farmer's field, pitched our tent, and spent the night. The next morning we were approached by a farmer offering us a job. He seemed to be disappointed to find out we were not migrant workers looking for work. I suppose that is what we looked like. He did not object to our camping in his field, but asked us to be sure not to leave a mess. We always would clean up after ourselves whenever we camped. We appreciated being able to use the property of others.

We left early in the morning. That evening we decided to stop in Fresno and to stay in a motel so we could clean up before going on into Riverside. We also wanted to get a good meal in a restaurant. First, we located a motel. At that time our youngest son was about eighteen months old. We put him down and he headed for one of the beds as fast as his legs could carry him. Larry started patting the bed and saying "home, home, home". Evidently he didn't care for the travel and sleeping in a tent because when we wanted to leave for the restaurant he started screaming at the top of his lungs. When Tom said "Come on, we're going to go to eat" he would not stop his screaming even long enough to eat.

He did not stop until we got back to the motel. When we put him down again, he said "home, home, home" and he ran to the bed and patted it again. The minute we opened the door and put him down he had instantly shut up. He really wanted a bed. I put him to bed and he went to sleep immediately. I wonder if he remembers anything about it. Judi and Jackie say they remember how he screamed.

September 7, 2014: Well, I don't need to wonder any more. I just phoned and talked to Larry and asked him if he remembers. He said he does not. It impressed us but it evidently did not impress him enough to make him remember. We all laugh about it now. He must have been tired of being cooped up in the car or truck while we were moving. That bed must have looked real good to him because he sure did not want to leave it once he saw it. He was OK the following morning and made no further fuss.

By the time we got into Los Angeles the truck was beginning to give my husband trouble. We decided it was likely we would be separated in the heavy traffic, but from there I knew the way to Riverside so if we got separated I was to continue on by myself, which is what happened. When I arrived at my sister-in-law's house I learned that my husband had gone up a small hill to get gas for the truck and just as he got into the gas station the truck threw a rod. Fortunately for us it happened when and where it did so we didn't have to pay a towing bill. By the time I arrived in Riverside Tom had phoned his sister from the gas station so arrangements were already made for him and the kids. Family members went into Los Angeles and picked them up. They made an agreement with the station for the truck and load to stay at the station and brought the family back to Riverside. I don't remember what arrangements had been made with the station, but I think Tom put a newly reconditioned engine in the truck right at that station. In those days gas stations were also repair shops for the most part. We all made it to Riverside safe and sound, and so was the truck with our furniture intact. The station attendant kept both truck and furniture safe until it was picked up.

After the truck was repaired and taken into Riverside we temporarily rented a house and looked for property where a car lot could be located. It was about six weeks later that we found just what we wanted to set up business. The idea of opening up a car lot in California did not turn out, mainly due to many different laws than were in Washington. Tom had a $10,000 bond in Washington, and California only needed a $5,000 bond. Fortunately Tom had made an escape clause in the lease on the business property so when getting the bond failed Tom decided it was time to change occupations. The bond requirements were entirely different between the two states and this encouraged Tom to go into Real Estate Sales. In Riverside, California my husband became a licensed realtor. This is what he did for the next fifteen years, and it worked out very well for us. Tom was Salesman of the Year several times in a row.

It didn't take long before we also found a house and traded a truck to the owner for his equity. That owner was glad to make the trade because he was in the process of signing the house over to someone because he was unable to make the payments. In fact if we had been fifteen minutes later, we would have been too late, it was that close. We had tracked his residence down and his daughter managed to reach the man by telephone. His family was, at least fifty miles away from Riverside. At the time of the phone call we were in Cabazon and the owner of the house was in Riverside. He actually had a pen in his hand and was ready to sign the papers to give the house away just to save his credit rating, when he answered the phone. He had been unable to sell the house, so this worked out for both of us. We got a house and the man got a truck that was now in good condition.

I had taken shorthand and bookkeeping at North Central High in Spokane. In Riverside, I continued on with my education of office practice by taking a college course in Accounting and did follow that profession for a few years. For several years I worked for a lumber wholesaler as a Secretary and Bookkeeper until he moved to Palm Desert. Next I went to work for the State of California at the Department of Motor Vehicles. I was there for seven years until we relocated to Portland.

After we had been in California for fifteen years Tom was offered a job in Portland, Oregon, helping his brother, George, run an automobile repair shop. Tom took his brother up on his offer. It was becoming obvious that too many kids of the same age as our youngest son were becoming involved with drugs so we decided a change of location would be a good idea under the circumstances. Our son finished high school in Portland without any trouble. While in Portland I worked as a Tax Preparer for several years. We lived in Portland for the next twenty-eight years until my husband met with that accident which ended his life.

HE LEFT HOME FOR THE LAST TIME

My husband, Tom, left home the morning of *June 22, 2001* about nine thirty, and by noon he was gone. He had fallen and had hit his head. He went into a coma and never recovered. The accident happened when he was closing a gate on some steps and evidently stepped off the edge of one of the steps, causing him to lose his balance.

In *November of 2001*, my daughter, Judi, and I decided to move back to California to be near another daughter and her family. I bought a home in Moreno Valley, lived in it for eighteen months, sold it and bought a mobile home in a very nice park. I have since written several articles for a small news letter for our manufactured home community. Since I like to write about a variety of things, I have contributed many stories and verses over the past few years. Somewhere along the line I will include the articles and the poems I wrote for the mobile home park news. I hope you enjoy reading this material as much as I enjoyed writing it.

As of this date in 2014, I am 92 years of age and it has become necessary for me to move in with my son. Tom and Karen live in Spokane for half of the year. They spend winters in Yuma, Arizona for the other half of the year. Judi still lives in California in a cottage on her sister's property. I will now become a "snow bird" with my son and his family. My legs gave out on me so it became necessary for me to have help. I still get along health-wise quite well. I am able to use the computer and I have written this entire book over a period of two or three years so I may skip around about my age in the stories. I have purchased a van so I can carry my scooter with me wherever I go. I prefer not to do my own driving (I have never liked to drive). I am always glad to let others do the driving. I also still like to travel and have taken several cruises. Right along with me on the cruise goes my trusty little scooter. When I travel by plane, I ride my scooter up to the door of the airplane and the crew takes it aboard somewhere and when the plane lands it is delivered right to the door of the plane and off I go on my way. Stories about my travels will come later.

NOW I TRY A COMPUTER

To start with, I was about eighty-four before I tackled trying the computer. I resisted it for a good long time. I finally went to an adult education school and took a course in the use of a computer. My daughter, Jackie, worked for the school district in Moreno Valley so she was able to get me into a good computer class. This in itself reminds me that when I went to high school they did not have electric typewriters, and now they are so obsolete that you cannot even give one away to a charitable organization. Finally, a neighbor took my beautiful electric typewriter off my hands to give to her grandchildren to play with as a toy. I will admit that the computer is easier to type on than that electric typewriter was—not for ease, but if you make a mistake it is easier to make a correction than to use correction tape although I sometimes find the computer can be very frustrating for me.

Enjoy my trip over memory lane. I will mention my friend Jane (name for computer only, not her real name) throughout as I had many an email from her. Even if I have never met her in person she has been a valued acquaintance by email over the past several years. I hope some day to meet her in person. I don't remember how I met her on the computer.

The time I spent writing and sending out my email and how things triggered memories just had to be written down before everything disappeared when I do. I am now ninety-two and my e-mail has reminded me of what happened at different times throughout the years. Some things are funny and other things may be sad.

Woven among the email articles are stories of my life experiences as I remember them. Entertaining or not, I have written them as I remember what happened, as I have found out we all have experiences that can be told if anyone will listen. Some might be dull but some others might be considered very interesting. Such is life as we experience it.

Every family should record stories told by the older members of the family while those older ones are still living. Otherwise you will regret it when it is too late. I wish I could have heard what my own grandparents experienced.

My advice to you is to deposit all the happiness you can in your memory bank. Time has a way of catching you unaware of the passing years. The years have flown by as fast as if time was a jet airplane. It seems like it was just yesterday that I saw people who were older than me and I never dreamed that one day I would be one of those older ones myself. I can remember thinking anyone over forty was really "over the hill" and were so very old. My friends, now retired, are showing their age with grey hair and aches and pains. I can't help it if I fall asleep while sitting still. A nap has become a treat. I sure didn't anticipate all the aches and pains and diminishing hearing, or the loss of being able to do things that I wanted to do. Just don't procrastinate. Accomplish whatever you would like to accomplish before you regret it. The way you live your life is your gift to those who come after you. You can never be sure about what will happen tomorrow because tomorrow may never come so do what you can today.

If there are older people in your family, I suggest you question them about life when they were young. You will lose out on many different life experiences if you don't obtain the information while they are still living. Don't wait until it is too late. While there have been a great many changes in the past one hundred years, there are still changes going on constantly today, and many of life's happenings can be interesting to read about at a later time. Life as we know it today will be very different tomorrow. Have your relative or friend compare things as they remember it from their childhood. Then maybe you will see the difference. Much of the information you hear about today comes from something someone in the past entered into a diary. It is those diaries that inform us of just what went on in the past. If there wasn't a written record everything from the past would be a blank. My grandparents could have told me many things from the era of the 1800's if I had known to ask them and listened. They had experience with the Indians and homesteaded in North Dakota before it was a state. It's too late now and I regret it. Use a tape recorder or other electronic means to get the information so you can go back and write it down as you have the time to do so. In this day of the computer, typing is easy and so very many gadgets available to record the facts of life that may be even easier than using the computer. Record their ordinary conversation, for you would be surprised what that can reveal. Don't be afraid to ask questions. They may be very happy to tell you what went on in their lives. Maybe they need reminders to help trigger their memory like the emails have done for me.

My memory bank may have been a complete failure if it hadn't been for the email reminders. Do you have an older relative that keeps telling the same boring story over and over? Just start asking him questions about his story and see if he doesn't have something more to add to it that he had forgotten about. That might keep it from being boring to you. There are changes going on constantly which you may not notice at the time. The changes are there and may come back to your mind at a later time, especially if you are reminded of them at a later date. Sometimes it only takes a very small thing to remind you of something you thought you had forgotten.

My mother's parents were born in Norway and emigrated here around 1865 as young people so they had a lot of experience, even with Indians in their time. They were very early settlers in the North Dakota Territory long before it was a state. Imagine what they could have told us. The hardships and experiences they had would be interesting to know about. I do know they lived there in a sod house. For how long they lived in a sod house I do not know.

In later years, my grandfather built several houses, really nice ones. Grandpa was a farmer and also evidently a carpenter. The last house he built now stands next door to the one they lived in at 1402 W. Buckeye in Spokane, Washington. My grandfather, Peder Enger, built this beautiful house when I was a child in Spokane. He wanted my grandmother to move into it, but she was quite a stubborn old lady and said the house she lived in was good enough. This was in their later years, after they had moved from North Dakota to Spokane, Washington, where they lived the rest of their lives. I don't know what year Grandpa left Canada and moved to Spokane where Grandma already lived. I do think he must have sold the Canadian farm after coming to Spokane, but I am not sure, only that I recall overhearing talk about having trouble getting the money out of Canada. I don't know why he would have trouble getting the money unless it was the amount allowed.

I don't even know why they or any other family members left North Dakota or why they chose Spokane to move to. They left the Dakota territory before the big exodus of the 1930's. There is no one left to answer the question of why. This is what I mean about listening to the older generation and recording their experiences. We need to ask them questions. If we don't, we permanently lose information about our heritage. They may have left North Dakota because of droughts killing crops. That is only a guess on my part. Many people left that area at the same time and probably for the same reason. That is the reason my husbands' family left Canada—either drought or the crops froze out during several winters. The year was 1928, when my husband was eight years old.

My grandfather seemed to take very slow short steps so I thought he couldn't run, or at least that he couldn't move very fast. I sure found out differently one time when I must have done something to cause him to chase me. I was probably about 6 or 7 years old at the time. I must have been aggravating him in some way. This happened when he was building the house next door to where they lived. It is the only time I ever remember of this grandfather ever being mad at me. He was a very mild mannered man. What I remember most about him was the time he chased me. I do remember seeing him sitting in the living room reading the Bible and singing songs in the Norwegian language. He lived to be 86 years of age. I don't remember what I did or if he caught me or if I was punished in any way. I only remember his very short steps when he walked. Those short steps sure didn't stop him, he could really run.

Although his name was Peder (pronounced Pedder) most people called him Pete. I suppose Peder was the Norwegian way of spelling the name which I took to be Peter in the U. S. He did not speak English when he arrived here, but now he spoke it well. He had a slight accent which I did not notice except he pronounced Job as Yob, as many European people pronounced the letter J as if it was a Y. Grandpa was about twenty-three when he arrived in the United States from Norway. Grandma was about seven when she arrived in the States so she didn't seem to have an accent in her speech. Maybe I was so used to it that I didn't notice, but I don't believe she did.

My grandfather went to Canada and must have homesteaded there at that time. I don't know what year he left North Dakota for Canada. He was a farmer and had a large farm in Saskatchewan. Evidently Grandpa was also talented in the building trade as he built several beautiful homes. I understand Grandma refused to go to Canada (she was very stubborn) even though he had built a very nice home on the Canadian farm there. Why wouldn't Grandma go with Grandpa? They seemed to get along real well when Grandpa moved back to Spokane in his later years. She evidently stayed in North Dakota when Grandpa went to Canada. Nothing I ever heard gave me any information about their life in North Dakota. I don't believe Grandma was ever afraid of the Indians. She made friends with everyone, no matter who they were. I do not know if Grandpa homesteaded in Canada. I imagine he must have in order to have that farm.

I don't know why the rest of the family ended up in Spokane. Even Grandma finally went to live in Spokane.. I don't know what year or under what circumstances, but they both ended up in Spokane for the rest of their life. She probably went to Spokane because the rest of her family left North Dakota and she would have been alone. The whole family of relatives on both sides of my family left from North Dakota, and ended up with some in Spokane and some in Idaho. Someone suggested that the families left North Dakota because of drought conditions. If only there was someone who could tell us. I would like to know for sure. Maybe they homesteaded in Idaho. I was surprised to find records of their names as homesteaders in the Benewah area, but I know nothing about any follow-up about those homesteads. I had never heard about them homesteading and the surprise came from records I saw that someone had at one of the Benewah Valley picnics a year or so ago. My fathers name was on one and my mothers name on another claim. They are not here any more for me to ask, and no other relative or person is alive either. Only what is on those papers to go by. I would like to know more, but that information is evidently lost. That homestead information was a very complete surprise to me.

That last house that Grandpa built is still standing next door to 1402 W. Buckeye in Spokane where they spent their final years. Since I am in Spokane in this year of 2014 I had my son drive over to 1402 W. Buckeye. The people living there now seem to be starting to remodel it. There was a new front door and the siding was being replaced in the front. The old garage was gone from the back. The side street now had sidewalks. What had been open lots in the neighborhood were now occupied with houses. As usual all over the country, everything has changed. After all it has been sixty-five years since my grandmother lived in that house, so I guess I should expect changes. I also wonder if there is still a trap door in the kitchen that leads to the basement, or if there is still an outside entrance to that basement from the rear of the house. I will just have to wonder. I doubt that I will ever get a chance to go over there and talk to the present owner. Actually the basement was only a small area under the kitchen, not a full basement.

Something just came to my mind. Grandma was afraid of cars. She said the first one she ever saw was painted red and she thought it was a devil and it scared her. I never learned why she was afraid otherwise. I think she was afraid of roads going over mountain passes as she had always lived in country that was flat and without any steep hills. The mountain passes and steep hills were a source of fright to many people who had always lived in flat country. In spite of being afraid of cars, she accepted a ride from a man who wanted to hire a friend who lived in Post Falls and needed a job very badly. During that ride they were in an accident and Grandma was injured. I believe she got a broken arm. That is all I remember and all I know of what happened. I don't even know if the friend got a job then. I only know the friend, Minnie Ryan, got married later and then when she was helping her husband, a building wall fell on her and it killed her. They were demolishing an old barn when it happened.

COLD WINTER TIME IN 1928

I was about five years old at the time we lived in Kellogg, Idaho for a few months. It was winter time and there was snow on the ground. I remember we had visited some neighbors and it was dark when we started for our house. My brother, Albert, who was only a few months old, was loaded into a wooden apple box that was fastened to a sled. Pulling him in that sled, we walked back to the house where we were living. It was night time and the only light we had was the bright light of the moon reflecting on the snow. I remember we could see quite well by that reflected light.

The next thing I remember is my mother driving back to Spokane from Kellogg in a Model T car with open or no windows. Or maybe it was just windows or openings that were covered by some kind of removable windows. I just don't remember, except it was very cold. I was holding my little brother, Albert, on my lap. On the way, as we came to the outskirts of the city and had just crossed the river, a wheel came off the car and rolled past us. Fortunately the car stayed upright and we did not go into the nearby river. I also don't know how the car was repaired so we could continue, or if someone came to get us. I only remember seeing the wheel go on past the car. When we got to my grandparents house I recall they placed my feet into a pan of cold water. The water felt burning hot, even though it was cold. Why cold water? My feet were evidently frozen and warming them up had to be done slowly.

This is the only time I ever knew of my mother driving a car. In later years she was trying to learn to drive again. It seemed to be too dangerous by that time as we were afraid she might go into a panic if anything went wrong. She was too easily excited over anything stressful. We discouraged her from ever driving a car again. She did not fight us about it and accepted that we would drive her wherever she wanted or needed to go.

Changes, oh how true. I am now 92 years old and I have seen tremendous changes in my short lifetime. Ninety-two may seem old to you, but when I look back it really has not been very long since I was a kid growing up around my paternal grandparents' farm in Idaho. Remember when you were a little kid, a year seemed to take forever. Yes, 92 years is an extremely short time, and it makes me realize what the Bible means when it says God considers a thousand years as one day or one day as a thousand years **(2 Peter, 3:8)** I took this from the New World Translation but it is in other versions also.

Cars were starting to become very popular by the 1930's. Horses had become pretty much obsolete, even for farm work. Horses are used completely different now from how they were used a hundred years ago. Now look what is used and is available—huge, motorized equipment. Now you would never see a horse working on a highway (as I did when I was about six) and now rarely even on a farm. (See Roads, later) Yes, time flies fast and faster and changes are made.

It was a luxury to own a manual typewriter when I went to high school. Even when I graduated from High school in January of 1941 there were no electric typewriters. Now just try to give an electric one away. They have been replaced with computers and the computer, too, is changing very fast. Seems the electric typewriter came forward around 1984. Shows how short a time it takes for something to improve, only to become obsolete and replaced by something better. Wonder what will replace the computer.

Back then the telephone had operators that assisted you to reach the person you were calling. "Operator," she said first, then she asked "Number Please". She was replaced with phones you could dial yourself. Long distance calls were a separate cost on your phone. Now there is the cell phone which can take pictures and act as a computer—what is next? Even the computer as we knew it at first is not the same. You can use the phone like you use your computer. The phone can even act as a GPS, which helps you find where you are going. You should never get lost that way. The TV today is not the same as it used to be. It looks and performs differently. There are constant electronic changes going on all the time, and that is also changing how we live our lives.

Future changes are fast knocking at the door right now, whether we want them or not. The Post Office replaced the Pony Express over a century ago. Now, can you imagine the Post Offices being gone? They are being replaced by Fed Ex, Email, and UPS. Junk mail and bills is what we get any more. Postage rates keep climbing higher. A few of us older folks can remember when postage was three cents. Plastic cards and online transactions are replacing the written check. With the written check also disappearing, it's causing further deterioration of the Post Office. Today the younger generation doesn't read the newspaper so newspapers are disappearing the same way the milkman and the laundry man and the ice man did. Mobile internet devices and e-readers have caused the newspaper and magazine publishers to consider developing paid news subscriptions to the phone. Books are heading towards being electronic so maybe we will not be seeing books to hold in our hands for much longer. The cell phone has replaced the land line telephone in many homes and businesses.

ROADS

I do remember the condition of the roads when I was so very young. Some roads were muddy when it rained and there really were not too many paved roads anywhere. For instance, up in Washington State from Spokane, driving east through Coeur d'Alene towards Montana, the pass, then known as "The Camel's Hump", was very steep, very narrow, and always very muddy when it rained. The car was very likely to become overheated so there were places beside the road where you could get water to cool the engine. I remember going over that road and someone having to help push the car when it was stuck in the mud.

Note: *Tuesday May 4, 2016*—We returned from Yuma, Arizona this week over this pass. There is no longer a "Camel's Hump" road. The old highway was completely closed off. I understand it was not preserved for anyone to travel over it to "remember the *GOOD OLD DAYS*" of muddy roads and overheated cars. That road has been relocated with a four lane paved freeway over the pass.

Many places along the highway that used to be called a wide spot in the road are now filled up with houses or businesses. One example is Post Falls, originally only a few houses, now full of houses and businesses. Post Falls can never now be referred to as a "wide spot in the road". Houses and businesses are spread all over the area where there used to be open spaces. Open spaces are now quite rare.

Around 1928 I remember seeing a main highway being built with horses for power, and they were moving a big scraper. This was on Highway 95 between Potlatch and Tensed., Idaho. This highway goes from Canada to Mexico. It is still a two lane road in most places. We use it when we leave Yuma and head back to Spokane until we get to Highway 15. Look what is available now. The only thing you see now is huge, powerful machinery. Changes. We just cannot seem to even catch up with what is going on and whoosh, it has changed again. No more horses for farm work or traveling to town or building highways.

Cars were starting to become popular and by the mid 1930's horses were completely obsolete for transportation. Roads had been improved and more of them had been paved. Cars were more plentiful and much more powerful. Yes, time flies and changes are made, and any more those changes are fast, fast, and faster. You could get a new car for $750. That is what my uncle paid in 1937 for a new Ford. Now a new car could cost you around $20,000 or more. It wasn't until around 1920 that the government started to pave and build roads so people could travel to the new National Parks. Before that the roads were mere trails that were dusty and unimproved. What a change.

EMAILS, STORIES & THOUGHTS
"YOU DON'T HAVE TO LOOK LIKE ME TO BE MY FRIEND"

The email I received pictured several different species of animals bedded down next to each other. One was a dog next to a spotted leopard. Both seemed to be smiling. One showed a sleeping fox with a bird (I think it was a parrot) cuddled and sleeping against him. Peaceful pictures of apparent friends. There were several more included, all similar.

I then received the following comment from my cousin *Elaine*: "We had a half moon parrot like the one in picture number 5 that rode on the back of Mandy, our little wire hair terrier. When Mandy lost her eyesight, the bird would let her know if there was another dog or something approaching that Mandy should bark at".

Animal watching can be entertaining.

CAN I COME WITH HIM TOMORROW

The story told of the time when a well behaved dog visited a neighbor and followed her into the house only to crawl into a corner to take a nap. He did this day after day until the householder finally put a note onto the dog's collar telling about the nap. The following day the dog returned with a note stating that the owner had six children, three under four years old, and the dog needed a rest. She wanted to know, "Can I come with him tomorrow?"

Having six children myself, I related to that story.

THE GOLDEN RETRIEVER DOG

My son and daughter-in-law got acquainted with a man who had just been newly married. It seems the bride was allergic to dogs, so the man was seeking a home for his dog. David agreed to keep the dog until a good home became available as he had a large fenced yard where he conducted his business. Of course the inevitable happened. They fell in love with that animal and decided to keep it for themselves.

One day Sue went out to the car and opened the door and the dog jumped in. When the dog didn't want to get out Sue just decided to let the matter drop and took him with her. The destination was to my place. I wondered about having the dog around in our small place, but Sue told the dog to lie down and he never moved until he was told he could. It was such a well-behaved animal it was a pleasure to have him around.

A few days later when Sue went to get in her car the dog was right there ready to go for a ride. When the dog didn't get out quickly when ordered, Sue got into the car, made a few circles in the yard, stopped the car, opened the door, and out jumped the dog. He'd had his ride. Sue quickly got back into the car and took off. After that he would wait patiently hoping to be invited to ride in the car. That dog was a smart animal.

He must have realized all he would get is a turn around the yard instead of the trip he had anticipated. David and Sue also had many other dogs through the years. I seldom take a strong liking to a dog, but I really did like that one. It had personality. I often wonder if the first owner ever realized what he gave up when he gave up that dog. He must have really loved the girl he married.

That story also reminded me of another Golden Retriever dog. My youngest son, Larry, kept having dogs that would run out onto the busy street in front of their house and would end up being hit. They lost several pets that way. They had a fenced yard, but the dogs kept getting out and getting killed.

It was different with the Golden Retriever. Even if the gate got left open, he never ran out into the street. Those Golden Retrievers must be exceptionally smart dogs. At least it seems that way.

MEMORIES KEEP RETURNING
EVEN WHEN DAYS ARE LONG GONE

March 3, 2013: I was watching TV this morning and the program was a reunion of the cast from the Walton Family. It seemed nice to be able to see the cast as they look today and comparing it to when most of them were just young kids when on the show. It also brought back many memories to my mind because I grew up during the years that this program represented. It was almost like I was reliving my childhood at times. My family went through those depression years and I was old enough to remember them. The program was really a true representation of the times.

As I write this I am now in my nineties and was a teenager during most of those years of the depression, the decade from 1929 to 1941. I will be 91 in a few weeks so I relate to the following statement by an unknown author: "Old age is like a bank account. You withdraw in later life what you have deposited along the way".

I wish to thank everyone for their part in reminding me of my memory deposits by sending me the emails that triggered my memory bank withdrawals.

My memory bank may have been a complete failure if it hadn't been for the email reminders. Do you have an older relative that keeps telling the same boring story over and over? Just start asking him questions about his story and see if he doesn't have something more to add to it that he had forgotten about. That might keep it from being boring to you. There are changes going on constantly which you may not notice at the time. The changes are there and may come back to your mind at a later time, especially if you are reminded of them at a later date. Sometimes it only takes a very small thing to remind you of something you thought you had forgotten.

I have received many comments from my E-mail friend OZ and a few others, which I include, as their comments also help me compare today with the yesterdays of the past.

OZ's Email: "I am amazed that you have seen so many changes in your lifetime. I never even look back to say 'I remember when'. The only difference is there really haven't been too many changes so far other than more wars, more people and more traffic, and that's about it."

Maybe the changes are going by so fast my friend OZ doesn't realize they are changes, but fast changes are going on constantly. I am sure she will look back some day and realize there really have been a great many changes, even in these days. They may be completely different from what I have seen. Electronic gadgets are an example. They are constantly changing. You buy one and before you get it home it seems to be obsolete.

The electric typewriter was a wonderful improvement in its day but now the great electric typewriter is now obsolete, replaced with the computer. The computer is gradually being challenged with the phone and the "tablet". What is next?

Changes, oh how true, and oh how many. As I write this I am 91 years now and I have seen tremendous changes in my short life-time. Yes, 91 years is a short time when you look back and can realize how really short 91 years really are. Remember when you were a little kid a year seemed to take forever. Well, at 91 a year rushes by like a jet airplane.

Cars were starting to become very popular by the 1930's. Horses had become pretty much obsolete, even for farm work. Horses are used completely different now from how they were used a hundred years ago. Now look what is used and is available—huge, motorized, equipment. You would never see a horse working on a highway now and rarely even on a farm. The horsepower on a farm today is in the form of motorized equipment. Yes, time flies fast and faster and changes are made.

It doesn't seem very long ago that the telephone had operators who assisted you to reach the person you were calling. "Operator", she said first, then she asked "Number Please"? She was replaced with phones you could dial yourself. Long distance calls were a separate cost on your home phone. The phone was connected to the wires in your home. Now you have the cell phone which doesn't have wires or separate charges for long distance calls. You can even take pictures and use it like a computer—so what is next? Change, we just cannot seem to even catch up with what is going on and, whoosh, it has changed again. There are constant electronic changes going on all the time, and that is also changing how we live our lives.

Future changes are fast knocking at the door right now, whether we want them or not. The Post Office replaced the

Pony Express over a century ago. Now, can you imagine the Post Offices being gone? It seems like they are being replaced by Fed Ex, Email, and UPS. Junk mail and bills is the kind of mail we get any more. Postage rates keep climbing higher. Plastic credit cards and online transactions are replacing the written check. With the written check also disappearing, it's less mail at the Post Office. Today newspapers are disappearing the same way the milkman and the laundry man and the ice man did. Newspaper and magazine publishers consider developing paid news subscriptions to the phone. Books are heading towards being electronic so maybe we will not be seeing books to hold in our hands for much longer. The cell phone has replaced the Land Line telephone in many homes and businesses.

Innovative new music is not being given a chance to get to the people who would like to hear it. TV and movies from their computers, and playing games takes up the time that used to be spent watching TV. Prime time shows have degenerated. Cable rates are skyrocketing and commercials seem to run longer than the story. Now our possessions are still in our lives, but we have them on a computer. There is no privacy any more. There are cameras all over and they are even built into your computer and cell phone. All we will have that can't be changed are memories. We have no choice but to accept the coming changes. The world changes as we walk on it… The only thing not changing is change itself.

LONG LIVES RUN IN THE FAMILY

In this present year I am not the only long lived one of my family. The following email was received from a cousin who stated: "I don't know how I got to be 99, but here I am and enjoying it. Lots of things I can't do, but so what? I am enjoying my life. God has been exceptionally good to me. I feel my health is as good as I could hope for and my family really treats me fine. I miss being outdoors a lot and I have quit driving and don't regret it. It was time. I enjoy your emails. Tell all "hello" for me. My best and God Bless you. Signed, Bill Horine.

Bill is a cousin of mine. He is the son of Earl Horine. I have only seen him twice in my lifetime; due to the fact we live so many states apart. Bill was a long time contributor to writing about outdoor life and had a great many articles published. This outdoor life and writing is really what he misses at this time. He is now 99 years of age in this year of 2014. I also have other cousins who are in their late 90's. I am 92 as I write this. We all have the same set of grandparents, John and Jenny Horine. At least one of us should reach the age of 100. I think there are probably a few more cousins who are in their nineties, but as I said, we live several states apart and I really don't know all of them.

In this present year of 2014 many people are wondering why folks do not congregate together as they did in the past. I believe I now realize just why they do not. Today people don't seem to "need" anyone else because they are "self-contained" by the many electronic gadgets in their homes. This is too bad. It would be very unbearable if all the modern gadgets were to suddenly disappear. Most people would not be able to handle it for very long if that happened. They don't realize now what it would do to them to be suddenly isolated and alone. Compare that to being locked up in a room all alone with no one to see or talk to. You might even compare it to being in jail. It is the gadgets that cause people to forgo congregating with others. Today they don't *"need"* anyone else any more. I think electricity would be missed the most for myself because it runs so many labor saving devices, including the pumping of water and running of machinery.

During the depression years between 1929 and 1941 we had no television, cell phones, nor electronic games. Some may not even have had a radio. Our sole entertainment consisted of dances at a school house, neighborhood picnics and potluck dinners. The neighbors would have a party at their home and many whole families would come. Sometimes they would play cards and other times they would play a fiddle or other instrument for the enjoyment of their neighbors. They seldom refused an invitation to the home of their neighbor. If you lived in a rural area without electricity you might be fortunate enough to have a battery operated radio. Most likely you did not have a telephone. Since you did not have electricity, you used either a coal oil lamp or a gasoline lantern for light.

You depended on your neighbors and you contacted them whenever you could. Neighbors were very important to you or else you were isolated and lonesome. All these gadgets like TV, cell phones, electronic tablets and computers have replaced people gathering together as they had in the past. People have become self-contained and don't seem to need anyone else for companionship as they did in the past. It's too bad, very much too bad. Gadgets really cannot replace the comfort of association with other people.

In the 1920 era, a lot of the country folks used horses, especially in the winter time. As I've noted, the roads were not paved to any extent and cars did not have the horsepower to go through the deep muddy, rutted dirt roads that might also be covered in deep snow. I remember the rural mail carrier used an automobile in the summer time but a horse and buggy in the winter months. The mailman also delivered groceries and at times passengers. The rural mail carrier would deliver a letter between houses if they were on his route and he came to their house before he got back to the post office. He would cancel the stamp and put it in the mailbox of the person addressed on the envelope. Oh yes, the postage at that time was three cents for a letter. You could write a penny postcard also. Of course the card had the stamp printed in the corner. Card and stamp was a penny. While the costs seem really low today, money was very hard to come by so the price seemed a bit high. The mail carrier went out of his way to help the people on his route and was a friend to everyone. You looked forward to his arrival each day. He was your contact with the outside world. Generally there was someone from the house waiting to visit with the mail carrier when he arrived. This is not the case today.

My grandparents had a good farm dog, named Rover. He would bring in the cows at milking time. All they had to do was tell him "Bring in the cows," and out he would go, hunt them up, and herd them into the barn. The cows never argued with Rover. Rover used to run out and bark at the wheels of the mail carrier's rig. He was finally broken of the habit one time when a tire blew out while he was pursuing the car. It must have finally scared the dog half to death. He learned his lesson and never chased a car again.

Speaking of lessons, Rover taught me one. I was sitting with Rover on the steps in front of the house and pointed at some chickens and instructed Rover to "sic 'em". If I had pointed at the cows or horses he would have brought them in, but he knew better than to chase chickens, but I must not have. Rover, instead of chasing the chickens, nipped at my hand. He didn't bite me; he just let me know in his own way that I was wrong. He knew better than to chase the chickens. I never tried that again. Rover was a good farm dog; evidently I wasn't so very good myself, only a bit mischievous at the age of five or six.

SOME GOT BY

How did some people get by fairly well during the great depression, while others did not? Those who had some land planted gardens, which made a lot of difference. Maybe they had chickens and would trade some eggs for seeds. If you had something you could trade you would find someone else who needed what you had. In return they would trade something for what you needed. A lot of bartering went on. I do remember also that people shared some of what they had with those who did not have. The farmer usually had meat because he raised cattle, sheep, chickens, and pigs. He did his own butchering. He did not run to the meat market for his meat. He had milk and cream. He sold eggs, and cream, which paid his property tax, gave him a few cents for essentials and plenty of food for his family. He usually helped others out very frequently. It was the city dweller who suffered the most privation. You could also rent a house for as low as five dollars a month. At 25 cents an hour, that took twenty hours of work to pay the rent. Some people would allow a family to move into their house, rent free, in order to have it taken care of. The one who moved in usually took good care of it and didn't do anything to destroy it. That is not the case today. Today people would be afraid to let someone into their house for free because so many are destructive instead of helpful. A big change of values now.

I do remember one destitute family who lived in the woods and used branches and leaves for shelter. They had woven the branches in such a way as to give some kind of protection. I do not know how long they lived that way, but I remember my grandparents gave them milk, eggs, and probably some meat when they butchered. The man of the family may have helped with the butchering at the time they gave them the meat. I also remember seeing they had a large cook stove inside that shelter. They must not have lived that way for a very long time. I do not know. I did hear that they moved to Spokane at some time. I never saw them again later.

There was also the fact of government "prohibition" of the manufacture and the sale of liquor. The demand for whisky then became "big business" and brought out the big-time gangsters back in the eastern states. Many a "little" guy had a still some place on his property and sold whiskey (sometimes called "white lightening, or "moonshine", or some other name) by the gallon to anyone who would buy it. They raised a lot of corn up in the mountains and the best way they could get it to market was in liquid form. They began selling by the gallon rather than by the bushel.

The "Recipe" (courtesy of "The Waltons") was quite a popular product. Whisky was not available in stores so individuals made and sold it, hoping not to get caught. A few were actually caught, but many also were not. All were afraid and were constantly watching for the possibility of a raid from what was referred to as "The Federals." Those who got caught with a still were sent to jail. Those who were making the whiskey were constantly on the alert for a possible raid, always afraid of being caught and sent to jail away from their families. The individual involved was usually a single family man making a small amount of alcohol to sell in secret. They would take it out to farms or at times into the city, always trying to be careful not to be noticed.

My knowledge of the "whiskey trade" is only what I discerned as an eight to ten year old kid. It seems like several "country" people either made the whiskey and put it into gallon or quart jars or knew someone who was making it. Seldom did anyone ever inform on them, maybe because they were either making it or selling it or using it themselves.

I really cannot compare it to the present day problem with narcotics. I cannot describe the difference between the two types of illegal action, but there is. Maybe the difference is the amount of violence involved with narcotics versus the making of whiskey by the small-time individual. The home brew was done on a very small scale two or three gallons at a time. Whiskey can ruin lives but not to the extent that narcotics do.

It all ended when the laws of prohibition were lifted around 1933 and it became legal to sell alcohol in the stores. It was no longer profitable to handle homemade "moonshine" and the trade died out. You soon began to hear someone say "If you boys want to take a drink, that's your business, but buy it in town, don't make it yourself. Maybe you don't agree with the government on all things, but a majority of us elected them, and it's up to us to stand by them and their laws."

CHANGES KEEP ON COMING

Since I was a kid small airplanes went on to become bigger ones and people started using them to get from one place to another. I have seen changes from horse and buggy used to travel where we wanted to go, to using automobiles for everything, and from horses used to plow fields, to large tractors that do the job, from telephones that required an operator, to cell phones that seem to do everything, and from typewriters to computers. Everything has changed and things I grew up with would be entirely strange to the kids nowadays. People have changed also.

When I was growing up most kids had to mind their parents or they had a trip behind the woodshed, now it seems like the kids are telling the parents what to do. I see many cases where a child as young as 2 years of age actually rules the home—not the parents as it should be. The parents are afraid to say no and the child is never disciplined. The child needs guidance, which he does not get. The parents do not seem to know how to discipline their children, You can talk to some children, others absolutely are too stubborn so other means are necessary to convince them. A paddling is a last resort after other means have been used. The parents are the ones who are put in jail if they have done anything like paddling the kids' buttocks to make the kids do what they are supposed to do. A paddling is not a beating. A beating is not discipline, it is abuse. Then some people wonder why so many young people end up in jail. It's probably why the jails are so full. *The kids never learned how to follow the rules of life. Discipline by the police is jail time. Jail is their way of paddling their buttocks. Jail itself is very cruel. A jail is a cage.* Too bad it ever comes to that. *A swat on the seat of the pants is much more kind to the kids than jail is; it is quicker and more humane than jailing in a cage.*

The problem seems to come from the parents not knowing how to discipline their kids. Some children can be talked to, but some are so stubborn that the only solution seems to be a swat on the seat of the pants. A child should be talked to first, but if that doesn't work it is not kind to the child to let them continue to misbehave. Many adults were raised without discipline in their own lives and now don't know how to handle their own children when they misbehave, making for a vicious cycle. Discipline is very necessary for everyone of any age, adult or child, or we could not survive.

EMAILS, STORIES & THOUGHTS

A WALK BACK IN TIME

Why do none of these nostalgia emails ever mention Mumbledy Peg? Did no one but my childhood friends play this game? If not, I wonder where they learned it. It must have been from someone's older brother. It was somewhat dangerous. It was more popular than marbles. And most girls did not play mumbledy peg. Maybe they just did not like the idea of a jackknife as the boys did. They also may have been afraid of getting cut with that jackknife blade. No one seems to play it any more. I don't remember how the game was played, except the use of a jackknife being balanced in some way. I don't believe I would like that game. It was a game for boys only. In this day any boy with a jackknife would be kept under observation and seen as a suspicious character.

Oz wrote: "I never heard of Mumbledy Peg, never wore gym clothes, thought they were ugly. I never wore sneakers growing up, in fact had my first pair when I was in my 40's. My parents never hit me I didn't have a dog and never got an allowance. My mother never wore silk stockings, heels, or jewelry, just a plain old house dress."

She also said that New Jersey still pumps your gas for free. There is a station around her house that still does that, which is extremely rare today (Oregon still pumps your gas for you. In fact it is against the law to let you pump your own gas. I like that law). Oz also wrote it was before her time to have glasses or whatever in soap boxes, only detergent inside the box. Her mother said they got a "depression dish" when they went to the movies. Now that "depression glass" is an expensive collector's item.

The closest she ever got to car hops is a fast food restaurant. She lived in the city, with tar and cement, and no one had grass. You still can get penny candy on the Net, and it doesn't cost too much to order. The Nuns at her Catholic School didn't believe in hitting, but "we got blessed with Holy Water". She says: "Would I like to go back???? You betcha."

That was in answer to the article I had sent to her. That item was showing girls dressed in shorts and shirts, and wearing gym shoes, sometimes referred to as sneakers. When I went to North Central High School in Spokane, we made our own gym suits. I thought they were quite nice. They consisted of a blouse and shorts—or sometimes called "rompers" as they were all one piece, not separate. You did not need to be ashamed to be seen on the field in those outfits.

Some of those old pictures and people's comments reminded me of more things past also, for instance, the car keys. We would leave the car out in the open with the keys in it, and the car was not locked. The car was rarely stolen either. We even went on vacation and did not lock the doors to the house. Sure would not do that today, unless we wanted to lose the car and our household furnishings. It did happen occasionally then but not to the extent it does today.

When we lived in Idaho in the1940's we had a 500 gallon gasoline tank. My husband was in the trucking business is why we had that big tank. Gas was rationed then and gas rationing stamps were hard to get. Anyway that tank of gasoline was left out about 50 feet from the road and no locks on it. It was on a platform, not underground—strictly out in the open. We never lost any gas, but we did not go on vacation while we had it either.

We never heard of drugs, other than prescriptions. Things have really changed since the 1940 era. People's attitudes, living styles, and the English language have been greatly changed, and not for the better in my opinion.

WHO CONSERVED THE ENVIRONMENT BEST?

The story goes: An older person was checking out at the store and the young cashier told the older lady that she should "*bring your own grocery bags* because plastic bags aren't good for the environment". She then went on to accuse "*the older generation does not care enough to save our environment for future generations, and they are wasteful.*" She thought it was a problem today and that the older generation was to blame.

We had our groceries put up in brown paper bags, and sometimes they were put into a cardboard box if the size of the purchase was large. We used the bags for many things like wrapping our household garbage. Those bags were used to cover our school books to protect them from wear or from being defaced with our scribbling. That way we could also personalize our books. The teacher would show us how to best fold the bags to fit our books. In fact it was one of our first lessons of each season, and required. If a person was at all artistic the covers on the books became very attractive, sometimes done in color and sometimes just in ink, and other times used to obtain friends autographs.

Who conserved the environment best? Those using present recycling or past methods? The email I received sure reminded me of how we recycled things in the past. I really do believe we did a much better job of recycling then than is done today. If there was a bottle laying in the street some kid would pick it up and turn it in for a candy bar or whatever two cents would buy at the time. The bottles were washed and reused.. Not so today. Today the bottles are plastic and are mostly thrown into the garbage can or left lying in the street. Only a few people turn them in now. Too many people won't be bothered to collect and turn them in even to get the refund they were charged for. If a penny is lying on the street, no one bothers to pick it up. While they can't buy much for a penny, a hundred of them makes a dollar and that will buy a little something.

I have several sheets of S&H Green Stamps. I kept them for nostalgia, loved getting them. They were a great incentive to shop at certain stores, which reminds me of my shopping ways, even today. If the container is one I can use after it is empty I will choose that item over another with "throw-away" containers. Too much stuff is thrown away that could be used or reused.

Back when I was young our milk came in glass bottles that were returned, washed and reused over and over. The milk bottle was worth ten cents at the grocery store if you turned it in. Do you remember home delivered milk with cardboard stoppers. Oh how I wish milk came in glass bottles now. Milk keeps better and tastes better in glass containers. It is hard to find anything in glass bottles any more. Everything is in a plastic container. We did the same with beer bottles. The store sent them back to the plant to be sterilized and refilled. That is really recycling. If we found a beer bottle we would take it to the store and receive two cents for it, and that two cents would buy us some candy. Bottles are thrown into the trash today because people don't want to be bothered with recycling them even to get the deposit refund. Today milk comes in a cardboard box or plastic jug, never refilled. More trash is the result. We spent summers riding our bikes. working the hula hoops, and visits to the pool. Eating Kool-Aid powder with sugar was fun, Soda pop machines that dispensed glass bottles were worth a visit. Soda pop machines were worth a visit. We didn't pay a deposit on the bottles but we returned them to the store and received a few cents for them. They were washed sterilized, and refilled. This is never done any more.

We didn't have an escalator so we walked up stairs. We walked to the grocery store, to school, the library, and we didn't climb into an automobile every time we had to go two blocks. When we mowed the lawn we used a push mower, not one with a gasoline engine. We washed the baby's diapers because we didn't have the throw-away kind. We even made our own diapers with flannel yardage. People today probably don't even know what a cloth diaper is. We dried clothes on a line, not in a dryer. In the winter we hung the clothes on the clothesline outside even in freezing weather. After they were freeze dried we brought them inside to finish drying the dampness out of them. Wind and sun did a good job with our laundry. We would wash the clothesline before hanging the clothes on it. You would walk the length of each line with a damp cloth around the lines. If you didn't wash the line the dust that had accumulated on it would leave a dirty line on your clothes. You would gather the clothes pins in when removing the clothes. If left out they would deteriorate, so inside they came. We did our best to conserve our resources. We didn't waste our money either as it was too scarce to afford to waste it. Kids wore hand-me-down clothes from their brothers or sisters, or cousins or other relatives, not always brand-new clothing. We were glad to get those 'new' items from someone else. When we did get new clothing they were plain and not name brand clothes called designer clothes. In fact, we never even heard of 'designer clothing.' If there was any kind of tear in the clothing, it was repaired, not thrown away. Today you seldom see anyone mending even a simple seam rip. Instead the item is thrown into the garbage can.

Back then we had one TV or one radio in the house, not one in every room if we even had one at all. The TV had a small screen, not a large screen of any size. In the kitchen, we stirred everything by hand, not by an electric mixer. When we mailed a package we used wadded up old newspaper to protect it. We never even heard of plastic wrap or plastic 'peanuts.'

If we got thirsty and wanted a drink we drank from a water fountain, not a bottle. We sure didn't buy bottles of water at the store. That was unheard of. At times we even drank from the water hose. If we were visiting a neighbor we didn't bother our friends mother for a drink, we just went to their water hose and helped ourselves. We used pens that were called a fountain pen that we refilled with ink instead of buying a new pen. We never threw a dull razor away we replaced the blades instead of throwing it away. When a pencil got short we even found a way to add something to make it longer and useable right down to the end. One thing I remember using was the shell from a bullet that the pencil fit into. That gave the stub of the pencil quite a bit more length so we could use it longer. Nothing went to waste. We couldn't afford to let anything go to waste so we either made do with what we had or we went without. It was necessary to conserve and we did it willingly. There wasn't as much garbage to be disposed of because we found a way to use as much as was possible.

When I was growing up we took the streetcar or a bus. Kids either walked or rode their bikes to school. No one drove them to school. In comparison doesn't it seem as if no one is doing the conservation now? Isn't it sad that the current generation laments how wasteful we older folks were? It takes the older generation to realize just who is conserving the environment and doing the wasting of everything today.

I recently bought a bottle of flavored water because the cap was one that was easily opened without removing it from the bottle. Just a twist and it was open or a twist and it was closed. I keep a bottle of water near the lamp where I read and that easy to use cap came in handy because it would not spill if tipped over and it is so easy to use. Now all I have to do is keep that bottle full of fresh water. Oh yes, I fill that bottle from the kitchen faucet, not from some store. If there are two identical items on a shelf and one has a container that I can figure out how to use again, that is the one I will buy. Today the trash bins are full to the top because there is so much non-reusable stuff. It seems to be manufactured in such a way that it cannot be mended, repaired, or used again.

SEPTEMBER 11TH 2001
THE FATEFUL PLOT OF TERROR

Criminals will find a way to cause terrible things to happen. They do not need guns to kill. Even airplanes can cause major problems when used by terrorists.

This event that happened was not memory triggered by email, but by Television. I was born not very long after the end of World War 1 and have lived during several more wars. It seems as if the wars never end as there are many kinds of warfare. This terrorism is simply another kind of warfare we are endurng now. The terrible events that occurred on September 11 in 2001, is now known as "nine eleven" (9/11). This terrorism simply and ironically became the same 9-1-1 number as the emergency number we call when we need help. It is becoming crowded by the never ending number of terror events going on in this and some other countries.

I will not say much about it except the way I learned what was going on. It was six am when I got a phone call from my son, Larry, who lived in Georgia. He said *"turn on your TV"*. I said *"Why"*. He said. **TURN IT ON"** and with a voice that indicated no argument. I turned it on to the awful events that occurred that morning. Airplanes, full of passengers, were hitting the World Trade Buildings that I had visited a few months before. Airplanes were being deliberately flown into many other buildings. All air flights were cancelled everywhere. Total confusion and sorrow. Something neither I, nor most people, will ever forget. The TV cameras were following it all as it happened. Everyone on those planes perished, as well as many of those in the buildings that were hit. One plane was diverted from a building when the passengers, who realized somethng was wrong, struggled with the pilot and caused the plane to wreck into a field instead of a building. This caused fewer deaths than would have occurred otherwise. Their news had been received over their cell phones. The pilots were deliberately causing mayhem, evidently knowing they, themselves, would perish. The ones flying the planes were not the commercial pilots the airlines had hired and the mahem was organized so several planes were involved at one time.

TRAVEL
LOS ANGELES, CALIFORNIA to RIO DE JANIERO, BRAZIL on to GREECE and back to LOS ANGELES, CALIFORNIA IN 27 DAYS

April 2007—I have returned after 27 days of traveling on a Cruise Ship from California to Rio de Janiero, Brazil to Athens, Greece then back to California. I made this trip with my cousin, Elaine Smith. She used her motorized wheel chair, and I took my electric scooter. We had a ball, got acquainted with a great many people, and when either of us tried to locate the other one there was always someone who said "Elaine went that way, or Peggy went that way awhile ago" – we didn't have to ask. It got so everyone recognized us.

I left on April 5th from Los Angeles, and flew to Atlanta, Georgia, where I connected with my cousin, Elaine, from Port Orchard, near Seattle. We boarded our plane there to go on to Rio de Janiero. No time was allowed for sight-seeing there in Rio de Janiero except from the airport to the ship. What we saw of the city was from the bus. What we could see was clean and neat and points of interest were pointed out. It is an old city. We had to have a visa to enter the country and it was the only country that did require us to have a visa to pass through their country. We stopped at the ports of Salvador and Recife. We did not get off the ship at either Port. It was on this trip that *we passed over the equator twice*, once on the way down on the airplane, and again on the way North on the cruise ship. There are no markers that pointed this out to us, but we were reminded by someone on the ship.

Our dining companions were a couple from Ireland, who immigrated to the United States and now live in Portland, Oregon. Another couple had lived in the Seattle area and now live in Massachusetts. The third couple, from Australia, was two neighbors who were traveling together. This made a very interesting group and all are potential friends. We were very glad to have been assigned to dine with this group of people on this trip. They were very interesting and we had many conversations during our meals.

On the days we were at sea we had time to read, visit with other people and hear their experiences, and see the very entertaining shows furnished by the ship. For the most part, the Atlantic Ocean was calm; although I would not want to be on the ocean in a rowboat. The ocean is too big and no land in sight would be very scary to me. The huge ship we were on felt safe enough. It never occurred to me not to be safe. That ship gave me a good chance to see what a life of luxury could be like. The food was outstanding and our rooms were cleaned daily. There was even a laundry on board. We didn't lack for anything.

Our only stop in Africa was at Senegal. This is where we saw street vendors selling clothing and wood carvings of animals. They were beautiful but I did not want to carry them with me. There were elephants, camels, sea creatures, bears, etc. that were very beautifully done. Everything was a temptation. Their goods were laid out on a canvas at the docks, and the only port where there were merchants in the open, not in a building. The area appeared to be poor. Of course the vendors were quite aggressive but they did understand "no" if you made it plain. Most spoke English even if some was hard to understand completely. No matter what though, you could understand their message.

We were thoroughly disappointed because they had to skip Morocco because of terrorism threats. Elaine had made arrangements with a school teacher whom she knew there to show us around Morocco. Needless to say, those plans had to be abandoned. Elaine has traveled all over the world and extensively knows people from many countries. She had made arrangements with this teacher ahead of time to take us around Morocco. He and his wife had planned to escort us together. They were at the port waiting for us, but because of the threat, the ship would not even go near that port. It was a disappointment to everyone. The country of Libya was not entered because of the possibility of threats there also, but we knew about Libya before we left home.

We stopped at Cadiz, Spain, then on to Lisbon, Portugal, and on again to Valencia and Barcelona, Spain. So many of these cities are built on steep mountains and an example of this is Monte Carlo, Monaco. Those who visited there had a lot of stairs to climb. We could not go because of the steps, being both of us, my cousin and me, had to depend on wheels. Elaine uses an electric wheel chair and I use an electric scooter.

Many people in these European countries take a "siesta" in the afternoons, so they close down for a couple of hours in the afternoons and stay open later in the day. We went into several ports in Italy—Florence, Pisa, Livorno, Rome, Naples, Messina, and Sicily. We took a tour in Naples. If you think traffic in LA is bad, you need to see Naples. Six lanes of traffic, plus cars parked at the curb. Two lanes going north, two lanes going south and then there were two lanes going in the middle, with a curb built up on each side, one lane each way, competing with trolley cars, automobiles, busses and small motorcycles, and pedestrians. Everything was going quite fast and bumper to bumper. Our guide said the driver was an "Arteest" and believe me, he had to be good to handle a large tourist bus and not have an accident. Hundreds of cars and hundreds of motorcycles were parked on the sidewalks. Believe it or not, everything there seemed to be orderly. The streets were clean. In the residential area streets were very narrow and the "Arteest" had to be good at his job. (I am not ridiculing the speech of the guide. Her English was near perfect and her pronunciation of Artist was interesting and very expressive.) We found most people speak English all over every country we ever visited.

We observed that there were few houses as we know them; everyone lives in flats that are touching each other. We noticed this all over the many countries. If we think housing is expensive here, ours is cheap compared to those countries. Europe for the most part is now using Euros for money and the conversion of one Euro equaled $1.35 US at that time.

Our last few stops included Messina, Sicily, and Italy. Then we had another day at sea and finally Santorini, Greece and to Kusadasi, Turkey. In Kusadasi, they use the Lira and will take US dollars as well as the Euro. We found they expect you to "bargain" for prices, and prices were much cheaper than elsewhere. The place appeared very clean and there was a shopping center near the port. They feature carpets, especially. Unless you travel by automobile, you don't get to see much of the country, and as I said they mostly live in what they call flats, which we might call apartments or possibly condos.

To take any tours cost $50 or more (much more) and hotel rates were around $300 a night, so we did not take many tours, which mostly consisted of a drive around the cities and a couple of those were enough for us. When we got off the ship we found many of the streets had curbs and made it impossible to get around with a wheelchair or scooter. We found plenty to do on the ship that was interesting, such as their nice large library. I read four books, which I never seem to get around to doing at home. When we went ashore in Naples we had a chance to visit some shops, but crossing the streets was dangerous and we were always in hopes the traffic would let us cross–they did and we did get home safe.

We got off the ship in Santorini. Just like the US cities, it has grown tremendously. They had a new airport and it was many miles out of the city center. The city has grown right up to the airport, just like here. We had no time to do any sightseeing as we had been scheduled to go straight to the airport to fly to Germany to board our flight from there back to San Francisco. We did not have a chance to do any sightseeing at all.

On Wednesday morning, May 2, we left Santorini, Greece, flew to Munich, Germany, went through their airport and security process, changed planes and started for home. We went straight through non-stop from Munich to San Francisco, went through customs, and got on another plane. Elaine headed for Seattle and I returned to LA for a total of 16 flying hours to get home.

It was hard to adjust after spending 27 days with my living quarters cleaned every day. The beds were turned down at night with a chocolate candy on the pillow, a different cute animal sculpture made from towels to greet us, and a basket of fruit on a tray each evening. We had food deliciously prepared and served elegantly for every meal.

I was glad to get home by then, real glad. I got home tired but I enjoyed the entire trip. My next trip is through the Panama Canal in a week.

AROUND THE PANAMA CANAL
IN SEVENTEEN DAYS

May 2007: Last month it was a cruise from Rio de Janiero to Greece. That one was for 27 days. This month it is from Florida around the Panama Canal to San Diego. This time it was only 17 days, but by the end of the second cruise I was quite ready to be home for a while. I was home only five days between the two trips. Don't get me wrong, I enjoyed both cruises but as usual there is no place like home. You manage to get a bit homesick, after being gone for almost two months with only five days at home in between the trips.

On this trip I was traveling with my friend, Margaret Fifer and her son and daughter-in-law. First, we drove to San Diego and stayed over night so we could leisurely board the airplane in the morning. This let us leave a car at the hotel while we were gone, giving us available transportation home after the cruise. In San Diego we boarded a plane to Atlanta, Georgia, changed planes there, and went on to Orlando, Florida for a nice stay overnight in a hotel there.

Margaret and I accompanied her son, and daughter-in-law on a search for a good place to eat. Margaret also uses a scooter for traveling. We used our scooters to go to a restaurant about a mile away from the hotel. We found a very interesting place and had a nice meal. The scenery around Orlando was beautiful and we got to see quite a bit of it because we had to search out places where we could get our scooters off the sidewalk.

In the morning we boarded a bus to take us to Port Canaveral to meet our ship. These big ships are about as long as a huge city block. We boarded the ship, went through security, which is the same as at an airport, and went on to our stateroom without any difficulty. We had a very nice room with a big window for a view of the ocean and scenery.

After a day at sea we stopped at Aruba for a day. Aruba seems to be a desert island, at least it appeared that way from the seaport. Those who took tours said it appeared to them that it was quite barren in the places they were able to go yet it is visited by tourists inland and is advertised to be luxurious elsewhere. It was originally settled by pirates according to stories. Margaret and I got off the ship and scooted around without going far from the ship. We found the shops were quite neat and clean. There are always shops at the ports with vendors selling their wares to passengers willing to buy souvenirs. I purchased a ring in Aruba that I liked and which I have worn ever since. It was made of silver with diamond appearing stones and cost very little. It was evidently a very good buy for the $5.00 I gave for it. (*NOTE: I wrote that information 7 years ago and the ring is still in good condition, with all the stones intact, even after seldom taking it off during those 7 years. I got my money's worth.*)

When we stopped in several cities I bought six beautiful opal rings. The bad news is they were stolen when our Yuma house was burglarized the spring of 2014 except for the one I was wearing. It never occurred to me that we would be burglarized and left all my jewelry in the house. I lost rings, earrings, class pins, necklaces, I would say at least $3,000 worth. Oh well, by now I can only regret not taking them back to Spokane with me and learned never to leave anything of much value in an unoccupied house again.

After another day at sea we went through the Panama Canal. The country was very lush and green. It took a full day to go through the locks, traveling from the Atlantic Ocean through the locks to the Pacific Ocean. Of course it rained as we went through. They have a very long rainy season. When the canal was built no one ever dreamed that the ships would ever be so large that they could not get through. There are plans to either widen the canal or build another one beside the current one. I could not see water beside the ship, so it must have been the maximum size to go through. I understand that it cost the cruise company the sum of $65,000 to use the Canal. I do not remember where I got that information.

The canal saves days of travel to get from one side of the continent to the other. Hundreds of ships use the canal so it must also be a very big saving to go across by the canal instead of going around the Horn. I think of our ancestors who traveled around the Horn in sail boats and the dangers they went through. The time it took from leaving the east coast when they were heading to Los Angeles and to San Francisco must have been a hardship and a miserable trip. The time it took also must have been weeks; compared to the time it takes now to go through the canal. Those who took the overland way across where the canal was built later had a very very miserable trip to navigate the crossing. They had to put up with rough terrain, humid climate, miserable mosquito bites and other obstacles. They walked they did not ride.

It was hard to get close enough to the rails to view the scenery because hundreds of curious people were crowding the rails to watch our going through the locks and our scooters do take up more than a little bit of room. There were several hundred passengers on this ship and of course everyone wanted to view the scenery up close.

Following the Panama Canal and another day at sea on the Pacific Ocean, we arrived at Puntarenas, Costa Rica, and went browsing at the flea markets. There were lots of vendors near the ship. My friend and I only went about 3 or 4 blocks from the ship. She had a gold bracelet on her wrist and a couple of policemen stopped her and told her to remove the bracelet or cover it up. We were warned about that on the ship, but forgot until reminded. She did as suggested and we had no incidents happen. We saw a beautiful beach and quite a few people were playing in the water. I was impressed with the ocean water that you could see to the sand below without anything to block the view. The water was crystal clear and not cloudy. The nearby stores were quite old, but neat. The vendors' set-ups were quite inexpensive as were their prices. They had a lot of silver items as well as hand made jewelry and knick-knacks. On May 22nd, we spent the day at sea, arriving at Acapulco, Mexico the next day. We had fun visiting the nearby stores and visiting with the people. The area was quite attractive and we ventured close to the ship. The area was clean and everything was neat and orderly. We were bombarded by taxi drivers wanting to take us places and several people offered to show us around. We refused until we found out the city pays them to escort people around the town. They also work for tips. Then we decided to take them up on it and went for a "stroll" with a nice lady guide. Her English was perfect so we did not need an interpreter. It was true in almost every place we went, that the people spoke plain if not the perfect English language. The guide we chose was very accommodating and took us to places that seldom see tourists. We got to go to places we would not have otherwise seen, like local markets with the goods the local people buy, not just tourist kinds of items. Clothing, jewelry, and food items were on display for us to either buy or just look at. In places the street was almost impassable for our scooters, but our guide managed to get us around the barriers. I should make a correction here. I had a scooter and my cousin, Elaine, used a motorized wheel chair so for convenience I will just call them scooters. It was a very enjoyable excursion, making the day memorable.

If you think any of the streets around your home are rough, you should see their streets other than the main thoroughfare. The roughness of Ironwood where I live is smooth as glass compared to what we saw. Our guide had us ride in the street as there was no way to get on or off the sidewalk with our scooter and wheelchair. We had chosen a very nice friendly lady guide. She was dressed in a simple uniform of a skirt and a blouse. She went out of her way to see that we had a nice tour of places that were not tourist traps or set up just for tourists. Everything was very clean and free of trash. The car drivers obeyed her signals and either moved over or stopped for us. It was quite a sight and quite a ride. We rode our scooters through poorer sections of town. The streets were very rough but our guide got us through it. It made us appreciate what we have at home. The tour was very interesting and we really enjoyed it. We visited several shops and being away from the general area catering to the cruise ships. The prices of goods for sale at the shops were reasonable in our opinion. We did resist buying too much though as it had to be carried home in our suitcases. The day went very smooth with our competent guide and we enjoyed it thoroughly. Somewhere on this cruise I managed to buy some opal rings (later stolen) that I enjoy wearing every day, along with the silver ring I bought in Aruba.

Another day was spent at sea between Acapulco and Mazatlan. We had a really nice time at Mazatlan without going far from the ship. The people were very friendly. I will always remember Mazatlan due to a nasty experience on the way back to the ship. Having exited the transportation provided for us, I decided to make a fast run up the gangplank. I should have waited and made sure an attendant was at the gangplank to help me but I did not. I started up the gangplank, which was very steep this day, and instead of leaning forward as I should have done, I leaned backward only to have the gangplank make a slight move just as I got on, and over backward I went. My scooter landed on top of me. I hit my head on the concrete and got a nasty sore and bruise on the back of my skull. I think the padding on the back of the scooter saved my back from injury. I received great attention from the crew and in the infirmary due to the head wound. It took several hours before I was able to return to my cabin due to being light-headed and faint. A cat-scan taken after I got home did not find any permanent damage.

It was the next stop the following day where we did not get off the ship as the tenders could not accommodate our scooters. It was Cabo San Lucas where the ships sometimes cannot get into port due to the weather. Still nursing an open head wound, I was very content to stay on board for the day. Between reading, playing cards, and visiting with friends, I kept busy. We played "International Rummy," sometimes known elsewhere as "Shanghai." It is the same game but probably a very slightly different version.

Saturday was at sea so I did my laundry as we were due in San Diego on Sunday morning and it was time to go through Customs and home from there. Staff from the hotel where we left our car met us and returned us to the hotel and our vehicle. Then we went home.

I enjoyed both the trips and will be home only a short time before going to Spokane to visit family. My homesickness will not last long. I get over it in a big hurry whenever someone says "Do you want to go" and I do. I practically keep my suitcase packed all the time. (A sad note, my friend, Margaret Fifer, who had arranged the trip for several of us passed away a few years after this cruise. We will all miss her and her arranging cruise trips for several of us. She would hunt up bargains so we could afford to go.)

THIS TIME I WENT TO SPOKANE

September 2007: I have just returned from visiting my family in Spokane, Washington.

I have no immediate plans for another trip in the very near future, but as I have said before, I will go at the drop of a hat. Maybe I should just move onto a cruise ship as a permanent resident. I read in a newspaper that one elderly lady claimed it was cheaper than an assisted living residence. Claiming better care on the ship was available, she made permanent arrangements to live on a cruise ship! I'd love to join her.

I took my mobility scooter to Spokane, as I do on all my trips. In Europe, I crossed many busy streets with no traffic lights. Many highways were like freeways, especially during rush hour. All we had to do was hold up our hand and they would stop and let us cross – everyone was very polite, in city after city during my travels abroad.

It was a very busy month for me. I was in Spokane only a few days when we all went to a convention in Kennewick for four days, In Kennewick, Washington I rode the scooter on busy streets as there were many sidewalks or curbs that provided no opening to get off the sidewalks so I drove in the bicycle lane, a little nervous but, again, everyone seemed to watch out for me and I made it back to my hotel without incident. With my scooter I find I have to watch out that the sidewalks have a way to get on or off of the curb, otherwise I can get stuck with no way to proceed. The same is true for anyone using a wheelchair.

After returning to my son's home, I called several relatives to visit. I invited them to come along with me to Benewah, the place where we had all lived in Idaho for several years, only to find that one cousin was now in a nursing home and quite ill. Another cousin was helping her daughter relocate after her husband had died and could not spare the time to attend the annual picnic. This was disappointing but this is the way things turn out at times; so just my son and I attended the Benewah Valley picnic. The picnic is now held annually in the old Benewah schoolhouse which has been turned into a community center.

Before the schoolhouse was turned into a community center, the picnics were held annually at the lake area called Rocky Point. We would all bring food from home and someone would make and bring the ice cream custard. The teenage youngsters would usually take turns at turning the freezer while the ice and salt made it really solid, or until it became frozen to the consistency necessary to become real "ice cream." Ice for the freezer came from someone who had cut the ice from the lake during the winter and stored it in sawdust until it was needed in the summer. We thoroughly enjoyed that ice cream. With no refrigerators, unless we stored ice in sawdust, we could only get ice cream in town.

This picnic is now held in the one room school where all eight grades were conducted in the same room with only one teacher. I would like to point out that the teacher had to be able to teach any of the eight grades, there was seldom all eight grades filled with students at the same time. This same Benewah school, is where all three of my older children started school before we moved back to Spokane. I attended the first grade in this school for a while although I had started school in another one-room school near Viola, Idaho. One woman who attended the picnic, Mickie Walker, was going to be 100 years old the following October. She was very alert and remembered me from when we had lived in this community although we had moved away fifty-six years ago.

I missed seeing the ones who could no longer attend the picnics any more. Some were ill at the time and others had passed away. I enjoyed visiting so many who were children when we lived in the community and now were parents and grandparents attending with their own children. It was nice to spend the time reminiscing and seeing old time friends. It was an enjoyable day.

When we moved to this area in 1943, there were no telephones or electricity available. During the years we lived there the neighbors got together and put in a telephone line. Talk about a party-line! This was one, with 20 phones on the one line, but it worked. The Forest Service furnished the line for the telephone, but the citizens in Benewah furnished the poles and the labor to get it installed. Each person also had to buy their own telephone. The phones were the kind you hung on the wall and used a crank to alert the operator to get the number you wanted to reach. The phones worked quite well and everyone cooperated in the use of the phone. If someone was using the phone and someone else wanted to use it, they would cooperate and end their own call as soon as possible. I never heard of any troubles over the use of the phone by the 20 families. At this time it was still an operator who said "Number Please".

We also petitioned to get electricity into our homes. A decision of whether to go to the Washington Water Power Company or the REA (public power) had to be decided. It took a while for everyone to decide which way to go as everyone had their own ideas of which way would be the better way to go. We ended up with the Washington Water Power Company as our electrical provider. Because we had to have so many people for the power company to install the lines, we were short one house, and the elderly people who lived there in that single house said they had never had electricity before and could do without it now. In order to get the line in for everyone else the man was told they would wire his house for free and pay the basic electric bill for a year. The basic bill was only $3.00 a month and only a minimal amount of wiring had to be done to the house, so we got our power without much cost to any individual.

When we had lived in the Benewah community, the old school had an outdoor toilet. Water had to be carried from a well. Since electricity had come into the valley they now had the convenience of what electricity could do for them. They bought a pump and installed water in the building so an indoor bathroom became possible. What used to be the two old cloak rooms are now used for a boys' and a girls' restroom. No more "outhouse."

A VISIT TO THE OLD HOMESTEAD AND MINE LOCATED AT ALADDIN

A group of us went north of Spokane to visit a community called Aladdin, where my husband's grandfather had homesteaded and built a cabin in the mountains. The town and post office no longer exist. It was located between Ione and Colville, Washington. Back in the 1970's the heirs of the property decided to sell the land. The grandfather had died in 1929 and his will had never been probated. With property being willed among ten children you can imagine the mess that ensued. Heirs had died and left heirs of their own, children had been born, and widows had remarried, etc. You can imagine the mess that had to be cleared up, but one man was willing to go through the process along with my husband, one of the heirs. After nearly two years it was finally given a free title so he could buy the property.

THE PROPERTY TITLE FINALLY
CLEARED AND SOLD

The buyer of that property, Dick VanderYacht,(1931-2014) invited me and anyone else I wanted to invite along, to come spend a day there. A group of six descendants (great grandchildren of Tarje Bergland, the one who had built the cabin) drove up there one day to see what he had done to the place. I was impressed and happy to see it all. The timber had been logged off several years before and it now had a new growth of trees. Mr. VanderYachts story follows later. We enjoyed a nice day there in that old cabin that had now been restored to its original form by the new owner. This property is now used as a tree farm. It is surrounded on three sides by a national forest. Mr. VanderYacht was very hospitable, supplying us with lunch. Also, he had come from his home on the Northwest coast of Washington State (a drive of 8 hours) so he could unlock the barriers constructed across the roads into the property. He left a key with my son, Tom, and invited us to use the property anytime we wanted. We enjoyed the visit and I finally met the man I had been corresponding with via e-mail for a long time. I do hope he and his wife will visit me some day. My husband had worked with him to get the property title cleared up, but this was the first time I had ever met the man. He is also the author of a few books, which I think are equal to Louis L'Amour. "*Camp on the Crazy*" is one of the books Dick has written. I have read it and found it very interesting and well written and I recommend it. Dick VanderYacht has written for trade magazines and has at least three books in print.

I received the following email from Dick VanderYacht. Tuesday, November 28, 2006. "Vivien Fosberg (a Bergland cousin) is a good friend of mine. She worked for my company as a receptionist and secretary for several years. I've kept in close contact since she quit. It was through her that I learned about the Bergland property north of Colville that her mother and others owned. It took 18 months to get the title cleared before I could buy the place. About 60 persons owned partial interest. Vivien gave me pictures and history. I wrote the "History of Meadow Crick" Lodge and tree farm and sent a book to Eileen Berger. I usually spend three or four weeks each year at the cabin. The main problem is that it takes eight and a half hours to drive to the place from my home in Blaine,Washington. I love it there. It's quiet, clean, and peaceful there. The whole place is forested. I've done some selective logging in past years—just finished another cut in September removing dead and dying trees and where they were too thick. We found a few pockets where all trees were infected with either beetles or root rot and all were removed. No logging is permitted in the basin where the cabin is located—it is just a big park."

Febrtuaty 28, 2001—"Regarding my profession as a broker: I fished commercially in local waters and Alaska for five years when first out of high school (family profession). Quite by accident I got a temporary job working for a Customs Broker, opening packages for US Customs inspection. I planned to stay six months and return to the frozen north. By then our first son was born and my wife wanted me to stay on the beach for that reason and because I'd nearly lost my life on the big sea water when we were dating. I stayed on the job and within months received a substantial raise and got used to shuffling papers instead of wading through dead fish. After I decided to stay, I learned all I could about the business and moved from package opener to document preparation and duty computation. It is an interesting business so I applied myself and kept advancing. The broker does all paper work and sends a bill for services to the importer."

Mr. VanderYacht kept advancing until he eventually owned the business along with a partner. There is a lot more to his story, but there is too much to tell here, even though it is very interesting. He is a very talented writer and I do recommend anyone to obtain any writing he has done—whether it is magazine articles or one of his novels. All are entertaining.

We were invited to visit with Mr. VanderYacht at his "Meadow Crick Lodge".

July 18, 2007. We took him up on his invitation and we met him at the property. He supplied us with a nice lunch and we had a very enjoyable visit. This visit gave me the idea of the following rhyme.

ODE TO THE MEADOW CRICK LODGE

The Bergland Brothers, many there were
Did not farm this mountain for Douglas Fir
But silver and gold is what they sought.
They found some silver, but it was all for naught.
Eventually they sold the property to Dick VanderYacht.
Old Tarje died, which was not what was planned.
Left to the heirs of the clan named Bergland.
Undivided it lay for many a year
Heirs there were many and title was not clear.
Dick worked hard to get clear title to this neglected land.
Now it's a tree farm with a nice timber stand.
Now VanderYacht was a man who loved the place.

Named it Meadow Crick Lodge, a name with such grace.
Restored the cabin to its original form
But the barn was ruined by a big snowstorm.
He's proud of this place where his friends can gather
Hunt and fish, play pinochle and do whatever they'd rather.
On July eighteenth two thousand and seven
Tarje's great grandchildren Tom, Clarion and Norman,
With Peggy, Judy, and Nancy (and her dog named Grace)
Accepted an invitation to visit this fascinating place
Explored the land, looked over the mines,
Ate lunch in the cabin, talked about old times.
Enjoyed the day thoroughly, as they surely ought
As the guest of the man named VanderYacht.

The Judy in this rhyme was the wife of Great Grandson Clarion Bergland, not the daughter, Judi, of Thomas Bergland. Nancy was Norman's wife, and Peggy is the mother of Tommy Bergland. Probably I should call him Tommy so he is not confused with his father, Thomas. Mr. VanderYacht was a very gracious host, and made us all very welcome.

I am sorry to have to add a postscript to this story about Mr. VanderYacht (1931-2014) He was a very nice man. We enjoyed our visit with him, and am very sorry to learn of his passing away on November 19, 2014. The great grandson, Clarion Bergland, is also deceased since that visit.

A VISIT TO THE MUSEUM IN TEKOA, WASHINGTON

On Tuesday, July 8, 2008, my son, Tom, and I started out from Spokane intending to visit the museum in Tekoa, Washington as our destination.

Of course we couldn't pass up stopping at the Rockford Cemetery on the way so we could visit the cemetery where pioneer relatives reside. My husband's great grandmother, his grandparents, Tarje and Charlotte Bergland, as well as an uncle, Christian Otto Bergland. are all residents of this cemetery. There is also a memorial headstone honoring his father and mother, Edisto and Ann Maria (Anmar) Bergland, which was placed there by a granddaughter, Eileen Jensen.

Some of the tombstones are dated before 1900. At the time Otto Bergland became a resident of the cemetery it was nothing but a huge weed patch. Now it is being cared for and is a beautiful, well cared for park that Rockford can be proud of. I want to say Thank You to those who have done such a wonderful job of restoring and beautifying and maintaining this cemetery. It is now one to be proud of.

I do not know why so many of the family came to Rockford, but my father-in-law, Edisto Bergland, worked in Hurds' store in 1906. This is as much as I know about it, and as most of those who might know more are undoubtedly deceased, it would now be up to those who have written information to find out anything more. I am now 86 so I realize how very important it is that young people ask questions of their older relatives and write it down. I did not realize how much interest I would take in family history when I was a young person. With recording devices and computers available it is not the big chore today that it was in the past.

After spending a short time in the cemetery, we proceeded to go on to visit the museum in Tekoa, Washington. We intended to look up a story about Dr. Abegglen, a long time physician in Tekoa. We had heard that he had written a book about happenings around this Palouse country. I wanted a copy if it was available. We found very little of what I wanted, although he is briefly mentioned in information they have. We were quite disappointed in not finding a copy of an article supposedly written about him in the Spokane papers. Unfortunately I have not found the information I wanted.

I was interested in anything I could find about Dr. Abegglen as he was the doctor who delivered all three of my daughters. I realize that Dr. Abegglen was the best doctor we ever had. You didn't need a separate specialist; he himself was a specialist. He knew exactly what to do for any kind of illness you had, whether it was measles, chicken pox, or whooping cough, or internal illnesses. I guess you can tell I had very much confidence in his ability.

March 1945: Dr. Abegglen came clear out to the Benewah where we lived when the snow was about 18 inches deep and the roads were icy and snow was drifting. We did not have telephones or electricity at the time so my husband had to drive the 20 miles into town and get him out of bed. By the time my husband returned, Dr. Abegglen was right behind him. I was hemorrhaging and Dr. Abegglen stayed all night at our house with me until the hemorrhage stopped. I had given birth to my second daughter ten days or so before and foolishly ran up and down the stairs against my mother-in-laws advice and it had left me in a dangerous condition. I don't know of any doctor today who would do what this doctor did for me, especially considering the dangerous road and weather conditions on this early March winter night, driving out twenty miles into the country during the middle of the night and over a mountain road covered with deep snow and ice. He stayed with me several hours until morning and I was safe. He did not even charge us for this house call if I remember right.

After looking around Tekoa we noticed it is not as large as it used to be. Like a lot of towns in rural areas people have left their farms and moved out to larger cities so the town shrinks down to nothing. There were fewer stores than had been there when we and others lived in the nearby area. Another example is the nearby town, Farmington, which had been thriving with stores and other businesses and now had none of the former stores.

Farmington doesn't even have old abandoned buildings to show there had ever been anything there in the first place. Only a community center and a bank remains in that town to show there had ever been a town at all. Most of the small towns in the Palouse farming area are now becoming close to being ghost towns. They no longer have the stores or businesses they used to have. Only a few of the community buildings are what is left of the formerly thriving towns. The farmers now seem to live in larger towns and commute to the farms.

We stopped in a little café and had a very good milkshake. They had an ad displayed for the Benewah Valley annual picnic, which we planned to attend the following Sunday. We enjoyed the day in Tekoa and Rockford and recommend visiting the Tekoa Museum.

It has many interesting facts about the early settlers of the area.

WE ATTENDED THE BENEWAH VALLEY
ANNUAL PICNIC

Sunday, July 13, 2008. This is the day of the big Annual Benewah Valley picnic, where residents and former residents get together to have a good time.

We left Spokane around 9 am and made a brief stop at the Rockford Cemetary before continuing on. As we headed on Highway 95 towards Worley, and then towards Plummer, we went around a mild curve that is unbroken for a distance of 1.3 miles. I had always heard that this is the longest unbroken highway curve in the world but could not find anything about it on the computer. This is an unusually long unbroken stretch of curve. Maybe it is just a local story on a historic highway. There is a lot of information about Highway 95, but nothing about the curve. Highway 95 goes from Canada to Mexico and we drive some of the way on it when we come down to Yuma as it comes right through the city. We continued past Plummer and then on to the Benewah turnoff. The road into the Benewah area was newly graveled although still like a washboard underneath. In case you young city dwellers do not know what I mean you might compare the road to the old washboard our grandparents used to wash clothes with—very rough. Do you even know what a washboard is? I keep wondering why that road isn't paved by now.

Before starting up the mountain, we observed the pretty rolling hills with green crops. In one meadow we saw a herd of four beautiful deer. They stopped for a while and looked at us and when we kept going, they also continued on their way. As we proceeded up the mountain we noted a

126

few nice new houses. Although the road had been freshly graded, again I say the road should have been paved many years ago. I say that every time I come here and hope that some day it will be true.

I have been acquainted with the Benewah area since I was four years old and that was around 1926, over 91 years ago. I can remember coming through on this road after there had been a big forest fire. I am not sure which year that fire was. There were people here, like the Hyde and the Fletcher families who homesteaded in the area in 1918, soon to be a century. Only a few of their descendants are still here now.

When I get anywhere near this area I think about the highway construction going on between Potlatch and Tensed with horses pulling the huge scraper. Now instead of horses, they have huge tractors. What a difference there is in the equipment they had then and what is available now. That had to be around 1927 when I was about four or five years old. What a difference between now and then. I think of these things when I go through this area. I-95 was an important paved road between Canada and Mexico at a time when paved roads were still quite scarce.

When we arrived at the Benewah Community Center (the former schoolhouse) there was a beautiful matched team of black and white horses pulling a carriage. The horses were like identical twins. I was really impressed with the great beauty of these two horses. Some of the people attending the picnic were being given a ride around the yard and evidently enjoying it very much. It reminded me of the ones I saw in New York City many years ago with people riding around

Central Park in the same kind of carriage. I was really impressed with the great beauty of these two horses.

As we were being directed to the parking area, we stopped long enough to deliver our part of the picnic lunch. This was not an ordinary lunch but a smorgasbord spread. It seems like everyone went all out to bring a variety of food. No one went away hungry as there was not only variety but, as always, a plentiful amount of food.

After lunch there was entertainment and then the annual auction started. The auction is for items donated to raise funds to maintain the building and grounds. Someone had freshly painted the playground equipment and it was in tip-top shape. Several children were enjoying the merry-go-round which many of us played on as young children ourselves.

The items being auctioned varied by quite a bit. The largest item was a cord of wood—in fact it ended up being two different cords of tamarack, wood that burns hot and is easy to split. I know how easy Tamarack is to split as I have split many a hunk of wood for my kitchen stove when we lived in the Benewah. That is why I especially liked the tamarack wood because it was so easy to cut and took very little effort. Included in the auction were items to wear, items for automobiles, coupons for beauty shop work, aids to make women beautiful, toys for children and some for adults. When a raffle drawing was held and a man won a doll, he donated it back for someone else to get. Someone won a log playhouse, built and donated by someone just for the auction; people really care enough to work to keep this area alive. There were several items that went into the raffle and two different people won dolls with handmade knit or crocheted dresses. One person won a small suitcase almost identical to one I bought two days before for $29. He got it on a ticket he bought for three tickets for a dollar, so he really got a bargain. The only difference in that suitcase and the one I bought is his was blue and the one I purchased was black. He may not realize what a big bargain he really got. They were very nice bags. It was at this auction that I had donated one of my books called "Who Cares Who Milks the Cow". The book is not about cows, but a young woman who took on the care of an infant whose mother was killed in a mud slide. The auction brought a high bid of $85. I offered to donate 20% of any further sales of the book that day and several were sold.

A VISIT TO THE OLD NEIGHBORHOOD

July 2005: On this visit to the Benewah Valley Picnic, my son, Tom, took my cousin, Betty Swofford, and me on a tour of the area around Benewah and Alder Creek. We noted the many changes made in the past 50 years. There are a lot of new people, a few of the old-timers, new houses, and old houses that were no longer there. Gone was the house we lived in; only the light pole still standing was left. The House formerly occupied by the people who had originally homesteaded early in the century—the Hyde family—and later owned by the Ray Pease family, was gone. The new barn built for the Pease family no longer existed. In fact, the old Post Office was located on the Hyde place, and now shows no signs of anything ever having been there. The old Marquardt mill left no clue of any kind. The "post office" building had been located by the entrance gate to the Hyde place, directly in line with the road branching off the Benewah Road to Alder Creek. There is no sign whatsoever of any of the buildings that had been there for so many years.

We had a time locating where my uncle, Ray Horine, had lived up the road about a mile towards Alder Creek. Everything had changed; buildings gone, trees and brush grown up, roads grown over with more trees and shrubs. They had lived there for a great many years with no water. They tried to dig a well but did not hit water. All their water was hauled in from elsewhere. About the only modern convenience they had was electricity when it was brought into the area. They did hit a spring one time but the water was full of iron—yellow and bad tasting. They could not even use it for washing clothes, or it would have discolored the clothes, making them look like they were rusty. There was a nice spring elsewhere but it was on someone else's property, quite a distance from their place. That spring was too far away to do them any good. After their daughters graduated from grade school they moved to St. Maries so the girls could go to high school.

There were also quite a number of changes in the Alder Creek area, just as it has been all over the Benewah area. With new people and new buildings the Benewah Valley and Alder Creek are now like a whole new country. It is hard to recognize anything other than the schoolhouse that is now the community center. The past fifty years have seen so many changes that it makes me wonder what the next fifty years will be like.

MORE ABOUT PEOPLE WHO LIVE IN THE BENEWAH VALLEY

July 13, 2008: I interviewed Billy Fletcher (who was the auctioneer, along with Benewah resident Mr. Hart) to get some of the following information. His grandparents, Georgia and Bill Fletcher, homesteaded in the area around

1918, raised chickens and sold eggs and cream to the creamery in St. Maries. It will soon be a century (2018) since the Fletcher family settled in the Benewah community.

The Fletchers had two children, a son, Esta, and a daughter, Alta. Their son, Esta and daughter-in-law Lucille also raised chickens and sold cream and eggs, not only in St. Maries, but to those neighbors needing eggs, milk, and cream.

I remember they had a beautiful Jersey cow. Jersey cows are known for the large amount of cream in their milk. This reminded me of the following verse that I had saved about twenty years ago and enjoyed it. There was no author shown at that time, and I do not have a clue as to who wrote it. I was fascinated by the quite surprising ending. Hope you also like it.

They strolled the lanes together;
The sky was studded with stars;
He walked her to the pasture gate,
And lifted for her the bars.
She raised her brown eyes to him—
There was nothing between them now;
For he was the farmer's hired man,
And she was a Jersey cow.

Esta Fletcher was a long time employee at the local Marquardt Saw Mill in Benewah. Esta and Lucille were a very popular and important asset to the Benewah community. It will soon be a century that the Fletcher families have represented the Benewah community. There have been a lot of changes in that century. I have pretty well repeated some of this information on page 199 with a small amount added about the Fletcher family. This was an important family for this community then and evidently the descendants of the original Fletchers still are. It will be a century next year (2018) that this family has represented the community.

Esta was one of the many residents who worked in the Marquardt Saw Mill, which was located on the Benewah Creek, about a mile east of the Benewah schoolhouse. Billy Fletcher was born to Esta and Lucille Fletcher in Benewah and has lived here all his life. Billy Fletcher now lives on the old Hans Sether place about half a mile off the Benewah Creek road. It had always been one of the nicest places in the area. I believe there is now a new home on the property.

I remember visiting Hans and Mrs. Sether when I was about five or six years old. I would walk past their place along with Alta Fletcher, on our way to and from school.

Alta was the daughter of Georgia and Bill Fletcher, Esta's sister. Mrs. Sether would give me some cookies and a glass of milk. Mr. and Mrs. Sether raised two boys, Archie and Frank Miller, but I do not remember their going to school when I did. A little more about Hans Sether later

The Marquardt Saw Mill employed quite a number of people in the area. This mill had a flourishing logging and lumber industry in the past. There had been several sawmills in this area at one time. They are all gone now and there is not much evidence that they ever existed. My husband hauled many truck loads of lumber from the Marquardt Mill to Spokane and Moses Lake that was used to build homes in both cities.

My son and I fully enjoyed both visiting with the old-timers and the newcomers to the Benewah Valley. As they advertise the annual get-together around the country, I recommend that everyone who wants to have a nice time should attend one of the annual picnics. These old fashioned kinds of get-togethers are fast disappearing so if you don't want to miss out on a fun way to spend a day, go next year. It is usually held the next Sunday after the Fourth of July. All it costs you is to bring a covered dish to share with the others who come. Visit with others and get acquainted with new people and become friends with them. A good time is guaranteed.

HOW I MET MY FUTURE HUSBAND

One time, in 1938, while on a visit to my aunt and cousins in Farmington, Washington my cousins took me over to the Alder Creek area in Benewah. We had an uncle, Ray Horine, and cousins in Alder Creek. While visiting that uncle I met Tom Bergland. It was two years later that a former Benewah neighbor. Frank Miller, came up from Benewah to visit our family in Spokane. Frank took my mother and me to visit the Berglands who had moved up to Spokane and were running a garage and gas station in Hillyard. Well, I liked that good looking Bergland fellow and when he called me for a date to come down to the Benewah for a dance being held in the schoolhouse, of course I accepted. A year later we were married and that marriage lasted sixty years until his fatal accident in 2001.

ANOTHER VISIT TO
SPOKANE, SEPTEMBER 2009

I got a phone call early in September asking me if I was sent an airline ticket, would I be interested in flying up to visit in Spokane. After all the arrangements were made and approved we found it was about $150 cheaper to fly out of Los Angeles instead of Ontario. So on the day of departure we headed for the Los Angeles airport. As it was in the middle of the afternoon, the traffic wasn't too bad. Of course we missed the right turnoff to make a smooth arrival at LAX, so we got a chance to see some of the city of Los Angeles as we tried to find our way back to the terminal. The exit into the airport is not marked very clearly so if you are not in the right lane of traffic at the right time you get a chance to try to find your way around. If you are not familiar with that area, you get to go sightseeing and hope you hit the correct street to arrive at your destination.

After we found the right place to alight from our vehicle, we found someone to help unload my scooter. As we had printed out our boarding pass before leaving home I had a smooth ride to the elevator and then through security. The security people were very nice to me here (not like the ones a couple of months earlier in Kansas City—didn't like them at all). I got to ride my scooter right up to the door of the airplane and the attendants took it someplace and loaded it on the plane, ready to ride right along with me to my destination. When I got off the plane it was right there waiting for me.

The timing of our arrival at the airport was pretty good, as I didn't have to wait very long for the plane to arrive at the gate. The plane landed in Sacramento and after everyone whose destination was Sacramento had departed from the plane there was about half an hour layover before the plane was reloaded to proceed on to Portland. I was invited to visit the cockpit and talk to the pilot. I asked him how he could handle all the instruments (there seemed to be hundreds of them) and he told me that was why there were two pilots flying the planes. I can see why an amateur couldn't just drop in and fly the plane. It must take quite a bit of training to learn how to handle all those instruments.

I was so interested in visiting with the pilot, that I didn't notice all the people boarding and walking behind me to their seats. This airline is Southwest and they don't assign seats—you pick your own. Your choice of seats is governed by the time you arrive at the gate and get in line after the priority boarding arrangements of people with children and the disabled. I nearly lost my seat. But one of the other nice passengers who was alert chased everyone away who would have taken my seat. I had chosen the bulkhead as it gave me more leg room. I really appreciated the concern of the other passenger as my legs cramp up to the point of not being able to stand on them if they are crowded.

When we landed in Portland, the layover was not very long and I stayed in my seat. The arrival in Spokane was very smooth and by the time I was ready to depart the plane, my scooter was waiting for me at the door. My son and daughter-in-law met me at the baggage area, picked up my suitcase, and we headed for their home.

I grew up in Spokane and it hasn't changed too much since I left there, except for the population increase, like most of the country. The increase has caused everything to spread nearly all the way out to the Idaho state line. I remember when I was a teen-ager going "out to the country" to pick strawberries. Now all I can say is, "Where is the country? There is no more country." All this brings back memories of what happened at one strawberry patch. My moher would pick a few berries in a row and then when it looked like the next row was better she would move there. Well, the owner, who was an elderly Italian man, told her "You Picka da here, picka da dere and picka all over the patch." Guess it impressed me at the time because I never forgot his telling her that she couldn't pick that way in his field. Now there are fewer strawberry fields. Instead there are more houses and more businesses.

After a few days, my son took us to a dinner show located at the state line called "The Rocking B Ranch." The minute you arrived you were invited to have all the coffee, water, and lemonade you wanted. It is held in a large barn, which I imagine may have been a dairy barn. Old farming machinery was throughout the building and tools hung on the walls. All was authentic old machinery now replaced with power instead of horses and cattle. It was very interesting and all brought back childhood memories of my Grandparents and their farm.

The entertainment started out with a family group playing country music. You should have heard the way two of the youngsters played all the instruments along with their parents. I had a chance later to talk to the younger ones and asked them their ages. The two boys were eleven and thirteen. These kids were very talented on all the instruments, but I was most impressed at how they played the fiddle. I really envy their ability. While the fiddle was especially good, they were efficient on the guitar and mandolin also. I had a chance to compliment them on their performance, which I had enjoyed.

The family group played for about an hour, then they announced there was a performance at the outdoor theater and all were invited to go outside to that show. It was a slapstick play about a great shoot-out. After the villain was slain it was announced that the dinner was ready to be served, buffet style. It consisted of roast beef, barbequed ribs, apple sauce, beans, salad, baked potatoes, greens, and desert. All the food was delicious and there was plenty of it.

After the meal, another group of entertainers came on stage. They were great and again they all performed with guitars, fiddles, base fiddle, and all the other instruments of a country band. The lady who played the fiddle was a fifth place fiddle Champion of the United States. In my opinion she should have been a first place winner. She could really make that fiddle sing. One performance she did was to make the music sound like a bird singing, even identifying which species it was. To say the least, the evening was one to remember. I enjoyed it immensely. This was real country music, not rock-and roll that is now called country music. One act consisted of the employees of the restaurant crew coming on stage and doing a lively square dance. Oh what the people of today are missing when they don't have the old barn dances and the great square dances and the very friendly get-togethers. We tried to go again the next year but it was no longer in business.

All of this brought back more memories of how my uncle, Ray Horine, and his family would play for our Benewah, Idaho community dances. My two cousins could pick up any stringed instrument and play it immediately, even if they had never seen it before. In addition to good music there was the potluck dinner. Sometimes there would be an auction of something like a pie and the person winning the auction would get to eat with the one who had made the pie. I miss this kind of good entertainment. It is very rare any more.

The old barn dances were fun, but for some reason you don't hear much about them any more. People nowadays really don't know what they are missing. Sure is too bad. All this good entertainment was free too. People were glad to volunteer their talents and didn't expect to be paid for it. The potluck dinners that accompanied the music showed off the ability of the cooks, who brought special dishes for everyone to enjoy. These are the kind of the "Good old Days" I would like to see returned. We did not have the convenience of electricity or even running water, but we had good neighbors and many good times. I miss them.

Too bad the people of today have become so friendly with their electronic gadgets that they don't "need" the association of other people like in the past. Without those gadgets as friends, their "friends" would be dead. Too bad, really, it is too bad.

THE TRAFFIC TICKET

We hear about people who get tickets through the mail after they have been photographed speeding or going through a stop sign. If you ever get a $40 ticket for that, do not do what one idiot did—by return mail he sent a picture of two $20 bills.

The police returned a picture of a pair of handcuffs. He got the hint and paid the fine.

To avoid a ticket, just obey the law and be careful how you drive, and don't be an idiot.

FIREFLIES

I saw fireflies for the first time one evening when we were traveling through the central states. I think it was in Missouri. They were quite fascinating to me. Fireflies can happily occupy an entire evening. Reminds me of the story of one little boy who told his grandmother that fireflies were just mosquitoes that followed you inside and needed a flashlight so they could see.

THE BLIND AND DEAF CAN BE AMAZING

Email Subject: A deaf-mute girl, sat on a horse that she had ridden for only three weeks!! She was training it for a client. She rides without a saddle, or halter and bit, and with no voice commands. She was using the method used by American Indians. Yet, having no voice and no hearing, she has persevered and achieved victory !!!

My Comment: Sometimes the deaf or the blind seem to accomplish more than those of us who have both good hearing and good eyes. First I want to tell you about Betty Palmer, and later I will write about a new device called the Deaf/Blind Communicator. The communicator should improve life for this handicap situation.

We had a friend, Betty Palmer, who was both deaf and blind and she did amazing things. She was very meticulous about her personal appearance and always looked well groomed and neat. She would stand in front of the mirror in the bathroom and fix her hair, all as if she could see what she was doing. She could see what she was doing only in her mind's eye, because she was totally blind.

Betty used sign language to talk to her friends by cupping their hands in her own hands while they signed. With us she would hold out her hand and we would write a message in the palm of her hand. We would only need to start a word and she would know what we were saying to her. She would repeat out loud what we were writing in her hand. She not only used sign language, but also used a Braille typewriter and would correspond with some others by that method. She was very bright and alert.

She must be well into her 80's by now. I have not seen Betty in several years. I do remember her and how she got around our house when she visited. We just had to be careful not to move anything around after she located where everything was placed as she had to know exactly where everything was. The first thing she did at our house was to explore the placement of the furniture and then took off walking like anyone with sight would do to get around. I never saw her stumble over anything. She also walked without a cane. At least I never saw her use one.

Melvin told us that when they were first married he had moved a chair without thinking. Melvin, moving the chair, had brought bad memories to mind and she had been very frightened for a moment. Someone in the past had evidently tried to hurt her by moving furniture around. She learned very quickly that Melvin was not at all like that. He would tease her though. I'll tell you about that a bit later. She was very patient with everyone and every situation.

During her first visit we had a swimming pool and Betty would get into the pool, feel around the edge to learn the size and shape of the pool, and then take off across the pool for a good swim. It was amazing how well she got around. I was a bit afraid she might drown but she evidently knew exactly what she was doing. She never let her handicap deter her from living a life that was as nearly normal as was possible under the circumstances. Betty was a delight to be with.

She could not even see shadows and was completely deaf (her deafness was caused by some childhood illness when she was around 18 months old). She did not lose her eyesight until she was about twenty years of age. She had evidently learned to "see" by touch. She got around very well.

She became blind when she was hit by a truck—someone alledgedly pushed her in front of a truck! The fellow who pushed her ended up in prison. While she did not lose her life, she did lose her sight as a result of the injuries.

Betty's husband, Melvin, tried several times to invent something to help her hearing but it did not work. He had hoped something could be done for her. When we went to Knott's Berry Farm one time we were standing by a train and when the whistle blew she jumped. I thought it was because it was so loud that she could hear it but her husband explained she felt the vibration instead of any hearing. Her deafness was complete and irreversible.

I still remember an incident that occurred another time when she and Melvin came to visit us in California and we took them on a trip to Mexico. Everything went smoothly until we came back to return home across the border. At the

Border an officer questioned all of us. The officer tried to talk to her. She gave no answer because she could not hear his questions. We tried to explain to the officer that she was both deaf and blind but he absolutely would not listen to us and was getting a bit too hot under the collar. He was starting to get nasty. Melvin finally got the officer to calm down enough to listen to him. That officer was finally convinced that he could talk to Melvin as her husband. It took quite a while to convince him that she was a US citizen, was blind, and could not hear him. Betty calmly sat back in the car while all of this was going on. Melvin was patiently writing notes in her hand telling her what was happening. In the meantime, as I said before, Melvin liked to tease Betty. Of course he could not miss an opportunity to tease her and tell her that she could not return to the US and would have to stay in Mexico while the rest of us went home. She just laughed at him. Being the good sport that she was she just grinned at us and took the teasing with good humor. The officer finally let Melvin answer his questions and we proceeded to go on our way home then.

Now, the way things are today, she would have to have a passport to get by the officer. A passport was not needed then. That was sometime before 1970 when traveling from the U. S. to Mexico or Canada was a simple procedure.

Betty outlived her husband. A newspaper in Spokane wrote an article about her. They used her to demonstrate some new invention which is supposed to help the deaf and blind to know what is going on better than what has been available up to this time.

Comment from OZ: What a story. With all the miracles that have happened in the medical arena, one wonders why there are still people who have these problems. You were fortunate to know someone like that.

That comment from OZ was written before I had the Communicator Article in my possession and before I wrote the second article, which follows.

MORE ABOUT BETTY PALMER

My husband first met Betty Palmer about forty-five years ago through her husband, Mel Palmer, whom he had known since he was a teen-ager. Melvin Palmer had noticed her attending meetings of Jehovah's Witnesses, reading her Braille Bible, and had decided to see if there was anything he could do to help her. Betty was highly intelligent and Melvin could communicate with her by writing messages in her hand. He would only need to start a word and she seemed to know what the word was and would repeat it out loud. Betty's speech was not too clear as she had not learned to talk as a child like you or I did, but was taught at schools for the deaf, but you could understand her once you got used to her voice.

To talk to Betty all you needed to do was write into the palm of her hand and she would repeat what you had written and answer you. When she corresponded with other deaf people she would use sign language and in turn wrap her hand around theirs and this way she corresponded with them. She could also use a typewriter to write letters. She was really quite a woman.

While Betty lost her hearing as a very young child, she was about twenty years of age when she lost her eyesight. We were told she was allegedly pushed in front of a vehicle that hit her and caused her to be blind. While she did not lose her life, she did lose her sight as a result.

After Betty and Melvin had been acquainted for a while, they decided to get married. I was a guest of theirs at lunch one day. Betty had cooked the dinner. Her house was very neat and clean and well decorated. Friends had taken Betty shopping for materials for her home and she had selected everything herself. She would feel the materials and decided whether she liked it or not. Her friend probably told her the color of the material. I believe Betty herself made her curtains. I never asked her or any of her friends about the selection of the colors, but everything was nicely decorated. She never let her handicap hinder her.

Melvin liked to travel and he wanted to make life more pleasant for Betty. The fact she was blind and deaf did not deter him. They traveled to many places. One time they came to visit us in California. (Originally we came from Spokane—and Melvin and Betty lived in Spokane). My husband, Tom Bergland, was a real estate broker in Riverside, California and Betty wanted to "look" at houses to see what they were like. We took her to empty houses that were for sale and she felt the outline of the kitchen and the layout of rooms in the house. As we neared the house she would feel the plants to "see" what they looked like. It was amazing. It also made her happy. She even "looked" at cactus. We warned her they were full of sharp stickers.

This did not deter her. She still had to find out what they all looked like.

One day, we took the couple up to Big Bear to see the country. This is a small town settlement in the mountains north of San Bernardino. Besides the scenery we saw some huge pine cones that were amazing. None of us had ever seen such huge cones like those. They were at least three times bigger than any we had ever seen before. I would say they were about a foot long. Melvin described it all to her as she examined one we had picked up. She evidently enjoyed this little trip immensely. I later got a thank you note from her, written on her typewriter. She had a typewriter with Braille keys. The area around Big Bear always reminded me of the area around Benewah. It is where we would go when we first moved to California, especially if we felt a bit homesick. In fact it was so much like the Northwest that if you blindfolded someone and brought them there they would swear they were back in the area of northern Idaho.

Melvin was a very inventive man, and he had tried several times to invent some kind of a hearing aid that would help her gain even a little hearing. He had hoped something could be done for her. Nothing he tried did the job

We went to Knott's Berry Farm one time and we were all standing by a train when the whistle blew loud and clear. Betty suddenly jumped so I assumed she could hear the noise because it was so very very loud. Melvin said it was only that she felt the vibration and jumped at the sudden feel of the vibration. To me it was a deafening noise.

While at Knott's we went to their restaurant to have dinner. We did not know Betty had had some kind of trauma about a chicken when she was a child, and she would not eat chicken. She would eat turkey, and Melvin tried to convince her that the meal was turkey. As I said, she was one smart lady and it did not fool her one bit. She would not touch that chicken. I do not remember what we ended up doing about it. This must have been around 1965. If we had known she felt that way about chicken we would have gone to a different restaurant. We never did find out why it bothered her to eat chicken.

About five years later, Melvin and Betty came to Riverside to visit us again. When they arrived Betty asked me if we still had the barrel shaped chairs we'd had at the other house. We had moved in between their visits. She remembered those chairs. During that time we had moved out to West Riverside. Again, she got acquainted with the house and took off just like the rest of us around there. After supper one evening, Melvin was washing the dishes and Betty was drying them. Somehow the same dishes were being done over a couple of times. Pretty soon Betty caught on. As I said, Melvin liked to tease, and Betty was one smart lady. We all had a good laugh, including Betty. She always took his teasing well.

At this visit Melvin made the statement that it was the "last trip they would make". It was a strange thing to say but it did not register what he was referring to at the time. It was not until several months later that we realized what he meant. Melvin had cancer and it was terminal. He had been trying to see that Betty had a good time. He spent several weeks, which turned out to be for the last time, visiting all their many friends who were scattered between Spokane and Southern California. He was an amazing man and was trying to be considerate of Betty's future. He wanted to leave her with pleasant memories to last her the rest of her life. He knew there was no one else who could take her visiting again. We enjoyed their visit, and it was the last time they came to see us. Even Betty did not know about his illness yet.

Betty had a severe handicap as far as most men were concerned. Melvin told us one time that her handicap never caused him any trouble. He had enjoyed her company and I am sure he made her life more enjoyable while he could. We had enjoyed their visits and it left me with many memories. Now there are only those memories left to two widows, for now, I, myself, am a widow.

I wrote this story about Betty a couple of years ago. I had hoped to look Betty up on one of my visits to Spokane. That never occurred, I never saw her again. I did not know how to find where she was living or who she was living with. It was not until I came back to Spokane at the end of May in 2014 that I learned that Betty had passed away. She was a delightful person to know and I am glad I knew her over the past years. That she and Melvin Palmer had visited our family several times where we lived in California has left me with great memories about both Betty and Melvin. She was an amazing woman. He was an amazing man. Both are now deceased.

ABOUT BETTY PALMER
AND THE DEAF/BLIND COMMUNICATOR

All too often people who are deaf and blind are isolated because of those around them thinking they cannot communicate because of their handicap. Everyone loses out when one group is isolated from the community at large

Sept 2009 My son sent me a newspaper article about a new device that has been invented to help the deaf and the blind. My friend, Betty Palmer, was featured on the front page along with the information about this new device called the Deaf/Blind Communicator, or DBC for short.

The Spokesman-Review on June 29, 2009 published an article about the Deaf/Blind Communicator, written by Kevin Graman. Betty Palmer was featured as a potential user.
My information came mainly from the computer. I was so very glad to see that Betty Palmer contributed to the story. The newspaper is where I learned of Betty's part in it..

The article explains about a new invention for the Blind and Deaf people who need such a welcome help in communicating with others. I recommend the article if you can obtain it. I found it to be interesting, and would be especially so to anyone who knows a deaf or blind person. I hope the device featured becomes financially available to those needing it.

Actual deaf and blind persons helped in developing the invention which should make life much more enjoyable for such handicapped people all over the world. Using computer technology is rapidly developing in so many ways and this is one that is welcome to those who cannot see or hear. It should release them from the world of darkness and silence. Those needing the device will have help in learning how to use it. Betty Palmer is written up in that story in the paper. Because of copyright laws I find I am unable to fully describe the part Betty Palmer played in the article. Look up about the Deaf/Blind invention on the internet, there is a lot there.

The device uses computer technology that transfers communication in Braille and is not large and cumbersome like the devices that have been available in the past. I went on the internet to find the following information: "Even one who is deaf and blind can have conversations with friends, family, bus drivers, waiters, and virtually anyone they need to communicate with as they connect to a wider world." There is a lot on the internet for you to learn more about this amazing device if you like.

The one using the device will be able to "talk" and to "hear" others around them by sending and receiving messages. "The device uses electronic Braille and texting technologies in one portable device light enough for deaf-blind persons to have with them at all times. The unit consists of two components: a DB Braille Note and a DB cell phone with a visual display and keyboard. Software is installed in both units, which connect wirelessly via Bluetooth. It provides text-to-braille translation. A wonderful improvement that will undoubtedly keep on improving as time goes by the same as other communication technologies have done in the past few years." Go to the internet for more information. This is a wonderful tool for those who are handicapped with deafness and blindness. You can imagine what it would be like to not be able to hear and also not be able to see. Loss of one is bad but to lose both eyes and hearing is tragic.

I thought it would be interesting to know a bit more about Betty Palmer, and hope you do agree with me. I had lost track of Betty and am happy that this device may make life so much more interesting and happy for the many other deaf and blind people who might otherwise live in a blank world of darkness and silence.

MORE MEMORIES
FROM ELAINE PETERS STOTSENBERG SMITH

"It wasn't until we moved to Rosalia in 1945 that we had a bathroom with an inside toilet. We used an outhouse in Farmington. Originally in Farmington we took our bath on Saturday in a galvanized tub placed in the dining room. Later Dad took a portion of the porch where he installed a claw foot bathtub and a small sink attached to the wall. There was no toilet. The outhouse was across the alley, probably 200 feet or more from the house. At first, we used old catalogs for toilet paper. The slick pages were the last to be used. I think later on we used store bought toilet paper, but I don't remember for sure.

I remember the days of telephone party-lines. We got our first phone in Farmington in 1944. It was a small black phone that hung on the wall in the dining room. Our number was 42, and we answered when the phone rang 2 short rings. We turned a crank to ring for the operator or to reach someone else on our party line. In Rosalia, we answered to a long and a short ring.

Oh yes, ten cents a gallon for gasoline. First you needed to use the long lever on the side of the pump to pump the gas up into a clear tube type measuring container at the top of the pump before inserting the nozzle into the car's gas tank, gravity did the rest. I even remember when cars were started with a crank. Yes, I lived in those days.

In Spokane, ice was delivered to some homes for their ice box. But when in Farmington, Dad brought big chunks of ice from Spokane and placed them in our cellar. We got our first refrigerator in 1941. Milk was delivered in glass bottles to the homes in Farmington, but we had a Jersey cow for ourselves.

Regrets, I have a few. I have regretted not singing. Chorus was not offered in Farmington. The school had too few students. By the time I got to Rosalia, I was afraid to expose my singing ignorance. The first time band was offered in Farmington was my freshman year in High school. I played the clarinet. But when I moved to Rosalia in my sophomore year, after a couple of months, I quit band because I just was not able to play well enough."

THE DAYS OF BLACK AND WHITE

Both TV and Movies were black and white and we enjoyed them. Actually TV wasn't seen in too many homes until the early 50's. Cities were not wired to send out the pictures where we lived. We saw our first TV in 1953 when TV came to Spokane. You didn't have to pay to get TV or radio. The screens of the TV were usually round or slightly oval. You could hardly see for all the snow. We still enjoyed it. We didn't need color to enjoy the pictures. TV's were much more simple then than they are now—I could repair ours myself when it broke down—no expensive repairmen to call when it went out. I cannot repair one today. They no longer have those large tubes that you could buy and replace yourself. Now they have much smaller components with larger screens, and take up less space. Pictures come in more clear now than they did formerly.

Red Skelton entertained us, and his jokes were not "dirty" either. They did not need to be laundered when he delivered them into our homes. That's not true of TV today. The same can be said about most books. It is hard to find a book today that isn't so full of graphic sex that they are mostly only fit to put into the garbage bin.

I remember a quarter was a pretty good allowance. You would reach into a muddy gutter to recover a penny. Five of those pennies bought a big candy bar. That same candy bar today would be about fifty cents to a dollar. People seldom bother with pennies today. They don't buy much, although a hundred of them amount to a dollar. A penny is almost regarded like a piece of scrap paper and is ignored. Remember the Candy cigarettes, and the wax Coke shaped bottles with colored sugar water inside? We chewed the wax after we drank the contents—they were fun. Boxes of laundry soap had free glasses, dishes, or towels hidden inside the box. The prize inside that box was also of pretty good quality, not junk. A lot of those prizes today are high priced collectors' items.

When you gassed up your car you would get free trading stamps. Today, all you can get at a gas station is gas and no extras are provided, and in most stations you even have to fill your own tank. The only exceptions are in Oregon and New Jersey where they have a law that you are not allowed to pump your own gas. At that time, you got your windshield cleaned, the oil checked, and gas was pumped for you, without asking to have it done. It was all for free and done every time you gassed up. You also did not pay for air or water, plus you got those trading stamps to boot. No tip was expected either. The gas station also included a repair shop where you could get help with your ailing car. Today all you get at the gas station is gas. If you had a flat tire you went to the gas station to get it fixed and did not have to go to a special tire shop like you have to today. They would really service your car all the way around. This service also came with a smile and was done willingly and fast. No freebees today. The freebees are a thing of the past.

DO YOU REMEMBER ANY OF THAT? Doesn't it feel good, just to go back to say, "Yeah, I remember that?"

Water balloons were the ultimate weapon (especially over a door so it caught you by surprise when you got soaked). Having a weapon in school meant being caught with a slingshot. Not today. Baseball cards in the spokes transformed any bike into a motorcycle. (*We loved the noise*) Saturday morning cartoons weren't thirty minute commercials for action figures. "Race Issues" meant arguing over who ran the fastest. Not that way today. Taking "drugs" meant orange-flavored chewable aspirin.

Today we have copy machines instead of mimeograph paper, computers instead of typewriters, ballpoint pens instead of fountain pens. Lead pencils that needed to be sharpened are now the mechanical kind.

How did we ever live through all of this?!!!

This is why older folks say, "I'm glad I grew up during the good old days...

If you were sent to the principal's office it was nothing compared to the fate that awaited at home. We were in fear of our lives, but it wasn't because of drive-by shootings, drugs, gangs, etc. Our parents and grandparents were a much bigger threat!! But we survived because their love was greater than the threat to our behinds.

If you don't know what all this means, just ask an older person.

I still can't keep from commenting when stories bring back memories—some good and some bad. You young folks of today will one day see your own "Good Old Days." I am wondering if there will be as many changes in the next fifty years as there have been in the last fifty. As fast as everything seems to be progressing there may be a lot more yet.

We kids would rather have gone swimming in a lake, than in a pool. No beach closures there. I played in the foot-deep creek running past my grandparents' farm. We had fun there in that creek. I look back and wish I was still there, enjoying it immensely.

The term cell phone would have conjured up thoughts of a phone in a jail cell, and a pager was the school PA system. We all took gym, not PE—and risked permanent injury with a pair of high top Ked's, only worn in gym, instead of having cross-training athletic shoes with air cushion soles and built-in light reflectors. I can't recall any injuries, but they must have happened because they tell us how much safer we are now. Oh yes, a pair of tennis shoes cost less than a dollar a pair, not close to a hundred dollars. So there. We also used them until they were worn out too. No throwing them away just because they had a spot on them. Flunking gym was not an option…. ever! I guess PE must be much harder than gym. Speaking of school, staying in detention after school caught all sorts of negative attention.

What an archaic health system we had then. Remember school nurses? Ours wore a hat and everything. Oh yeah…. And where was the Benadryl and sterilization kit when I got that bee sting? I could have been killed! We had fun playing "King of the Hill" on piles of gravel left on vacant construction sites, and when we got hurt, Mom pulled out the 48-cent bottle of mercurochrome (kids liked it better because it didn't sting like iodine did) and then we got our butt spanked. Now it requires a trip to the emergency room, followed by a 10-day dose of an expensive bottle of antibiotics, and then Mom calls the attorney to sue the contractor for leaving a horribly vicious pile of gravel where it was such a threat.

We didn't act up at the neighbor's house either, because if we did we got our butt paddled when we got home. I recall Danny from next door coming over and doing tricks on the front steps, just before he fell off. Little did his Mom know then that she could have sued like they do today; instead, she picked him up and swatted him for being such a goof.

How did we ever survive? Love to all of us who shared this era; and to those who didn't, sorry for what you missed. I wouldn't trade it for anything. Remember that the very best of life's pleasures are the most simple. I just can't recall how bored we were without computers, Play Station, Nintendo, X-box or 270 digital TV cable stations. We found simple things to play with, like a sardine can became a boat, or some can could be made into a car or truck. We used our imaginations, and were happy with what was available..

Any parent roday that paddles a kids buttocks is sent to jail and the kids are sent to some place that lets them do whatever they want to do, even if it is wrong! Oh well, I suppose that's what is called "progress".……... And just remember, since I am now ninety years of age, I wonder how I ever survived such a lack of parents being punished for making their kids behave. Why my parents would have been thrown in jail and we kids would have been sent to some government institution for kids whose parents abused them by making them behave. Guess that is why there are so many kids ending up in jail nowadays.

One last thought: One of my adult sons thanked me one day for making him behave (yes, he did get his behind paddled a time or two.) He said it was what kept him from doing things that made others go to jail. Also, there is a very big difference between a spanking and a beating. A light correction to the buttocks can do a lot of good if the child is not let to continue his misbehaving. Sometimes just turning the child over your knee is all it takes—he gets the idea. At times while the child is lying over your knee all you need to do is slap your hands together and the noise does the trick. One of my children could be talked to and a spanking would not work for him at all. The others would not listen to you trying to talk to him or her. Each child is different and it takes different methods to correct him or her. Many children of today just are not taught to be good citizens or to follow the rules. If they don't follow the rules they end up in a cage. (jail).

All that brought back the memory of a spanking my sister and I got for something we had done one morning. I do not remember what we did but I do remember the punishment we received. Whatever it was, it was something that caused my father to feel the need to punish us. We were probably about five and seven years old. Mom helped to put a pad under our underwear so when we got spanked, it didn't hurt. I didn't say a word, but my sister spoke up and said something like, "Ha ha, we had padding." Dad asked her "Is it still there" and of course it was gone, so he turned her over his knee and paddled her again. She then cried and told him that "Peggy also had padding" and when he didn't paddle me again she protested to him. He told her "She didn't say anything". I hadn't told him, but she had. That ended the punishment. I know he knew at the time that we were padded. He couldn't help but know. My sister just could not keep her mouth shut. I think whatever we had done had to do with the one room school that we lived by, and had happened earlier that morning. My father had been up at the school to start the heater to warm the building up before school started that morning.

Comment from OZ; "Memories are what makes us 'us.'" Even the bad ones don't seem that bad now. I just hope the changes are for the good in the next 50 years. Star Trek comes to mind, just hope it won't be like Star Wars. Yes! I agree the good old days are here for a lot of us."

TRUCKS AND EXPERIENCES

An article about long truck road trains---multiple trailers pulled by one semi-tractor in Australia brought to mind that you can see a triple unit in Oregon, but most states do not allow more than a double. In Australia, you might see a caravan of five or six units being hauled behind only one truck. The highways there were isolated and these long road-trains are allowed. Two trailers behind a truck are usually the most you will see in this country. A big long train of trailers would be a little dangerous on the crowded highways in the States. The most my husband had behind his truck was a long trailer loaded with logs, lumber, or telephone poles. What he drove in those days was called a truck. Now they are called tractors and are very much larger in size also. To me a tractor is still a farm implement. The language has changed drastically in the past few years. The new language is a bit confusing and hard to understand, many words meaning the opposite now from what they used to mean.

In the 1940's my husband, Tom, was in the trucking business in Idaho until he sold out and moved back to Spokane in 1951. There are a very large number of homes built in Spokane and west to Pasco, Kennewick, and Moses Lake that were built with lumber he hauled from Marquardt Saw mill in Benewah, Idaho (an area located about 60 miles south of Spokane, and half way between St. Maries, Idaho and Tekoa, Washington). There is really no comparison between his truck and those in use today. The cab on his truck was about like a pickup truck cab is today—no sleeper or any of the fancy do-dads like today's "tractors" have. The lumber was stacked high and long. When he wasn't hauling lumber, sometimes it would be logs or telephone poles that were about 90 feet long that he had on his load. In those days they used wood telephone poles. Some days he would be out in the farming community during harvest time and would haul loads of grain. What he hauled would depend on the season or the demand for whatever needed to be transported.

A few tales about the experiences Tom had while on the road were not bad, but some were frightening. One time he picked up a hitchhiker and it wasn't too long before he realized the guy might not be a safe passenger. I don't know if it was what the man said or the way he talked, but Tom figured there was something wrong so he figured out a way to get him out of the truck before anything did happen. I don't know any further details, or I don't remember them, but he never picked up a hitchhiker again. He said he was scared and he wasn't a man easily scared. It had taught him a lesson. No more picking up hitchhikers. Too bad when someone needs a ride, giving one might not be a safe thing to do.

Another time, over towards Pasco, Tom saw a vehicle over a bank into a deep ditch and no one was around. There was no way for the vehicle to get out without assistance, so he figured they probably had gone to seek help. He fastened the vehicle to his winch and pulled it out and set the vehicle onto the highway. He says they would probably always wonder how the vehicle got up there. Tom also always wondered how they acted when the owners found their vehicle out of the ditch when they had left it way down below. If they brought someone out there to help them, the helper may have thought they were hallucinating—there was no jeep in the ditch, only the one sitting up on the highway. The email picture showed a large load of logs with one log rolling down the highway. The fasteners must have come loose. This triggered the following memory:

Log hauling can be very dangerous if anything goes wrong with the loading or with the fasteners. One time a load of logs prematurely started rolling off the truck when my brother-in-law, Leroy, was unloading it at the sawmill and it rolled onto him. Fortunately it did not kill him, but he spent some time in the hospital with a crushed ankle plus other injuries. The logging business can be quite dangerous. He and my husband had quite a few very close calls.

One time Leroy's truck suddenly lost its brakes going down a steep grade. The load was helping to speed the truck faster and faster. There was a bad sharp curve coming up at the bottom of the hill with the possibility of traffic being in the way. He didn't know whether it was safer to try to jump out of the truck or to ride the load to the bottom. If he jumped, he would try to turn the load so it would go into a ditch and not wreck anything except his truck. He decided it was just as dangerous to jump out of the speeding truck as to stay in to the bottom of the grade. He hoped he could make that sharp turn and also that there was no other car coming around the bend. If he hit any other vehicle it surely would be fatal all the way around. On top of the danger from the runaway truck, this happened right at the entrance to a resort area where quite a number of vehicles could be in the way. The entrance to the resort was right on the curve itself. Very fortunately everything worked out all right. Both truck and driver stayed upright and no other cars appeared on the highway right at that spot. He had made the right decision to stay with the truck.

There are times when a load of finished lumber can create quite a dangerous situation. If anything goes wrong with the fasteners the load can shift and lumber can go flying all over the road. Hopefully, any time something like that would happen there would be no cars or people in the vicinity to be hurt or seriously injured. I don't believe Tom ever had a load of finished lumber get lost. He always had to be alert to load and road conditions so he could discover any problem before it was too late. He would check his load of lumber quite frequently to make sure none of it had shifted.

Sometimes there is an occasion when something humorous or even embarrassing can happen. The driver can be caught unawares if he isn't really careful. I guess I can tell of one occasion that happened to my husband. He was unloading a load of logs into a lake and he thought there was no one around so it was safe to answer the call of nature. He was zipping up his pants when he heard a voice call out, "Thank you, I've always wanted to get a moving picture of a load of logs being unloaded." The man with the moving picture camera turned and left. My husband did not know who the man was and only hoped that no one who knew him ever saw the pictures, although he also didn't know how much picture was taken past the unloading of the logs. He only found out the cameraman was from California (the event happened in Idaho). Being a small world it could happen that the film could show up in California after we moved there, and a member of the family or neighbors could see it, but very hopefully not. Strange things can pop up unexpectedly and in strange places at strange times.

THE WEATHER WAS BAD
FOR TRUCKS AND HAULING

The following two stories occurred while we and my husband's brother, Leroy Bergland (1910-1964), lived in the Benewah valley. Both brothers were in the logging and hauling business at that time. Each had their own business but worked together on a few jobs.

This experience happened when winter was approaching. When Tom and Leroy left home the roads were clear, the sun was out, but that was early in the morning. The weather was chilly as it was late Fall and Winter weather was due at any time.

Tom and Leroy drove east of Spokane toward Kellogg, Idaho. They went up a river road to pick up a load of telephone poles. These poles were probably 90 feet long. The logging road was winding and next to the river. Well, with 90 foot poles behind the truck it was a bit tricky to maneuver around the bends and in one place a wheel hung over the river with nothing under it. I assume it was probably one of the dual trailer wheels, not the truck wheels, and the poles would have steadied the vehicle. There was no backing up or other maneuvering so they carefully moved forward and continued on their way.

I told you he and his brother were not easily scared (I sure would have been). Both men were also experienced in solving truck problems. I don't know how they handled the wheel hanging over the river, but they got the truck out and also the load of telephone poles intact. They sure didn't want to dump a load of poles in order to save the truck or themselves if they didn't absolutely have to. The poles were worth a small fortune. They did solve the problem and headed on into their destination. The family livelihood depended on that truck so there was no way of not solving the problem if at all possible.

All this had taken several hours so it was late afternoon by this time. The weather was clouding up and getting colder as they headed back to Spokane. By the time Tom and Leroy got to Post Falls (25 miles east of Spokane) it had started to snow quite hard and visibility had deteriorated to nothing. They came upon an underpass with traffic stopped due to someone fishtailing under the pass and ending up cross-wise under the viaduct, blocking the road. The men got out of the truck and Leroy went back up the road and tried to stop the traffic, but everyone refused to stop. The people seemed to panic and it got worse to the point that the underpass was completely plugged up and no way out. When people panic they do not use reason. If they had stopped like they were asked to do, the equipment on the truck, in spite of the load of poles, would have let them pull the stranded vehicle out of the way and everyone could have gone on.

It ended up that the storm was a blizzard and approximately a hundred people had to be crowded into the basement of a nearby parsonage. Among the people stranded was a telephone lineman with equipment and he and my husband went to a telephone pole, climbed it and tapped into a phone line, making phone calls to each family to let them know that loved ones were safe. Elsewhere, some people who

163

abandoned their cars ended up frozen to death. That winter turned out to be about the coldest on record for the area.

Lots of experiences occur in our lifetimes, if people could only tell about them. There were many other experiences to tell and maybe I will write more about them some day.

NO MORE LUMBERJACKS

NOTE: The email video I received shows some very interesting machinery that does the work of ten men, modern machinery that is now used to log timber, replacing men. The newest equipment is more than amazing. It also puts men out of work. Being a lumberjack is not necessarily just a job for a man, either.

In order to get a very much needed new house, my sister-in-law (by this time a widow of my husbands brother, Leroy Bergland), went out into the woods and felled trees She trimmed those trees, then sent them to the sawmill to be cut into lumber. Since she owned the property that the trees grew on she had done the best thing in order to get that new house that had been planned for a long time. The year was 1964.

She didn't have the equipment that is shown in that email video, but she had her own physical labor and a saw and an axe, and plenty of determination.

When the lumber was delivered back to her property, she made arrangements to have the house built. She worked with an architect, and realized that doing much of the work herself was the only way she could afford the new house and she really did need it. Not a whim of any foolish desire, it was need. She put in a lot of hard work that was very time consuming as she also had a large family to care for at the same time, but she made it. The home turned out very nicely done. She herself is no longer with us but the house stands as a tribute in honor of what a woman can do if she either has to or really wants to do something. She and Leroy had planned to build the home before, but cancer took his life at the age of 54 before their plans could be realized. She fulfilled the project on her own. That home is among one of the nicer ones in the Benewah Valley.

This morning, *October 7, 2017* I was talking to Karen Foster, one of Dorothy Bergland's daughters, who told me she was about six at the time her mother was cutting the timber for the house project. She was with her mother who asked her to run get "PeeWee". She wondered why her mother wanted her to get her brother. What her mother had asked her to get was a *peavey*. A peavey is a logging tool used to turn logs or grab them to hold them. PeeWee is her brother's nickname and peavey sounded the same to her.

Comment from OZ: "She sounds like a woman who gets what she wants or needs by doing it herself. You didn't include a date, but I would guess it was way back when? Early 1900's? I think those who came through the depression were stronger people because of that hard time."

I answered—I think I remember it was around 1964 shortly after her husband died.

Comment from an email pal "Your sister-in-law was a brave lady to say the least! It took a lot of guts to do something like that on her own."

I remember getting stuff for my father and watching him when he built on to the house where we lived in Des Moines, Washington when I was about 5 years old. He built the fireplace in there too. Of course, he had that knowledge because his father was a mason (either brick or concrete) and had worked with him for a lot of years before he went into the military. It was beautiful when it was done. The fireplace had a raised hearth with flower places on each side. Between the main wall and the big room he built was a buffet style cabinet with doors on either side.

I really liked that house. We lost it because my dad got ill so we moved in with my aunt and uncle on my mom's side of the family. Take care,"

My answer to both of my Email pals: She was my sister-in-law, married to my husband's oldest brother, Leroy. He died of cancer in his throat, and nearly starved to death. She had eight living children. Leroy died in 1964 at the age of 54. They had planned to get a new house but his health broke down before that could happen. She actually did go out and fell the trees, trimmed them, and sent them to the saw mill.

She was still fairly young when she herself died of heart failure many years later. She had a date to meet one of her daughters for lunch. That was the daughter who was three years old when her father died. When she did not show up, the daughter, who lived in another town about sixty miles away, called someone to go check on her mother and they found her in bed. She had died peacefully in her sleep.

To email pal I wrote: You asked about my husband's work and the variety of jobs he had and how we met. I'll tell you a bit. By now you know we both grew up during the years of the Depression, which has affected our life throughout the years, both his and mine.

Oh yes! My husband was into a lot of different professions. When I met Tom Bergland, it was while on a visit to my uncle and his family in Idaho. I was 16 and he was 18 when we met. The year was 1938. The Bergland's were into the logging business, felling trees, cutting cordwood, also making fence posts and hauling them out to the farmers so they could fence their land and pastures. A couple of years later he and his family moved to Spokane and opened up a gas station and auto repair shop. Tom helped his parents with the station, did mechanical work, and worked as a carpenter building houses and anything else he could do for work. This was in late 1939 and it was still Depression years, so work was still very hard to get.

One time, according to Tom, he was in the woods cutting logs and bumped into a hornets nest, with the resulting stings. The hornets got into his pants legs and were taking revenge on him for disturbing them. Of course the stings were painful and he really danced while removing his trousers to get rid of the hornets. Those little insects are tough to deal with and sometimes are very thick in the forrest.

It was through another friend from Benewah that we met again and started dating. By this time I was 18 and Tom was 20. A year later we were married. Times were still hard and the Depression was not yet over with. Tom did whatever he could to find work. One job was at an Armours Meat Packing Plant cleaning up the "kill floor." He didn't like the job, but work was work at the time. It was a very nasty job cleaning up a bloody floor. He invented a way to do the job better. The wages were 65 cents an hour. My husband had told the supervisor about his idea, which the company did use. He was supposed to get a bonus for ideas to make improvements. Who got the bonus but the supervisor? He should not have told his idea to the supervisor before turning it in.

From that job he went into the mines in Metaline Falls, a city north of Spokane. He worked in the mines for several months. He did not like mining as it was underground. Again, work was work. When the opportunity came up to change jobs, he took it. He got a chance to help my uncle run a sawmill in the area known as Benewah in Idaho. It was then war years and at the time when jobs were "frozen" and you could not change jobs without government permission. He was able to get permission because lumber was a needed commodity. He did like logging and lumber because it was outdoor work. He had been raised around that kind of work.

Later when my uncle closed down his small sawmill, Tom bought a truck and went into the lumber and log hauling business. Quite a number of houses were built with lumber manufactured at the Marquardt Sawmill which he hauled to Spokane and also to Pasco and Moses Lake. As that kind of work was seasonal, Tom would find work elsewhere as a carpenter during the winter months. During harvest season he would go out to the farmland area and haul grain, and a few times he hauled furniture for people who were moving to a different area. He would keep himself and his truck very busy.

In December 1951 we sold our house in Benewah, bought a house in Spokane and moved to Spokane. After several jobs there he went into the used car business with my brother for a few years. In 1959 we sold out and moved to be near relatives in California. There Tom went into the real estate business and bought and sold houses. He was successful in the Real Estate business but opportunity opened up in Portland, Oregon so we left California in 1974. Along with managing his brother's garage in Portland, we again invested in Real Estate. We lived in Portland for twenty-eight years until Tom had an unfortunate accident one morning. He left home about 9:30 and an hour later, I got a call from the hospital that I should come to the hospital immediately. He had fallen and hit his head. He never recovered. He died June 22, 2001, five months before that fateful day now known as Nine-Eleven. That winter Judi and I moved back to California.

Email pal wrote back: "Wow, what a neat story you tell, but what a very sad end. My uncle got out of the lumber business! After a while they were using helicopters to pull logs off the sides of the mountains over in the west coast area! My uncle thought it a widow maker's job for sure! Which it was. But he 'choke set' for a long time until one day he almost bit the dust! It really opened his eyes, believe me.

My father was born just before the depression (1928) so he is a little younger than you, but he tells me stories about being raised during that time, etc. I used to love looking at all the cars back then with him. He would tell me how his folks would rent 5 acres of land, plant a garden on it, harvest it, and then when the neighbors would come over and ask for help my dad's father (Grandpa) would have something to help them with. Sometimes they would have the veggies and sometimes they would have the meat so they put it all together and ate dinner together! (her father is now deceased)

My mother used to ask my grandfather if they were poor. My grandfather used to say it is just a state of mind and "no, they weren't poor". However, they were just as poor as the next person! My grandfather didn't have any work so he would go fishing instead, and tend to the garden, along with the chickens that they had etc. When they got tired of Salmon my grandfather would butcher a chicken. They lived in the Shoreline area of Seattle, but it was called Forest Park before it was Shoreline. There were woods there at that time and they used to go mushroom hunting, etc. My mom and her sisters used to play in the woods and back then it was safe to do that....not now!

My father's folks lived in Lansing, Michigan when my father was born. They moved to Jerome Township, Ingham Co. Mi or a place called Sanford, Mi. My father was a paper boy by the time he was 10 years old. One day my grandpa went in to pay his house payment and the guy told him that it was paid off. My father had paid it! Well, my grandpa was madder than a wet hen. When my father got home he said to him, 'I think you have something that belongs to me.' My father went and got the title to his house, gave it to him. By that time he was 17! Then he went into the military.

A FEW GOOD HELPFUL HINTS

Pin a small safety pin to the seam of your slip and you will not have a clinging skirt or dress. Same thing works with slacks that cling when wearing panty hose. This really works. I have tried it. I don't bother with removing the pin during laundry either.

To warm biscuits, pancakes, or muffins that were refrigerated, place them in a microwave with a cup of water. The moisture will keep the food moist and help it reheat faster. This also helps if items are a bit dry and you want to freshen them up. OK, I tried this too.

Do you buy loaves of bread when on sale? Cool them down in the refrigerator before freezing them. To use put them back in the refrigerator to thaw and you won't have soggy bread, and they will be like fresh loaves. I have also tried this one and it does work.

Store your opened chunks of cheese in aluminum foil. It will stay fresh much longer and not mold. I have also tried this and it worked for me. Refrigerate it though.

TRIVIA

Did you know that a mosquito is just an insect that makes you like flies better?

An adult is a person who has stopped growing at both ends and is now growing in the middle. That describes a lot of us today.

Dust is just mud with the juice squeezed out

THE GREY-HAIRED BRIGADE

Sometimes we are referred to as senior citizens, sometimes as old fogies, at other times we are called geezers, and in some cases "Baby Boomers." Many of us have been retired for some time. We walk slower now, our eyes and hearing are not what they once were. We worked hard, raised our children, and grown old. Some refer to us as being over the hill. but there are a few things that need to be considered. We led America into the technological age when we studied English, history, math and science. Many of us had firsthand experience with outhouses. Oh, those outhouses! They were hateful, inconvenient, and stinky, but absolutely necessary.

We remember telephone party-lines and 25 cent gasoline. Milk and ice was delivered to our homes and put into an icebox. The iceman would not only bring the ice inside the house, but he would put it into the ice box for us. An ice box then is now a refrigerator that makes its own ice. Remember when cars were started with a crank? You could get your arm broken when the crank kicked back at you. Yes, we lived those days. We really don't want to go back to a lot of it. It was hard, very hard work.

We are probably now considered old fashioned and out-dated by many. But there are a few things you need to remember before completely writing us off. We do not apologize to anyone because we have lived through all that you only read about in history books. Yes, we are old and slow these days but we have several good fights still left in us.

That reminds me—my mother said the city lights from a distance made her feel very lonesome. I never asked her why. Wish I had. It must have reminded her of something sad in her life. My mother was raised in North Dakota and the farm was isolated. Personally I love to watch city lights. To me the city lights are very beautiful. A train whistle at night is a lonesome sound to me. I really don't know why, unless it is because it is a long drawn out sound. I suppose everyone has something that subconsciously reminds them of some sadness or unpleasantness.

*I'LL JUST CALL HER MARY***

We had a friend, I'll call her Mary, (not the email Mary) who had been married four times and been widowed each time within a few years. One time, soon after the fourth loss, she complained to my husband. She said, "I fall in love and get married and then shortly I lose my husband. I don't know why this keeps happening to me and don't know what to do any more." She asked for his advice. He jokingly told her, "Just marry someone younger." She was around 60 at the time.

Several months later, Mary was asked to help a man, Daniel*--whose wife had abandoned him and his two small children. The wife had evidently felt she could not handle the fact that the baby, who was only a year old, was diabetic and needed special care. Daniel also had arthritis and was disabled at times, but he was a hard worker who earned a comfortable living. Mary moved into his house and became well-liked by this family. Being the family lived in a very small town where everyone knew everyone else, some busybodies started talking about the fact that Mary was living in the house full time. No matter that she was twenty years older than the man of the house. It had worked out well for the man and his children as well as Mary, as she was a very loving person with the children and a good housekeeper. When the rumors reached Mary and Daniel they decided that they had a lot in common and decided to get married. She helped raise the children to adulthood although the child who had been the baby was severely diabetic and died around the age of 20 from the illness. Mary was in her 80's when she died. Daniel told my husband one time he never regretted having Mary as his wife even though she was about twenty years older than he was. It had worked out well for both of them.

** True story, but names changed. They are all deceased now.

IN THE KITCHEN

Email story reminded me that we all did this--chop eggs on the same cutting board and with the same knife and no bleach, but we didn't seem to get food poisoning. My Mom would defrost hamburger on the counter, spread mayonnaise and make our school sandwiches on that same cutting board, then wrap the sandwiches in wax paper, put the lunch in a paper bag, not in ice pack coolers and we never got sick from it that I ever knew of.

COMMENT FROM MY SON LARRY: "Very interesting Mom. You could trust the milk and eggs that were delivered, too, eh?"

When we lived on a farm we had lots of butter and cream and milk and eggs, all we could eat. I remember years later when we were not on a farm, the price of butter went up to

50 cents a pound. I was so upset I went to buying Margarine, which was white (by law) and had to be colored with a little packet of coloring enclosed in the package—and you mixed the color in yourself. I paid 20 cents a pound for margarine, sometimes less if it was on sale. Now that butter is so costly, I use it in preference to margarine. Now I only buy butter and it is anywhere from $3 a pound to $4.50 a pound. Kinda backward isn't it?

Yes, at that time, the laws would not let margarine be sold already colored so we had to mix the color ourselves. They were afraid it might actually be mistaken for butter, hence the white color. Now it comes colored and looks like butter, but is clearly marked as margarine. Because of the difference in price, margarine probably outsells butter.

DO YOU HAVE LEAD IN YOUR BOOTS?

I contributed quite a few verses for our news letter, hoping those with lead in their boots would pay attention and slow down. Lead in their boots is referring to those who drive too fast in a park where the tenants are over 55. Here are a few of them.

Residents with scooters and wheel
chairs are close to the ground.
So get the lead out of your boot so they can still be around.
This is not a speeding rink.
So please do stop and really think.

Even though we're now over fifty-five
We really still want to stay alive.
So please do stop driving so fast.

Make that fast drive be your last.
Now what's your hurry anyway?
We love this park so all I can say
Is slow that car so we stay alive in it.
Speeding doesn't save you even one minute.

VARIOUS VERSES AND STORIES

I have written several news items presented by and for the special residents (my neighbors) where I lived at the Mobilehome Park in Moreno Valley, California over the past eleven years. The response was very encouraging. Many volunteered to make life more pleasant for all of us, and need to be remembered. They did not expect to be paid for their many hours of work. There are many still alive who are spending many hours on our behalf. We really appreciate them and they need to be remembered also.

Our wonderful volumteers. What would we do without them. They are the ones who help make life better for all of us.

DONUTS AND COFFEE ON WEDNESDAYS

Every Wednesday we met at our clubhouse in the "over fifty-five" mobile home park where we live. We would have a good visit and drink coffee and eat donuts. I thought it would be a good idea to encourage everyone to join us for a nice visit and to have donuts and coffee with us so they could get better acquainted. I sent out the following invitation.

COFFEE ON WEDNESDAY you will all agree
Works best if shared with company.

Talk with others or just listen to the chatter
Which you do really doesn't matter.
Visit with Virgil and Mary Jo
Helen and Bill and others you know.
There's Jerry and there's Dolly
There's Verna and then by golly
You must not forget Marie and Fran
And all the rest who really can
Enliven your lives by being a friend
You will enjoy yourself you can depend
Donna and Bob and some of the rest
Come each week and enjoy the best.
There's Ingrid and Jim, Lorna and Louise
Even Alice and Peggy if you please
Come join us now and enjoy the fun
We'll welcome you so please just come.
Maryland and Richard enjoy fixing it ready
So come on down and be a steady
Have coffee and donuts with all the fun.
Doesn't that make you want to run
On down to the clubhouse on Wednesday?

EARTHQUAKE TROUBLED RESIDENT

Richard and Maryland Nygren have been the hosts of the donut and coffee meetings at the clubhouse for several years. It was Richard who made the good coffee we enjoyed every week. Maryland served the donuts and cleaned up afterward. An earthquake inspired me to write about what happened to Maryland when she was startled one morning by the sharp jolt of the quake.

MARYLAND NYGREN & THE EARTHQUAKE

We had an earthquake the other day
So Maryland decided to be on her way
Up she jumped and headed for the door
Tripped and fell down on the floor
Broke her hip it is sad to say
Went to the hospital that very day
Now that news is so very sad
She spends her time in the rehab
That is no place to spend your time
We hope to see you soon, looking just fine.
To have our donuts without our friend
Makes us sad right to the end.
Our Maryland is missed there is no doubt
Wednesday is not the same to be without
Our Maryland, who fell onto the floor
Now when we see you coming through the door
Again fixing donuts and coffee, our spirits will soar.
Come home quick. Wednesday is not the same
When Maryland is missing from this donut game
We miss you friend. Get well and come back soon.

Maryland came back and resumed helping every Wednesday morning as usual. Her hip kept bothering her until she had it replaced. She recovered nicely from the replacement. *The following memorial is written with a sad heart.* Maryland Nygren was always cheerful and never missed a Wednesday meeting with those of us who came to the clubhouse to enjoy her company while we ate donuts and drank coffee. Sad to say, she had a stroke that ended her life. She will be greatly missed'

IN MEMORY OF MARYLAND NYGREN

Maryland hosted our Wednesday morning get-together
For the past few years, no matter the weather.
Rain or shine she was always there
Now we are sorry to see an empty chair.
Smiling and happy she would always appear
Rewarding us with her smiling good cheer.
She broke her hip a few months ago
After an earthquake frightened her so.
She jumped up and ran, a fatal mistake
It caused her to fall and her hip it did break.
She still came to the clubhouse to let us all know
It is a good time to gather together to show
How friends can enjoy visiting with each other
And learn to know our neighbor is not a bother.
Maryland came to help us every week
Friendly gatherings she always did seek
So enjoy your coffee and donuts my friend
Our grief at her passing will not soon end.

ACCIDENTS DO HAPPEN

I had an accident in December 2011. Here is the report of what happened. I wrote about it to a friend the same afternoon: "I went down to the clubhouse this morning and had my usual Wednesday coffee and donut break with other residents of this park.

I picked up a few library books to read. Another friend came with more books. I kept all but two of those and headed home. That was a very big load of books. As I got to my driveway I headed across the drainage ditch on my scooter and missed the very *narrow* ramp. Over I went with the load of books throwing me off balance. The scooter landed on top of me. I couldn't move. Very fortunately, John, the neighbor across the street, had been just ahead of me. He had not gone inside yet and heard me calling for help. If he hadn't been there, I don't know how long I would have lain there, as no one else came by for quite a while. My arm hurt and was sore.. I couldn't get up. John's wife helped me get my legs straightened up so I was a bit more comfortable. They could not get me on my feet until someone else came by and stopped. Between everyone they finally got me onto a chair. Then someone called my daughter, Jackie, who took me to the emergency room at the hospital. X-rays showed no broken bones, but I was really bruised and swollen and in pain. The good news is the soreness and bruising will heal. I can put up with the pain with the good news of no broken bones. I can hardly move my arm and I've used all the energy left in me to type this out, so bye for now.

Oh yes, I got myself a wider bridge across the ditch, which I should have done sooner.

MORE NEWS
FROM AROUND THE PARK

Whenever someone was ill in our Mobile home community it was reported in our news letter. Falling is always a danger to us over 55, but we seem to do it anyway. For some reason a great number of us managed to fall or trip recently and down we went.

Some of us fell it's sad to say
Sure hope it doesn't happen every day.
Falling seems to be among us here in the Park.
Though we really aren't trying to set a big mark.

Bad news last month for Pat Janitell
Injured his arm when he slipped and fell
We saw him later with his arm in a sling
Hope he is now rid of the pesky thing.

Peggy using a walker like it was a wheel chair
Went over backwards and flew through the air.
Learned a walker isn't to be used that way.
So folks don't try it is all I can say.
A nasty bang on the head is not worth the ride
Unless you want to have bruises and lose some hide.

With Velma, a chair went out from under.
Felt like she'd been hit by lightening and thunder.

Sadly, Pat Janitell fell again
I'm sure he's in a lot of pain.
Fell down this time and broke his foot,
Now he's wearing a cement boot.

OUR DRIVE THROUGH CHICAGO

Summer 1953: One time in 1953, we were traveling to New York and went through Chicago at the rush hour. It was a brother-in-law's turn to drive. Instead of my husband taking the wheel, he insisted that Howard could drive, but the traffic was bumper-to-bumper. That was over fifty years ago. That one time I was in Chicago all I saw was the heavy rush hour traffic. Guess that did not give a fair picture of the whole town. We did not stop except at stop lights or signs, or even to eat there. The only thing I really remember was who was driving our car.

If you can drive through a large city during rush hour, you can probably drive anywhere. Maybe that is why I am not afraid of busy freeway traffic. I feel it is safer than on the side streets. It was on a side street in New Jersey that we got broadsided. We were going from New Jersey into New York City. The guy who hit us was the dispatcher for a manufacturing concern and was trying to catch a driver. We had the green light and the dispatcher went through the red light, hit us, which caused the car to spin around and roll over.

Comment by OZ: "Chicago is one of the prettiest cities in the U. S. We drove through Chicago at night, with no problem. I lived in Philadelphia. Talk about rush hour, it lasts 24 hours a day on the freeway, and you better be able to drive on the side streets, or if not, you won't survive the city. Of course the downtown area is worse.

I think downtown Dallas is beautiful at night, especially at Christmas time, you know, after the rush hour. We traveled across the U. S. at Christmas time from San Diego to Philly every year for ten years. Sometimes we traveled during the summer. The cities were prettier at night when you could see them from a distance. There are a lot of pretty cities across the U. S. I wish I could see them all."

OUR TRIP TO ISRAEL AND GREECE IN 1978

SPRING OF 1978: My husband, Tom, and I went to Israel in 1978 and shortly before we made our final arrangements we were offered a chance to go on to Greece for $50.00 additional airfare, plus the ground arrangements. At first Tom thought that we shouldn't, I told him it was something we just could not pass up, that it was a chance of a lifetime. He did finally agree with me. We spent a week in Israel, and another in Greece. Best bargain we could have taken advantage of. Never regretted it either.

Only half of the original group who went to Israel took advantage of the Greek portion. There were twenty of us in the group that went on from Israel to Greece. We spent the week touring Greece for $400 for the ground arrangements. It was one of the best $450 each we ever spent. The tour included hotel, transportation, meals; everything was complete, even including a cruise to one of the islands on a ship. It was worth every penny it cost us and was a very great bargain. I am so glad we did not pass up the opportunity. We lived in Portland at the time, but some of the group we were with happened to be from around Riverside and San Bernardino. It was not by special arrangement but by accident that we were paired with people from that California area that we were very familiar with. We had a wonderful time. Really it is a small world. One man was in his eighties and he kept up with everyone with no trouble. The youngest in the group was about ten years old. Wonderful group, wonderful trip, wonderful time had by everyone.

On our Israel guided tour there were places where we were instructed to pull the shades over the windows of our bus.

In one place our guide just instructed us to not take any pictures of the area and he would let us keep the shades up. He let us look around but no pictures. It was probably in military areas. Everyone in our group was cooperative and we had no trouble at any time. We made quite a few tours around Israel. All went very smoothly during our whole visit. There were armed soldiers everywhere, but we saw no trouble. Some of those soldiers appeared to be quite young, and many of them were young women.

GREECE

One evening in Greece after we ate our evening meal some lively music started. I guess I started to dance with the music and the waiter joined me. The waiter and I entertained everyone by dancing for them. When I started dancing it wasn't with the idea of entertaining anyone, it just was something that happened. Maybe that is why it turned out so well. It was fun. If the waiter started to touch me, I would dodge and turn, which made it as if it were rehearsed. Our group soon left for our next destination after eating.

In Greece, we toured many of the places mentioned in the Bible. We also visited where the Olympics were held and where some of the Christians were used as bait for lions and other persecutions. In one of the auditoriums we went to the top of the auditorium while someone in the arena talked to another person. The acoustics were amazing. The sound carried up to us as if they had a microphone.

What a trip. Our Greek guide spoke broken English but we could understand him if we listened closely. Since our arrangements were made at the last minute he was the only one the company could get on such short notice. He was an older man who had spent five years in the U. S. Most students in other countries are required to learn English and speak it quite well. I found this to be true on my later travels and on cruises I have taken since then. Some speak with barely an accent, others no accent at all.

We got to spend a few hours in Switzerland when the plane landed between New York and Israel on the way there. I purchased some Swiss music while waiting for our plane. That is where we saw hundreds of bicycles used for transportation on the streets—instead of automobiles. There wasn't time to venture far from the airport, so we didn't get to see much of that country.

At the time we boarded our plane in Switzerland and left for Israel, we went through a thorough security check, both personally and our baggage. After boarding the plane, I noticed the plane itself was thoroughly checked inside and out. It didn't mean too much at the time, but now I can understand why—it was for our own personal security as well as for the plane. All inspections were done quite a distance from the buildings. After they inspected our personal bodies, they bussed us from the airport out to a building away from the airport buildings to go over our luggage. At the time of all inspections, wherever they occurred, starting in New York and ending in Greece, we were asked if anyone had asked us to bring something like a package along with us. I guess that is how someone could possibly get a bomb onto an airplane secretly. Well, someone did ask me to take a package with me and wanted it mailed in another country, but I sent them to our group leader who turned them down. I don't know if it was an innocent request or a dangerous one, but no one should assume anything these days and we didn't then either.

After the week in Israel, we were guarded, along with our baggage, by armed guards all the way to the airport. The armed guards rode the bus with us. Some time earlier there was a case of someone boarding a bus load of tourists and setting off a bomb. This is why we were accompanied and so closely guarded all the time we were in that country. It was quite strange to see very young men as well as girls on the street with automatic rifles. They were in military uniforms. In many places we saw bombed out buildings. Even though we saw all of that, for some reason I never felt threatened personally.

Our room accommodations were very nice and our meals were very good. One incident I remember when we went into a restaurant and was handed a menu. At the top of the list was "calf brain croquets." Well, of course I was NOT going to order or eat such a thing as that. Nobody came to take my order, but a plate was set in front of me with what I thought looked like Chinese egg rolls, so I ate it. I then turned to the lady sitting next to me and told her it was very delicious and wondered what it was. She said it was just what I was not going to order, "calf brain croquets." It doesn't pay to prejudge something like that. I got over my prejudice about the croquets in a hurry.

This in turn reminded me of what I had told a neighbor boy when I fed him some lunch one time. Without tasting what I had put on the table, he said "I don't like it," and I told him we tasted things before we said we don't like something. The dish he didn't like was what he ended up eating all there was of it and wanting more. Well, I really did like that dish I was not going to eat. Lesson learned. The menu was a courtesy only to let us know what was being served. I enjoyed all. I got to enjoy several different foods. One thing that was so very different one time was radishes. They were huge and tasted very good and they were not hot like I have tried at home.

When we got home, Tom gave talks about the trip and we got to take part of the cost of the trip off our income tax. When I took all of the cost off, of course I got audited, but they allowed a great portion of the cost for both of us. They were very nice and I really didn't expect to be able to take the entire cost off but they allowed a very substantial amount. Wonderful experience that trip—I even enjoyed the IRS audit—I got to tell them about the trip. The cost of the trip was deductible because Tom gave lectures about the trip to several congregations when we returned.

Many of the pictures we took in Israel were taken through the windows of the bus while it was moving and came out surprisingly very clear. I still have that camera, but because it takes film, it is very obsolete now. It was a very, very good camera. Too bad it is obsolete. Sometime when I get in the notion I will remember things that happened in Greece— like the experience of having to go to the public restroom. It sure was a very different kind of experience from what we have here. Instead of a sit down toilet, you had to stand up and hit a hole in the floor. Not too pleasant an experience. Quite different and difficult for women.

The restroom in restaurants is referred to as a water closet. The restaurant rest rooms were equipped with toilets. In Greece, I didn't realize the people in the hotel earn their living by tips from carrying your baggage and I wanted to carry my own. I had a run-in with an elderly woman who insisted on carrying my suitcase up the stairs to our room. If I had only known ahead of time she needed the tip money, I would not have insisted on carrying my own suitcase—I had only one case, but the woman was quite elderly and I thought it was too much for her. Too bad I had no knowledge of the custom. I have learned to pack light and put everything in one medium size suitcase. I was used to carrying my own all the time. A person really should learn a few of the customs of other countries before going there. I even goofed up when we went to Hawaii. There we insulted our hostess by renting a car and when we left we laundered the sheets, all not knowing when you are the guest of a native Hawaiian you are really a guest that she had planned on doing all those things for us. We were following our customs, not hers.

WE VISITED THE MASADA

When in Israel, I had to ride a gondola in order to visit the Masada. The gondola went from the vicinity of the Dead Sea up to the top of the mountain where the Masada was. I had to close my eyes in order to make it. About that ride up to Masada, it was worth it even though I was so nervous about the height. The ride was in a car run through the air on a cable. It was a wonderful experience on top. I just had to make up my mind that I could ride that gondola. That is part of the trip I won't forget either. On the back side of the Masada was a ramp built at the time the Masada was attacked. That is the way the invaders got to the top themselves. They used the surrounding materials in the vicinity to build that ramp. Without the ramp they would not have made it up the mountain. That must have been quite a job as they didn't have equipment like we have today. I would call that a very large landfill job..

I am not nervous in an airplane, but cannot take a sky ride like the one over near Palm Springs in California. I have been on that gondola ride near Palm Springs once and that is more than enough for me. I can't even take the sky ride at Disneyland without getting a panicky feeling. That is the way I felt riding the gondola from the Dead Sea up to the Masada. I am glad that I did get up there though. The panic I felt didn't ruin the trip for me. It would have been a shame if I had missed the experience due to a foolish panic over riding in that bucket up in the air. I guess that is the way some people must feel about airplanes, but I love flying in airplanes. Can someone explain that to me? I guess I am just a coward when it comes to not having my feet on the ground. Even a tall ladder floors me, although a small one doesn't bother me. I cannot figure myself out on that. Fear is strange. Actually that is what panic is—simply only fear.

You may wonder what the country looked like around the Dead Sea. If you have ever been around the Salton Sea in Southern California, that is what that country looks like. It is quite similar with the water and the desert with the mountains in the back ground.

The whole trip took us a little over three weeks. First to Israel, then to Greece, and then we rented a car when we returned from Europe and spent a week driving around parts of New York state. It was a very memorable vacation, one to last a lifetime. The part we saw of New York State was beautiful.

*Comments from an email :Peggy,*I've taken that ride to the top of Masada in 1973 and have never forgotten it. On one of our trips Arne and the two girls took the ski ride up a mountain side—I stayed behind—couldn't do it but when it came to Masada I thought—gotta do it—and glad I did. One gal fainted on the way up. That trip to Israel is one of the best—Arne said "I'm not going to any desert—I'm going to stay home and fish Lake Minnetonka (close to home and his favorite fishing spot) – but you should go—you will never have a chance to be with a group you know like this"—the minister who married us and baptized Laurie was the group leader. For our trip to Israel we got an extra 3 days free because we were supposed to land in Amman, Jordan. A plane was shot down there at that time so the trip was postponed. For our inconvenience the 3 days included a trip to Alexandra, Egypt and Cairo—yes, I rode a camel at the pyramids. In the extra 3 days we also got to Iskenderan, Turkey—took a trip up the side of the mountain where Christians had their services.— We took communion there and I still have my little wood communion cup. There was an escape route on the other side of the cave that was closed off by weather and rocks over the years. Just like Masada—people were not left to their own ways and had to be destroyed. Sounds like today, doesn't it?"

(Thank you, for the input)

THE HUMMINGBIRDS

Someone sent me a video showing the eggs in a hummingbird nest. Keep in mind the egg is smaller than a tic tac and a quarter fits the opening of the nest. This lady found the hummingbird nest and got pictures all the way from the egg to leaving the nest. It took 24 days from birth to flight. It was a wonderful experience that she shared with us.

At one time I, myself, had at least six hummingbird nests in the vines just outside my windows. It was awesome to watch the progress after they hatched. The eggs were about the size of a green pea. The tiny nests were well-hidden among the vines. There never seemed to be any more than two eggs to a nest. There is no more than room for two birds. Even two eventually got very crowded. Sad to say, I had to cut the vines down and no longer have the pleasure of seeing so many hummingbirds. It was a treat to be able to sit inside the house and to be able to see everything through the windows.

Response from pal: "Beautiful. We had a pair of hummingbirds last summer and I kept the little feeder filled at all times. I read that the hummingbird and the Cooper's Hawk can live in the same area because the hummingbird is too fast for the hawk. The hawk has moved on to another territory because the robins and cardinals and bluejays are back. The hawk has wiped out our adorable little chipmunks (had 12 at a time on our deck). The rabbits, many birds, and who knows what else, are gone. Keep on writing. I sure enjoy!"

THIS TIME IT'S CANARIES

My daughter, Jackie, bought two canaries a while back. They were both supposed to be male. She left them with me for a week one time and shortly I heard one singing. I knew that by putting two males in the same cage they would not sing. After about a week we noticed they were trying to build a nest. Jackie took them home and the bird continued to build the nest and then soon there were four eggs in the nest. It took only two weeks until there were four little birds. After a few weeks the birds were too crowded in the cage and she sold the babies to the person she had bought the parents from. Very shortly the canary had built another nest and laid 4 more eggs. Jackie tried to help out and the eggs were lost by something happening to the nest. That little canary turned around and laid five more eggs.

Now, Jackie doesn't try to help the birds who know how to care for themselves.

At one time Jackie had an outdoor aviary with twenty-seven birds. They were doing very well until a neighbor put hot ashes into their trash can. The ashes caused a fire and the smoke killed all her birds. These birds were not canaries but another variety. She has never replaced them.

SCHOOL LUNCHES
AND THE TERRIBLE WASTE IT CAUSES

I was shocked one time when I attended my granddaughter's school during lunch time. Thi nothing compared to what the markets toss daily...Such a waste when you think of the hundreds of people who don't have enough to eat.

BEFORE CHAIN SAWS

It was only 125 years ago when the Northwest logging industry was still young. The email pictures were of Redwood Trees being cut. These were extremely huge trees, bigger than most garage doors of today. The cutting was done by physical labor, not machinery. No chain saws then. The caption under the picture called the saw a "hand saw." It looked to me like it was several saws fastened together. We always knew them as "cross-cut" saws. To me a hand saw is what a carpenter uses to cut lumber into sizes he needs. They may have meant that they were cutting the trees by hand. Those trees were really huge. I remember on our first trip to California we visited the Redwoods and drove our car through the base of a hollowed out Redwood tree. A memorable experience

To those wondering what a cross-cut saw is, it's a long saw with a handle at each end for two people to use while they stand, one on each side of a log, and cut across the log. One will pull the saw towards himself, and then the other one will pull it back again. This way they are cutting across the log, back and forth, back and forth, until the log is cut in two. This is why they call it a cross-cut saw—it cuts across the log. They keep this up until the log is cut into the length they want it to be. It is very strenuous work. That kind of work is probably done now with what is called a chain saw, which is much faster and sure is a lot less strenuous. A "hand saw" is the one a carpenter uses to cut lumber while building something. The use of the term bow-saws and cross-cut could have been due to the area where someone lived and what they grew up with.

I have personally been on the end of a "crosscut" saw when we lived in Idaho. I had to help cut the wood from a felled tree. It took two people to handle the cross-cut. Then to add insult to injury, I also had to chop the wood into pieces that would fit into my cook stove. No, I don't want to go back to such primitive living. I even like the gas stove I have now better than the electric stove which I was so glad to get when we got the electric line in. This is just an opinion from someone who has lived through experiences quite similar to our ancestors who first settled this country.

Try living with no electricity, no paved roads, no indoor plumbing, carry your water in from a creek, and then the dirty water back out again. To wash clothes you carried the water into the house and lifted it up into a boiler on the stove to heat. Then you carried it to your washing machine, if you had one, otherwise you used a washboard and a tub. If you had a modern convenience like a gasoline powered washing machine and the motor balked you ended up scrubbing diapers on a washboard—well, you have never lived until you have tried it. Oh yes, and during the winter you hung those diapers and other clothes on a clothesline outside. The clothes would "freeze dry" and then when you brought them in they were damp and you had to hang them up to finish their drying—oh boy, you know something? I don't miss all that "fun" for some reason.

You also know what—I have a wash tub and a scrub board in my shed if anyone would like to see it. I will even let you try it out if you'd like (I won't let you bathe in it though). Bring on your laundry. Since I have already done my share of scrubbing on the washboard, I'll let you do it on your own. I'll even furnish you some water from a faucet so you won't have to carry the water in. Yep, we carried the water into the house, put it in a boiler on the stove to heat so we could wash clothes, and then we had to carry the dirty water back outside to dispose of it. Fun, Fun, Fun. This was also the same routine for bath water. Try taking a bath all scrunched up in a small tub. You did the best you could. Oh yes, when the water was hot, you carried it to where you needed it. Lots of water carrying.

One of the first things I bought when we got electricity was an electric cook stove. In case you wonder why my husband didn't help carry the water in, it was because he was working fifteen to twenty hours a day hauling lumber up to Spokane and to Moses Lake from where we lived in Idaho. This was during the war years and things were not only rationed but very hard to get. But we survived. It was hard, but it also didn't kill us. When we got the electric line in my husband dug a well and piped water into the house. Also, now I can talk about the "Good Old Days" that actually were not so good, even if we didn't let it bother us at the time. For some reason, the whole family survived it. Now I have a telephone, television, indoor plumbing, (real bathtub, shower, toilet) running water and *the bills to pay for it all.* What more could I ask for.

OBSERVATION SEVERAL YEARS LATER

This happened one day at the mobile home park where I lived in California, probably in 2012. It was really inconvenient not to have that electricity so I wrote about it.

"My electricity was just turned back on. They had to repair the transformer. It now reminds me of the "Good Old

Days" the first few years that we lived in Idaho. We had no electricity until my husband and several neighbors got together and built an electric line. While we did not have some of the conveniences we have today (some had not been invented yet) here is what I learned today: I don't want to go back to those *GOOD OLD DAYS at all."*

Here is what I did not have today—No TV or Radio, use of my washer and dryer, no vacuum cleaner, no night lights, no porch light, no iron (who irons any more) no computer or printer, no automatic electric igniter for my gas range (I used a lighter gadget to ignite the burners to fix breakfast) no lights (and no gas lantern to see by) no record player or CD player, my electric clocks would not work, neither would my sewing machine. The ceiling fans would not go on, the furnace defied me to try to get it to turn on even if it was cold. (Yes, it does get cold here in California) I did not need the air conditioner so I did not miss it as it would not have gone on anyway. My cell phone would not charge without electricity. The microwave defied me to try to use it. The coffee pot sulked. The can opener, blender and toaster dared me, so I glared at them. I have one of those electric beds that will raise up if I want to sit up, etc. It was completely lazy, and wanted some juice I guess. When I turned the water on it reminded me that it takes electricity to run the pump too. My electric typewriter would not work if I had tried to use it (it's obsolete anyway, even if they did not have electric typewriters when I went to high school, and of course you can't even give them away any more, so there). No one could use their computer either while the electricity was off.

I could go on and on, but you get the idea. Appreciate that little convenience you have, *it's called **electricity***.

A NEW LANGUAGE

The language being used today is like a foreign language. Try finding something in the phone book under the terms you used to use and you cannot find it. You have to learn a new language or you don't find what you need. The terms used on a computer is an example of a "new language". It means something completely different to us older folks than to the younger generation. To us a mouse is a rodent, a virus is illness, a worm is what is used to bait a fishhook. Confusing isn't it? It goes on and on and on.

BEFORE CHAIN SAWS
HARD WORK

FROM OZ: "You always have an interesting story to share. You speak of long work hours back in the day depending where you live I guess. I think it made your generation tough and endure more than the kids today. I don't think we'll ever see a generation like yours again, in my lifetime anyway."

I answered: The fifteen to twenty-hour days were because logging and lumbering is seasonal work and our livelihood depended on most income coming in during the summer months. It was feast in summer and famine in winter so your income came from summer work. In the winter, Tom would go wherever he could get work as a carpenter. Sometimes that was scarce too and it meant he would be away from home for long periods at a time or had to go a long distance to get work.

OZ "I remember my mother hanging clothes outside. She said they dry better and smell nice, even in the winter. She didn't have a dryer at the time, in fact she didn't have a dryer until the '80's—that's 1980's, ha. My mother, who was born in 1924, was one of ten, said she had to carry water from the sink to the bathroom upstairs if she wanted to take a bath. They all did. She didn't chop wood but they had coal, living in Philadelphia, PA which is a city and not a rural place.

The people in the Pennsylvania Mountains had outhouses and those people had it hard. I guess that some people forget about the "good old days". Mine were nothing like yours and my kids didn't even know what a record was. I took them to my aunt who was 90 at the time and she let them pick a record out and play it on a record machine. They thought that was neat. I heard they are trying to bring the old vinyls back.

I've never seen the Redwoods. There is so much to do in this country; I would have to live 5 life times to complete a journey through the US. I have had electric stoves for ages; I prefer a gas stove the same as you.

Well thanks for the story. Oh yes, the term 'hand saw' probably was used because most of us would have to have cross-cut saw explained to us. I have a cross cut shredder, and to me it means that it chops up the paper in little pieces. I would be wondering why they did that to a tree. The new language is using older terms in a new and different way".

MORE ABOUT CHAIN SAWS
HARD WORK

FROM email pal: "I remember trees like this too! I never was in a logging camp, but my best girl friends grandmother was a cook and so were my mother's great aunt and those great uncles used to make a living logging around the Enumclaw, Washington area. They used to call those saws either cross cut or bow saws, but the term bow saws seem to stick in my mind better for some reason. I remember seeing pictures of my mother's family in tents that were made from split logs and then canvas tops. I had always imagined that life was not fun back then and a lot of hard work! One had to be strong to survive whatever came that way! At one time I had always thought that life was simpler back then. I surely do not think that now. It took courage and a lot of hard work to live like that!"

My comment: This happened during one of our "moves" that my dad seemed to always require. The logs that were covered with canvas reminds me of the time when I was quite young when we went past the area where Bonneville Dam was being built and I saw where people were living. They had floors with wood sides built up and a large tent fastened on top of the framework. I thought it was quite a clever way to house people. I have often wondered why the same idea wasn't used for temporary "camping" quarters. It gave more room than an ordinary tent and kept you off the ground at the same time.

I recently read a book about the early travelers and pioneers. They used a lot of tents as living quarters until they could get some kind of a shelter built. Some even had to live in them during the cold winter months. They would also dig into the ground for shelter. They would make bricks of sod and build a house with those bricks. Digging into the ground for shelter was a good protection from the extreme winter weather. Anything to survive. Many times the floor was only packed down earth. In this day we probably cannot imagine the living conditions of our pioneer ancestors. I wonder if we would be able to survive even one winter if we suddenly had to do so in this generation since we don't even have an idea of how they lived in those days. Do we realize how privileged we are?

WE TRAVELED A LOT

My husband and I did a lot of traveling when we were younger. We could afford to do so only because we took a tent and cooking equipment. We didn't have the luxury of a motor home at that time. The kids were small and I believe we did most of this traveling when we had only three children. We didn't do so much after the 4th one came along.

I think the last camping trip we took was when we were returning back toward home after going to New York. We stopped in the Black Hills and toured Mt. Rushmore that has the statues of the Presidents carved into the mountainside in South Dakota. That evening we pulled into the yard of a closed country school, pitched our tent, ate our supper, and went to sleep in our tent. In the morning I crawled out of my sleeping bag and found out I had had company during the night—a little lizard crawled out of bed with me. That ended it. I refused to ever sleep on the ground again. We didn't do as much traveling after that and when we did we had either a travel trailer or a motor home, and sometimes the luxury of a motel room.

We made a trip to California once or twice a year but stayed in a motel. We also didn't stop much on the way either. Motels were around $10.00 a night, which we could hardly afford (now those same motels are closer to $100 a night). I am so glad we did all that traveling when we did. We were young enough to do so, and we would not be able to do it when we got older. Now I go by airplane or go on a cruise whenever I can. Even the cruise I just went on shows me that most of my traveling days are over.

At 91, I find it a bit too hard to get around any more as my legs are giving me plenty of trouble. Otherwise I do really well, everything else considered.

STILL MORE ABOUT HARD WORK

From email: This isn't about chain saws but we lived in the area where they were used. It is about hard work. My Father was in the trucking business but hauling of a different kind than lumber and logs. I remember those old days. Mom and Dad bought a refrigerator in 1941, just before the war, but before that, Dad would bring back from Spokane a 2 foot by 4 foot by 12 inch chunk of ice for our halfway in the ground cellar on his weekly, Thursday, 60 mile trips to Spokane and 60 mile return trips to Farmington.

Each Thursday, Dad would haul cattle to the Spokane stock yard, or anything else Farmington people wanted to send to Spokane. Then Dad would wash out his truck and haul groceries from the URM supply center back to the Farmington stores. Dad had a common carrier license that allowed him to haul anything. Many times, during WW2, he moved people from Farmington, to the Seattle, Bremerton, or Portland area so they could work in the war effort. I recall he often stopped near North Bend to pick up a load of shingles to bring back. I don't recall him ever returning with an empty truck. He could always find a load.

There was an old fellow who wanted to ride up to Spokane and back with him each week. The rumor was the old fellow visited the Coeur d'Alene Hotel and a special lady or maybe a different lady regularly. I remember the fellow and his name but prefer not to use it. Other Farmington people also hitched a ride occasionally but not for the same reason. I rode along sometimes, but most often in the back of the truck. I recall several times riding high up, on the load, above the cab of the truck. I don't remember what I laid on up there, but it was something Dad was delivering. I was quite young then.

Oh yes, Dad got the first electric stove brought into Farmington after the end of the war. We couldn't use that stove in Farmington, but used it in Rosalia when we moved there in August 1945. We let the sellers of the farm we bought stay until August. Dad wanted to stay in Farmington until after harvest because his business also included hauling grain sacks to the Farmers Warehouse in Farmington or bulk grain to an elevator in Salteze, Farmington, Tekoa, Garfield, Belmont, Oaksdale, or some other place in the area."

MORE TRUCKING NEWS

Now I want to add to this. My husband, Thomas (1920-2001) also would haul grain sacks in the summer. Mostly the grain was dried peas. They were harvested and left in the field until loaded. Those sacks of peas probably weighed at least a hundred pounds each and had to be loaded by hand, onto the truck and then hauled to their destination to be unloaded again by hand labor. It was long hours of hard work. By having two men lifting the sacks from the ground up onto the truck bed, it was easier on the back, and faster, to load the truck. When he got to the place where the peas were stored, he also had to unload by hand. There was no machinery to do the heavy work. The farm areas he worked were Salteze, Tekoa, Garfield, Oaksdale, and other farms in the area. Tom was very tired when he got home. I think his back hurt extremely bad too. The pea harvest and hauling only lasted a few weeks each year. This was back breaking work to say the least. There were times when he could not get help that he would load and unload the sacks by himself. Needless to say he was extremely tired when he got home. Undoubtedly his back was also in extreme pain.

My husband would hire a helper if someone was available. He hired one young man, who was about twenty years of age, and part of his wages was for me to fix him supper when he was working. Hauling peas was very dirty work. This young man was a hard worker, but my husband had to strongly remind him to wash his hands before meals or he would have sat down with his dirt and all. It was evident that he never bathed. He sure looked muddy even when he came to work in the morning with the same dust and dirt acquired the day before.

We heard later that he was in the military service and the other soldiers had grabbed him physically and saw to it that he got a shower. He lived with his father and I don't believe he grew up with a mother to care for him. They had not been very long as residents of Benewah and no one knew anything about the father and son. They had evidently been temporary in the area. When the job was over, I never heard much more about the young man and I never saw him again after the job Tom had hired him for was ended. It appeared to me that something had been missing from his life before then. You can imagine what someone looks like who never had a bath. I don't remember though if he had an odor to him—just that he was dirty and muddy appearing. I believe if he had been odorous I would remember it. That really would have impressed me enough about him to remember.

I WATCHED THE CHILDREN

Another time a man with three young children came by looking for work and needed someone to watch the children while he searched for a job in Benewah. I volunteered to watch them for a few hours. I don't remember why I volunteered to watch the three of them. The little girls were dirty appearing. I bathed the little girls and all three children played outside until I fed them. The children minded me when I asked them to do anything. The father did not find work in the area. I never saw them again.

A MOOSE IS HARNESSED

In a Power Point group of pictures, I had an article about a moose that was harnessed and used as a farm animal. I expressed my opinion that it was probably a fake. But other animals are harnessed up and used as work animals, dogs are used to pull sleds and camels are used as beasts of burden, so why not a moose I wondered.

REPLY FROM email pal:That animal is in fact real. I read about it a few years ago, the whole story. He was orphaned and he hung around the reindeer that this guy owned so the guy started to feed it. The moose decided to stay and be friends and one day wanted to be harnessed just like the others of his clan, so to speak."

On our trip to Canada in 1966 we saw farms where they raised wild animals like Elk and Moose so the story may be true.

FROM OZ: "I did find an article about the taming of the Moose. It started in 1949. They have Moose Farms where they breed them, because of their low numbers, and they do give milk. I didn't find anything about a fake photo."

4/12/17—Someone sent me an email picture today of a farmer and his moose harnessed. Guess it can be done after all. I think the moose would have to be one that was domesticated. Oxen were harnessed, so why not a moose.

1949 COST OF LIVING
VERSUS 2012 COST OF LIVING

I found the following information which I thought to be interesting, comparing 1949 prices with 2012 prices. Boy! Do I ever remember those prices. Makes it hard to adjust to the prices of everything today.

Average new house in 1949 was $7450. In 1955 we bought a new house for $14,000. Now it is about $250,000 or more for either of those houses. Inflation isn't it. Wages, $2950 (that is per YEAR) vs. now it's more than that per month

Gasoline was 27 cents. Now we hope it doesn't go higher than today's $4.39 a gallon.(that was the price in California at the time)

Average cost of new car $1420. Today an old almost worn out one costs that much.

Same brand of new cars that sold for $1420 in 1949 probably sells now for $20,000 or even more. We bought new cars when we moved to California and paid about $4000 for them. That was around 1960

Minimum wage 70 cents per hour then is now around $9 (depending on which state)In 1941 my husband had a job that paid 65 cents an hour. Fairly good job and that was not minimum wage. I do not remember that there was such a thing as minimum wages then.

Bacon per pound 50 cents (oh, how expensive that was). Now it's about $4 per pound.

In 1934 my grandfather built a beautiful 3 bedroom home with hardwood floors and a full basement in Spokane and sold it for $3500. Today, that very same home would sell for $250,000 and more and would be snapped up in a hurry. Yes, that very same house built in 1934 would bring that price today. While in Spokane last year, I looked that home up and it looks as good today as it did then. It was quality built.

FROM A 1957 MENU

I believe these were prices that Woolworths charged, but others were about the same

A ham and cheese sandwich was 60 cents, (no extra charge to have it toasted)

A toasted cheese sandwich was 30 cents.

An ice cream soda or a sundae was 25 cents.

A banana split was 39 cents (kinda expensive wasn't it?)

A malted milk or a milk shake was 25 cents

Orange juice (regular size) was 20 cents but a large was 30 cents.

Hot chocolate was 15 cents

Apple pie was 15 cents per cut (wasn't that something?)

A cup of coffee was 5 cents and sometimes it was even free. Yes, free with a meal, and no charge for as many refills as you wanted.

You could buy a cup of coffee alone if that is all you wanted, with free refills too.

In fact, you could get a whole meal for 40 cents.

Compare those with prices of today on your own. Today the prices have reached the sky.

I used to go to Woolworths to eat occasionally and those were the prices I paid. I could not afford to eat there or any other place very often.

MORE SURVIVAL WAYS

The following is from one of my email pals, after I had sent her an email called "America in Color from 1939 to 1943," with comments by me at a later time.

"Wow, this is a wonderful piece of footage. I can't go back that far, my dear, but my father can and has often told me about his younger days during the depression. My grandfather used to rent a five acre plot for a dollar, where he grew vegetables not only for his own family but for his neighbors as well. My grandfather was a mason, which only means that he worked with concrete and bricks. But he was the best mason around and everyone wanted him to do their steps, homes, or whatever they had for concrete, etc. He knew the value of good hard work; after all it was for a dollar a day!

My grandparents on my mother's side were fishers. They owned a boat called "the Wave". When my mother and aunt were old enough to walk on deck he sold the boat for a house in Forrest Park, now called Shoreline, Washington. He was a Reader's Digest sales person, a silverware salesman, etc. etc. Now my grandmother's side is a little more interesting as her family was some of the first settlers in Auburn (Green River) and they had brought horses (Norman War Horses) from England to the US. They had the last herd until my great uncle sold it off. The last time I heard they were in Snohomish somewhere. My mother and siblings used to ride Big Red (fondly known as Old Soldier) who was taken by Teddy Roosevelt to Cuba to fight in the rebellion there. Big Red was grazed across his rump with a bullet and received a ration of oats for the rest of his life; he was 45 years old when he died quietly one summer afternoon. He is buried on the south knoll where my great great grandparents are buried in a little fenced off place on the farm they bought for a nickel down!

My grandfather's parents were from Missouri, came out West in about 1900 sometime. I find them on the census in 1910 in Palouse, Whitman County, Washington. By that time they had 9 children born to them, 13 children total that I know of. A few of them not only married here but a couple of them died here as well. Interesting, yes, but then again when a person is so into genealogy, like I am, I can't help myself."

JUST OBSERVATIONS

During the depression years, if you had an income of $100 per month you could really live "high off the hog" as the saying goes. You were considered wealthy.

I remember in 1934, a family friend tried to join the military because he could not get a job. The military was not taking on anyone as there were too many volunteers from people out of work. By 1941, wages were still way under 65 cents an hour if you could get work. Then World War 2 arrived and men were drafted into the military.

The war made for many changes. Men didn't have to volunteer; they were drafted. Yes there have been a lot of changes over the last hundred years. There will undoubtedly be a great many more in the next hundred.

Before World War 2, very few married women worked outside the home. The war did cause a drastic change to that picture. Women went to work and have never returned to being "just a housewife". Instead of caring for their own children they hired baby-sitters to care for the children and now it is common for other than the parents to raise the children. This has upset the balance of family life to the detriment of the family.

When I was in high school I tried to get baby-sitting jobs. They were scarce, very scarce. The few times I got a job it was for 25 cents for the entire evening, not an hour. For that

25 cents I was expected to clean up the house and was never allowed to go to sleep no matter what time the parents got home, even if it was 2 a.m.

After my mother was able to get Aid for Dependent Children (ADC) help from welfare, she got $30 a month for four kids. When I became 16 they cut that in half, expecting me to get a job. I don't know how they expected me to get a job if I couldn't even get a babysitting job for 25 cents an evening. If I did get a regular daytime job, it meant I would not be able to go to school. Mom ended up going to the Welfare department and talking to the Case Worker. She told them they would have to put us kids in an orphanage because that way she knew we would be fed and have shelter. It really was no fun to be on welfare. They restored the grant back to $30 a month. I finished high school. We also got off Welfare's ADC then and my mother got work at Kaisers that fall after the big war started.

MY SUMMER JOB

During the summer of 1939 I worked as a maid for a family. I was required to "live in." I had a very small bedroom upstairs. It was probably six by eight feet in size.

By 6 in the morning, I had to get up and fix breakfast for the man of the house. He must have had ulcers, as the Cream of Wheat had to be cooked in a double boiler the night before. Then in the morning it had to be heated up in the double boiler and made sure there were no lumps in the cereal. I don't remember if he had anything else for breakfast.

Their daughter was visiting with her baby (who was less than a year old). I had to keep the baby fed and quiet until the mother and grandmother got up. Then I made their breakfast. They always ate all meals in the dining room. I ate in the kitchen (thank goodness). If they rang a bell it was to come serve them something else they wanted. After breakfast and cleaning up the kitchen, I had to clean the house, do the laundry and do the ironing. They even wanted their cotton anklets ironed. I didn't see the sense of that, and still don't, but I ironed them. Once, while cleaning the living room, I saw a lizard come crawling into the house and I thought it was a snake when I first saw it so I screamed. They didn't like it that I screamed, but it had startled me when I saw the long tail which appeared to be a snake.

They saw to it that I earned every cent of the **$4 a week** I was paid. I was supposed to have two afternoons a week off of the seven days I had to be there. It actually amounted to 7 days a week with only a few hours off. They always saw to it that I had work so I couldn't leave until after 3 in the afternoon. When school resumed in the fall they wanted me to keep on working for them. I found an excuse that I couldn't work any longer, that I was needed at home. I hated that job and it haunts me to this day. They were not very nice to their hired help. I purchased the first new coat I ever had with my earnings of that summer.

THE NEXT SUMMER WAS DIFFERENT

The next summer I did the same kind of work. I got my jobs through the Washington State employment office. When I went to the lady's home at the appointed time and she opened the door, it scared the daylights out of me. Who was it but one of the teachers from the Junior High School I had attended. She was the one I had had a run in with when I had taken a note sent by the principal to one of the students. I guess I was supposed to see the teacher first before giving the note to the student and she told me so. She also had a reputation for being strict. She wasn't nasty to me, she only explained it was proper to see the teacher first, but it scared me at the time and I felt intimidated.

If I had known who was to be my employer before I had gone to her house, I most probably would not have gone there. The reason I did not know the name is because she had married during the summer and now had a new name. The man she married was a widower with two daughters.

As it turned out, she was a wonderful employer and I had the opportunity of learning a lot from her. She was kind and thoughtful. The daughters were required to do the dishes in the evening. I only had to supervise them. She didn't pile a bunch of extra chores onto me. Mrs. Kirk worked right along with me. The lady was very nice to me. I always ate with the family. Oh what a difference that was. I was treated like one of the family.

When school started, the job was over. A few weeks later she called me to see if I could help her out during the time she was having a party. I was glad to go. And, believe it or not, after I helped serve her guests, she served me.

I repeat: if I had known who was to be my employer before I had gone to her house, I most probably would not have gone there. I am very glad I did not know at the time.

WHERE ARE YOUR PICTURES KEPT?

THE STRANGERS IN THE BOX—I received a poem about how people will put their pictures in a box and not put information about the person on the back. This causes their names and memories to be lost. If someone had taken the time to put the information of who what, where, or when the picture was taken it would bring back memories of their heritage. The faces and memories would pass away without information on those pictures and then you and yours would become the *Strangers in the Box*. How many times have we experienced the feelings expressed by the unknown writer?

I was browsing through a bunch of genealogy material that I had put away a few years ago and came across an envelope of pictures I don't remember looking at before. These all brought back memories of different people, some are now long gone, but most of all the biggest surprise was a picture. On the back was a note: *"TAKEN ON HIS 100TH BIRTHDAY"*. Just who was he, which relative was he. I am sure it was a relative, but who was he related to? When and where was the picture taken. I would like to know, but the information is lost because no one put the information on the back of the picture. No name was noted on the picture, but with so many family members now living to be close to 100, it is likely through the family of my grandmother. We only have a little genealogy of her family and very little of my grandfather. Just who was that 100 year old man. I just have to guess that he was my great great grandfather, judging that information on the fact there are so many long lived ones from the same grandparents. Very unfortunate it was not identified.

A poem from an unknown author fits the occasion of the picture without information that would have been nice to have.

It should move us to identify our own pictures for those who follow after us. I do not know who the unknown author of that poem was. I got it from someone by email. Pictures are important. They help us to see what our ancestors or friends looked like. Pictures are stories that are visible. We really need them and they should always be identified, for others if not for ourselves.

WHERE HAVE ALL THE YEARS GONE
LONG LIVED ONES

Where have all the years gone? Once I thought thirty-five was really old. Barring illness our minds stay almost the same as they were when we were twenty years of age. We are seldom prepared for the aches and pains and loss of strength that goes with aging. Life goes by too quickly. Now there are many in my family who are heading to the age of 100, When you look back one hundred years is not a very long time.

From a cousin who writes: "Hi Everyone, I sure received a lot of greetings for my 97th birthday. Thanks so much to all of you. I am feeling a lot better these days and with the weather changing to nice days, I have been out a lot. I don't know how I got to 97. I must have sneaked in the back door. I was down to Des Moines yesterday and helped open the Eagle part of the program. It was something I could do. There were a lot of people coming to the fair. I have never seen so many baby carriages with small kids. Again, thanks much for the greetings. I sure appreciated them—Bill Horine."

Update in 2014: That was written in 2012. This same cousin is now 99 years of age and still going strong in this year of 2014. I have another cousin who is 97 and another is 95, another one who is 92 and about two months older than me. All five of us have descended from the same set of grandparents. Mark and Jennie Horine.

January 25, 2016—Update. It was bound to happen that my updates ended up outdated.

Bill Horine has passed away without quite reaching 100. So has my cousin Artha Bennett who reached 97 and Donald Horine who only made it to 97 and Helen Miller also expired at 96. They only made it to 2014 and 2015. Still it was quite a feat. I am still here at 93 and so is Lois Johnson at 93. It won't be long until the two of us will be 94. Don't plan on either of us being the next, so keep expecting to hear from us again soon. All of us the grandchildren of Mark and Jennie Horine. One of my father's sisters, Ruth, lived to be 93 and her daughter, Irene Enger, passed away past the age of 95 (two more descendants of Mark and Jennie Horine). No wonder I am now 93 and still going strong with relatives and ancestors like that.

Guess I can look forward to a few years yet. Now, on my mother's side of the family, my mother was almost 94 when she passed away. My uncle, her brother, was 91 when he expired. My husband's only sister was 96 at her passing. My husband, Tom, had been going strong at the age of 81 until he fell and hit his head. He did not survive that fall.

I have been surrounded with "old" people who don't seem to know any better than to keep living towards 100. Why should I break that kind of record?" See you all when I reach *ONE HUNDRED*. Hope you are not too confused by this list of "old" people. Since I have not yet reached 100 all I can say is "see you later" as I am not yet "old" although all of us are long lived on both sides of my family.

JOY Another cousin, on my mother's side of the family, wrote to me: "Peggy, you are adorable! I love your genealogy report! My mother, Clara, lived to be 90 years and seven months. My husband said all he ever saw her do was eat and sleep – she was busy in her younger years but exercise and diet were not for her. I had a cancer removed at the age of 48 in 1975. I went through chemo and now still going strong at 87."

She signed off with "Keep your emails coming!" (Clara was a first cousin to my mother.)

NOTES FROM email pal (in 2012): "Well, I do declare, that you are only 90 years young!!! My great aunt lived to be 109 years young. Her sister lived to be 103!! So, yep, the Rhoades side of this family also has strong genes for longevity!

Well, my dear, I do hope that you have the back of those pictures marked as to who they are, so that whoever is doing your genealogy can get some very good use out of them about now!!! Actually that is a treasure trove of discovery for the person doing the family genealogy and especially if you can identify them!!

I know my grandfather would have out-lived his wife if he had not had cancer that couldn't be treated properly. Basically it was in too late of a stage to get it all. All the chemo etc. did was buy him about ten years or so. But through it all, all he would ever take is an aspirin. I can't imagine the pain that he was going through but do know that the doctor had made a cocktail for him to take if he was bad enough off!!! He never did take it and later we had to dump that stuff. I do believe that longevity of life is in the genes that you inherit from both sides of your family. So never get old my friend, getting younger is much easier cuz getting older isn't for wimps!! Have a great evening!!"

TRAVELING BY AIR TO NEW YORK

In 1950 we went by plane to New York. Then we got stranded for a while. A group of people had chartered a plane for a trip to New York City. We had all planned on that trip for several months. Because the Korean War had just been declared the government suddenly cancelled all civilian plans for air travel on anything like chartered trips. This had unexpectedly changed all our plans for the trip. Because the larger plane had been cancelled our group was too large for the smaller plane that had become available. The charter had been through a regular company and it had now become necessary for them to limit the number who could go on the trip to New York. Since the war squelched our plans, when the plane that would carry 50 passengers became available from Seattle, there was room for only that many. That this plane had come to Seattle from Florida with a load of some kind, and was returning to Florida empty, is the only reason we even got a plane at all. The charter company had it fitted with seats for fifty.

217

It was required to have at least two flight attendants on this plane and two young women volunteered in Seattle to do the duty in order to get a seat. The rest of the fifty people who were selected boarded the plane in Spokane upon its arrival. The plane was a prop plane, not a jet. It was a bit scary as the weather was very turbulent and we bounced around quite a bit. After a few rough bumps I decided it would not do any good to be so scared. I decided if the plane went down it would be quick, so I just relaxed. I would have plenty of time to worry later if anything went wrong. Some of the other passengers were extremely air sick from a combination of fear and severe turbulence and the volunteers had to assist them. I felt sorry for the two young women who had volunteered in order to be included on the trip and were not paid for their work. They never complained though. It surely must have been hard under the circumstances. No one on the plane panicked as the plane bounced around. All were quiet, even though evidently very frightened.

We made it safely to Minnesota where the plane landed to refuel. Unfortunately the weather was working up to a tornado is why the flight was so turbulent. The FAA required the plane to be taken on a test flight before they would let it be taken up again with passengers. I was told by someone that the plane had been required to be taken up for a test flight, but I do not remember who told me or if the information was true. I just know the plane was taken up and none of us were allowed to accompany it for the test. While we were at the airport, and the plane was being put through the test flight, we had lunch. Then we were allowed to continue on. We made it on in to New York without further incident.

We were told that we would have to take a train home as no planes were available back from New York. We were stranded in New York for two weeks. The hotel we had been in was quite expensive, so we ended up moving to one a little less costly. After moving to the lesser cost hotel we still could not get a train back home. Even trains were hard to get passage on because of the war declaration. It was costing us to eat in restaurants and with the hotel to pay for we ran low on money. We finally got passage on a train. By the last day on the train we were completely out of money. Someone else helped us out for the train meals that last day. Not a pleasant situation. We did arrive home OK after all.

PLANES HAVE GROWN UP

Why are planes so fascinating to view? I have seen the progress of changes in planes over the past 95 years. My first plane ride was in a biplane—that is a plane with two sets of wings. I was probably ten years old at the time. That would have been about 1932. We just went for a short ride over Palouse, Washington. In my 95 years of life, I have seen a great many changes on both the ground and in the air. Planes have "grown up" from small planes to huge jumbo jets. From "slow" to breaking the sound barrier. People are still very fascinated with airplanes. One grandson is going to college to learn about planes and he makes videos about them.

FAMOUS AVIATORS

Charles Lindberg, Amelia Earhart, and Douglas Corrigan all were Aviation Pioneers from 1927 to 1938. I don't want to forget Howard Hughes and his famous plane the

Spruce Goose. They were the kind of people a person could remember and not easily forget. They were the firsts of their kind and day.

LINDBERG FLEW OVER SPOKANE
And I remember seeing it fly over

Charles A. Lindberg--I recall the time when I was five years old living in Spokane when everyone crowded onto the Monroe Street Bridge to watch Lindberg fly over the town and the Monroe Street bridge. He had completed his famous solo flight over the Atlantic Ocean in 1927 and was very popular in the news. It seemed like there were thousands of people on that bridge at the time wanting to get a peek at him and his famous plane. Lindberg was on a nationwide tour which included landing in Spokane on September 12, 1927. During his stay in Spokane he made a low level flight over the St. Luke's Hospital so the crippled children could see his plane. This must have been the time and place where I saw this event as the hospital is quite near the Monroe Street bridge. I clearly remember the tremendous crowd. There was standing room only and no cars could have gotten on that bridge that day. I do clearly remember seeing the plane fly over.

Another thing I remember from a later time was the Lindberg baby kidnapping. It was in the news, making headlines every day. Such a terrible event. This kidnapping caused the law to invoke the death penalty for kidnapping. The news was kept going about the trial of the man accused of the deed. I was probably about ten or eleven years old at the time but it was such a crime that I never forgot it. The baby was found dead and the man named Hauptman was convicted.

It was not the internet that reminded me of the Lindberg flyover but driving over that Monroe Street bridge a few days ago—*October 2017*. I made the remark to Sherry, who was driving my van, that it reminded me of the event. She suggested I write about it. Memories, memories, and more memories come to mind with small occurances to jog that memory.

Now airplanes have gone from the relatively quiet and small size planes that Lindberg flew to big jumbo jets that can fly around the world and fast planes that can break the sound barrier. What is next I wonder.

AMELIA EARHART

Another famous flyer was *Amelia Earhart*. She was the first female to fly solo over the Atlantic. She set many flying records, wrote books, and received the Distinguished Flying Cross. She was adventurous as a child and was fascinated with airplanes after she was given a ride one time. While on that ride she decided that flying was what she would do with her life. What I remember about her is the fact that she was very famous about her flying ability. She disappeared on a flight on July 2, 1937. Fascination about her life continues to this day. An extensive search was made but no trace has ever been located. It is still a mystery as to what actually happened to her. It also seems to pop up in the news that they would still like to find her remains and to know what happened to her. There was all kinds of speculation about what happened to her, from running out of gas to being shot down.

Even after 80 years has passed, people wonder about her disappearance. In fact a search for her remains still goes on. Everyone wants to know—just what happened to her.

HOWARD HUGHES AND HIS SPRUCE GOOSE

Howard Hughes made the first flight around the world in 1938. He was an aviator, movie producer, inventor, engineer, and big businessman. He designed and built planes, and was a test pilot. His inventions made him wealthy along with his other enterprises. He became very famous with his flight around the world. He had many close calls on that flight. He made it to Paris with his plane coming in on nothing but fumes.

He later made headlines with the plane he built entirely of wood which made it very heavy. Someone called it the *Spruce Goose*, a name which stuck to the plane, which it is still called to this day. Hughes hated that name. When someone claimed it would never fly, Hughes took it up and flew it to prove that it would fly. On November 2, 1947 he took it up and flew it for about a mile. That was the only airborne flight it ever made. He had proven his claim that the plane would fly.

The plane was put on display in California for many years and was a big tourist attraction. We visited the display one time. A few years ago it was moved to a museum in McMinville, Oregon, a city near Portland, as a museum piece for people to view. The plane was built near the end of World War 2 with the idea that it would be big enough to transport war materials and large items. Being made of plentiful wood, it would save scarce materials in plane building. It went no further because the war ended and they no longer needed it. However, it was the forerunner of the large transport planes we have today. This plane has the biggest wing span in history. It is attractive in appearance.

Mr Hughes was a very brilliant man, who, at the end of his life, became very ill and died a recluse.

WRONG WAY CORRIGAN

Douglas Corrigan—was born in 1907. Corrigan was an airplane mechanic who had earlier helped build the plane that Lindberg had flown over the Atlantic in 1927.

On *July 17, 1938.* he took off from a Brooklyn airport in a tiny single engine plane supposedly heading for California. He had filed a flight plan to go to California, but 29 hours later his plane landed in Ireland. He claimed his compasses had "failed" him which caused him to "*accidentally*" fly the wrong way. This caught the attention of the public.

Aviation Authorities had turned down Corrigans request to make a Trans-Atlantic Flite, so when his compasses "failed" he crossed the Atlantic and he ended up in Ireland. The public hailed him as a hero, and treated him as such. That is when he became known as "*Wrong Way Corrigan*". After that anyone who made a big mistake or did things backward, was given the nick-name *Wrong Way Corrigan*. It seems like there is more than one way to "skin a cat,"

ENTERTAINING FLIGHT CREWS

I have flown a lot in my travels and on some airlines the attendants help pass the time by telling stories or jokes. One time I was on a flight from California to Spokane and the flight crew was entertaining us. I believe the flight was turbulent. It helped to pass the time and it also was unforgettable. Besides the jokes, they had a contest. Among the things that qualified you in that contest was if you had a hole in your stocking. Well, of course I had a hole in the toe of my stocking. I got the prize of a bottle of wine. (Good wine) That hole had developed after I had left home. It worked out good under the circumstances. I enjoyed the flight and remember it to this day. Maybe I got the prize because no one else would admit to having a hole in their stocking.

They made this announcement, which I think is a great one: "Ladies and Gentlemen, if you wish to smoke, the smoking sections on this airplane are on the wing so if you can light 'em, you can smoke 'em." I really like this one.

All this made us forget about the turbulence. As we were landing the flight attendants reminded us to gather all of our belongings. If we were to leave anything they suggested it be something they might like to have and it would be divided with the employees. The only thing they really did not want was our children or our spouses because they could not share them. The flight was enjoyable and we left laughing.

CELL PHONES

The days of a phone in the home, sometimes referred to as a land phone, are all but gone.

There are times when you might wish there had never been such as thing as a cell phone. Personally I hate to be traveling along and someone unnecessarily uses the cell phone in the car. It is as irritating in the automobile as it is in a restaurant. I feel the time in my car is my time, which I do not want to share with a cell phone. I fully wish someone would invent something so it would be impossible to use a cell phone in the car unless it was an emergency. In other words a gadget that could be either turned on or turned off.

AUTOMOBILE DRIVING & ROLLOVERS

If you wish to drive alive, stay in the right hand lane except for passing. Left hand cruisers cause more accidents and deaths than drunk drivers according to a police report.

If cars are passing you on the right side it means you are driving in the wrong lane and need to move over. In describing the rollovers I go from the last one to the earliest ones.

As usual, this reminds me of the accidents I have been in. They do happen extremely fast. I have been in four cars that have rolled over. You do not have time to avoid what happens. In two of them I got broken ribs (they are very painful, especially if you need to cough). The last car that rolled over happened in 1985. It left scars, but no injuries that were cripling.

ROLLOVER #4 --This accident happened because of "black ice" on the highway. The highway looked dry, and the ice was entirely invisible. Black ice is quite dangerous and extremely slick. It is deceiving and unless you get out of the car and try to step on it you don't know it even exists. That was how I got my second set of broken ribs. Now I personally know how it feels to have a car skid on ice.

On December 19, 1985, we were going to Spokane from Portland and the weather was cold but beautiful with the sun out and no clouds. The highway appeared to be nice and clear with only a small amount of snow along the edge of the highway. Everything was going along beautifully well, but as we were going up a hill halfway between Umatilla and Kennewick through an unpopulated stretch of highway the car suddenly, but slowly, started to turn around. We went over the edge of the highway into a ditch and the car rolled over. My husband figured the cause was that the car automatically shifted gears as we were going uphill. The shift changed our speed, causing the car to slide sideways on the slick ice, and we went over the bank and rolled. The car was totaled. Fortunately I wasn't.

A truck driver stopped and used his radio to call for an ambulance. He had first aid equipment, as well as a neck brace and a blanket which he used to help get me off the snow. I was lying with my bare back on the snow. My blouse was up under my arms and my slacks were down around my hips. Fortunately only the middle of my back was exposed, but that snow was cold.

This accident happened on a stretch of highway with no houses between the Columbia River and Kennewick, Washington. I really appreciate the help of the long-haul truck driver. The closest town was about 15 miles in each direction. Without him and his radio to call for help we might have been in big trouble as the area was quite desolate.

He also must have been trained in first aid. With the help of others who stopped they got me off the snow. I never learned who he was so I could thank him for his help. He probably never got his blanket back either. My husband lost his glasses and never did find them although we looked when we went past the accident scene on the way home.

I spent five days in the hospital in Kennewick before my daughter arrived from California to rent a car to take us the two hundred miles back home to Portland. By that time there was no more ice.

It wasn't until I had been home a few days that we noticed my foot was turning black. My daughter took me to the doctor and all he did was see me from the doorway and shouted at someone, "Call an Ambulance." He wouldn't even let my daughter drive me the few blocks from the clinic to the hospital. He had immediately recognized it as gangrene. Gangrene had set into that scratch I got when I went through the sun roof—yes, the sun roof. Because it was winter the sun roof was closed until I opened it with my body. There was evidently broken metal where my body had forced itself through that closed sun roof. I felt my foot being scratched on the broken metal, but it did not hurt—maybe because I had broken ribs which did hurt. Because of the other injuries, no one noticed that scratch and it didn't bother me either until later after I got home.

I have a big crease from lost flesh at my ankle but I did not lose my foot or leg and the crease does not bother me in any way, for which I am very thankful. It took a full month in the Portland hospital to clear up the infection in my ankle.

That kind of ice skating is no fun. We sure did not make it to Spokane that day and are very fortunate the damage was not more. We came out of it alive, thankfully.

COMMENT FROM email pal: "We only hear about the ones who pick the pockets of a passed out drunk or somebody who is hurt so it is nice to hear about all the people who stopped to help. My husband always warned me---drive slowly on bridges in the wintertime—sometimes they're treacherous—ice. As our granddaughter used to say when she was so little, 'I be reel keerful.'"

WE WERE HIT BROADSIDE IN NEW JERSEY

Rollover #3 happened in 1953 in Rahway, New Jersey. With all our nomadic traveling we went to New York several times. We had just left our clothes at a laundry in Rahway and had to kill time to give them an hour to wash our clothes for us. We were driving very slowly and as we approached an intersection we could see the light was green. We were planning on going into New York City after picking up our laundry.

We had the green light and the truck dispatcher for a large manufacturing company went through the red light, hit us broadside, and caused the car to spin around and roll over. The guy who hit us was trying to catch a truck driver. Being in a residential part of town, he probably thought there would not be any traffic. We were far enough through the intersection that he caught us near the back fender or there might have been more very serious bodily injuries than there were.

The other car hit our left rear corner by the back door so Judi got the brunt of the impact and then both she and I got the impact when the car spun around and then rolled the opposite way. The dispatcher went up to a nearby house to use their phone before we could do anything ourselves to call for help. A police officer took Judi and me to a nearby hospital to have X-rays taken. The X-rays were fuzzy and they refused to take them over. Judi was the one with an injury and bruises.

We got caught with a crooked insurance adjuster and repair shop. We spent two weeks in a motel waiting for the car to be fixed. We were caught afoot two miles from a grocery store or restaurant on a highway with no sidewalks. We ran low on money and when the repair shop finished "repairing" our car it was late on a Friday evening. When my husband pointed out they had not done a good job on the car they said we would have to wait until the next week to redo it, as all the repairmen had gone home for the weekend. Of course this was deliberate. They knew we would be delayed at least another week or even longer. We took the car and started for home. It was raining and the car leaked. The windows didn't work right. It was a lousy job they did on the car. All we could do was head for home, back to Spokane.

The car should have been totaled in the first place, but the "adjuster" and the repair shop insisted the car had to be repaired, that it was good enough that it should not be totaled. Tom told the repair shop and the insurance adjuster that he would take the amount of the cost of repair and call it even. It was about that time they tricked my husband out of the office. By handing him some coins and asking him to go out to the shop to get them all some cold pop (the day was very hot and humid). When he returned to the office, they had locked the door. We should have called our insurance company right then and there. Locking him out was evidence that something was wrong, that they were up to mischief. I suppose they thought it wouldn't matter because we were so far away from home. I hope our insurance company did something about that crooked adjuster. Our insurance company was not active east of the Mississippi River at that time is why they had to hire an independent insurance adjuster.

We had three kids with us and the lady running the motel was kind enough to take us to an amusement park one time while we were there. Another time, she invited us to eat with her family. That was so very welcome as we were eating by warming up cans of soup by filling the wash basin with hot water and setting the cans of soup in the water. It was too far to walk (two or more miles) to a restaurant with three small children on a highway with no sidewalk. We had tried to get a motel closer into town but with no car to move around with, we were stuck. With three kids several motels didn't want to "take a chance" to rent to us. We had a couple take us around to several places to get the motel we did end up with, but they couldn't do any more than that. They also had to get back home on the West coast with their family.

Three years later, we had to return by train to New Jersey for a trial, where things happened to make me believe that a lot of bribery took place that day. There had been an eyewitness who testified for the insurance company at the trial. We didn't know we should have joined the insurance company at that time for our personal injury. Of course, the insurance company won the case and collected for the damage to the car. We had trouble locating that witness because it was three years later. By that time, the eyewitness was in the military.

Because, at the trial, the word Insurance was used, a mistrial was declared. As all the extra jurors had been in the courtroom and had heard "insurance," they could not be used. The judge would not order a new bunch of jurors, as it was June and would have taken a lot of time, etc. We could not afford to stay in NJ any longer. We finally settled out of court for practically nothing. What we got did not even cover the expense of that trip back for the trial. We'd have probably won, but it was too traumatic and too expensive on our part to pursue any more. The insurance company collected for the car and we settled for $1000. After the mistrial was declared, I talked to a young man who seemed to be there for the manufacturing company as a witness. He had an accent, so for some reason I asked him where he was from. He told me he was from Puerto Rico. He worked for that trucking company. The company would fire him if he didn't testify he saw the accident and that we went through the red light. I asked him when he came to the United States and he wasn't even in this country at the time of the collision. He was being forced to lie in order to keep his job.

When we got home to Spokane, our insurance company representative did a good cussing job when he took a look at the lousy work the repair shop did on the car. They redid the car so it was satisfactory. I don't know if they did anything about the way the adjuster handled the claim, but they should have. After the second repair job the car was OK, but the cost of repairing it again must have been astronomical. There was nothing mechanically wrong with the car; only the body had been damaged.

ROLLOVER ON THE WAY TO YELLOWSTONE PARK

ROLL OVER #2 Summer of 1949. We had first planned to leave on vacation to Yellowstone Park seven years earlier, but the morning before we would have left, Tom suddenly had an attack of severe pain. He ended up with an appendectomy that morning.

He decided that while he was already in the hospital it was also a good time to get his tonsils removed. Afterward, he told me it was a mistake to have two surgeries at the same time even if it did save the price of another hospital bill.

When we finally had time and money to try again in the Summer of 1949, we were within a very few miles of the park entrance when this accident occurred, the result of foolish kids driving too fast. My son, who was eight years old at the time, says he saw that the girl driving the car that hit us was passing another car at the time. I remember it was at a curve in the road. Tommy remembers his dad's boots hit him in the head as we went over. Judi says she remembers the girl was coming around a bend in the road and was heading right at us. She also remembers the girl was passing a line of cars.

The two girls, Judi and Jackie, were in the back seat with their grandparents. Judi was not quite six years old at the time but has a very vivid memory of what happened. She also remembers that I showed the kids how close we were to the river and explained to them that if we had rolled over one more turn onto the side of the car instead of landing on the top that we might have gone into the river and drowned. Thankfully no one died from that collision.

My husband avoided a head-on collision by his quick action, but it caused us to roll over when the right front wheel hit a rock. The momentum and the weight of the other car hitting our car, along with a rock in the right place at the wrong time, caused our car to flip over onto its top. The girl side-swiped us from the front left headlight clear to the back fender. If a head-on collision had occurred all of us might have been killed, especially if the force of the collision had caused us to go into the Yellowstone River.

The girl driving the car was 18 and working away from home. This made it so her parents could not be held responsible according to the insurance company. She had no insurance herself and the owner of the car she was driving immediately took an airplane out of the country, trying to avoid any responsibility. He probably also did not have insurance. When we asked them to pay for what our insurance did not cover, they literally told us, "You can't get blood out of a turnip." You can't. We didn't either.

Fortunately we had insurance that covered our car as the car was totaled. I don't know what damage happened to the other car. I don't remember anything about the car that hit us. This was in 1949 and we were fortunate to be able to get a new car a dealer had just gotten in. Cars were still scarce since the start of World War 2. The dealer told us it had been promised to a local farmer, but let us have the car due to the fact he could now get another one for his customer. We had looked at a used car at one dealership but it had very high mileage on it, was fairly old (pre-war) and the price was almost as much as a new car. We were very glad to find the new car.

Our insurance company called the girl "insurance proof"— no insurance herself; she was 18 and claimed she was not living at home so her parents were not liable, the owner of the car left the country and probably did not have insurance at all himself. They were right—"you can't get blood out of a turnip" and it was useless to sue.

Tom's mother is the one who was really hurt and did suffer from the damage for several months. The injury triggered some kind of arthritis pain. She spent five days in the hospital and never did get to Yellowstone Park. My father-in-law and our family went on to the park and spent a few days visiting. This was the time Ed Bergland, Tom's father, chased a small uninvited bear away from our camp. Thankfully the bear left and did not turn on him. Bears can be very dangerous. Those bears try to join you for food. Only the foolish feed them.

It was also on this trip to Yellowstone that we witnessed an older man try to entice a bear into a car where two elderly and utterly frightened women were sitting. They were almost paralyzed with fear. Someone should have shot that darned fool. (I mean the fool, not the bear) That man seemed to think it was funny. It looked to me almost as if he was trying to get them killed. He was laughing all the time he was trying to entice the bear to get inside that car with the two ladies. The stupid jerk was not funny in my opinion. It made me hope that bear would turn on him instead of those poor ladies. Those bears in Yellowstone Park are not tame and they can be very, very dangerous. But there are always fools who won't listen or pay attention. GRRRR.

That was the last time we ever had a two door car. My in-laws were in the back seat. A two door car is absolutely dangerous in my opinion. They are almost impossible to get out of in an accident and especially one that is sitting on its top. Anyone in the back seat of a two door car is trapped in an accident, especially if the car is upside down.

A strange thing about this accident was that all day long from early morning I had been thinking that if I saw an accident I would take pictures, never dreaming that we were the ones who would be in an accident. I crawled out of that upside down car, grabbed my camera, and while others were aiding the injured, I started taking pictures. I no longer have those pictures except those in my memory. If the pictures are in existence, they are with Judi, as I gave all of my pictures to her for safekeeping.

Along with everything else the police officer who arrived had to hitchhike to the scene of the accident! I don't know why he had to arrive that way; I only remember someone saying that is the way he came. I can only assume he was off duty at the time, and that he may have been close by somehow. We were quite a way from the city of Livingston, Montana. That morning we had visited some caves and by the time of the accident it was mid-afternoon.

ROLLOVER #1 The year was 1944. If I remember right, it was in September. My cousins were home on leave. They had joined the Merchant Marines. We wanted to join with them in visiting one of their cousins and to go out to dinner. Since we also knew their cousins we thought it was a nice idea. It would be a pleasant relaxing evening.

My husband had worked in the woods all day and I had been canning plums. We were tired, but going to another town and letting one of the others drive our car seemed like a good idea. We ate dinner and danced to the music the restaurant provided. Instead of heading for home, which was fifty miles away, we went over to the home of one of the other cousins. After visiting with their parents for a couple of hours, we started for home.

By this time it was past midnight. My husband knew he was too tired to drive, so he asked one of my cousins to drive. That was a big mistake. Everyone was tired and no one should have driven home at that time. We had been invited to stay overnight. We were within fifteen miles from home when the driver went to sleep at the wheel. One cousin's wife was in the back seat and wondered if Vern, the one driving, was getting sleepy, but was afraid to ask for fear of offending him. By then it was too late. He went off the road and we went over a bank and rolled. Tom got a broken nose. The others were shook up, but fortunately they were only bruised. That was the time I got the first set of broken ribs. No fun at any time. It could have turned out a lot worse though because my cousin, the driver, was thrown out of the car and could have been crushed. As it was the car had made a complete turn over and landed on its wheels. He was lying beside the car. That ditch we went into was about fifteen feet deep and straight down from the highway. When the car turned over like a summer cartwheel, I hit the steering wheel with my ribs. No wonder they were broken. I don't know who got the worst of that deal—the cars' steering wheel or me. I had bent the steering wheel with the impact to my ribs. To top it off, I was four months pregnant. Fortunately there was no further injury to any of us. Relatives ended up finishing canning my plums. I was unable to do much for a few weeks. The insurance company would have totaled it but in 1944 it was impossible to get a new car and a good used car was extremely hard to find so we had to get this one repaired even though it cost an immense amount.

See why I prefer to travel by airplanes? I think they are much safer than an automobile. Not so many foolish ones flying an airplane as those driving an automobile. Besides, in an airplane, I wouldn't need to tell the story, would I?

Comment from OZ: "Peggy, I think you had your fair share of accidents. I only had fender benders, nothing serious. A cop broadsided me and my car wouldn't start, so I was without a car for a while, so I sued the city and won, got a car. Of course it messed up my left arm, couldn't move it, it was stuck. I had to endure months of therapy, but all was well. My 4 yr old son was in the car, and he was fine, thank God."

THE OLD WEST

I received a video of old pictures that really represented the "Old West" as it really was and found them to be very interesting. It was during the 1930's and 40's that Western pictures were popular, then the number declined and very few are made any more. The Western today is mostly seen as re-runs on TV. Too bad, as I really like old Westerns.

Of special interest was the picture of "Calamity Jane" as she really was, not as she is pictured in the movies. She was not the slim, very pretty girl pictured in the movies, but an ordinary woman who had to work for a living, and who dressed in men's clothes to do hard work that was usually done by men. This made her become the subject of men who wrote stories that they were selling to the public. She was not what most would call pretty, but was a very ordinary looking woman. Her real name was Martha Jane Canary.

I found this information in a non-fiction book written about Wild Bill Hickock. Very interesting lives the early pioneers went through. "Wild Bill Hickock" was murdered at the young age of 39 only a short time after he had been married, but not to Calamity Jane. Evidently the "romance" of Calamity Jane and Hickock was someone's story telling ability. Hickock had been a lawman in several cities throughout the western states, and kept "law and order" Western style. The man who murdered him shot him in the back of his head while he was playing cards. The man was tried twice for his murder and then executed by being hanged.

In an article on the computer, the information was different about his marriage. There seems to be different information about the man's marriage between the book and what the computer tells. The book called the woman Hickock married a Society Matron, while the computer claims something different. Some stories about them state that both Hickock and Calamity Jane were unsavory characters, that they were the heroes of fictional stories of writers of the day trying to sell their stories based on real live people. Hickock and Martha Jane Canary were never married to each other.

Evidently not lovers either. I guess they made good story telling tales because they were both known people.

I LIKE TO READ

I have always loved to pick up a book. I used to make my mother upset because I would be up very late while reading. Still I would get to school on time in the morning, even if I was reading until after midnight. I do that even to this day. Get a good book and keep reading because I just cannot put it down. Sometimes I read a complete book in a day, or a long book in a day and a half. Guess I'll go turn the TV on again to see who is being shot or knifed—in real life, no less. Don't have to read fiction about it, just turn on the news and it's there in quantity. Bye for now.

VANCOUVER, WASHINGTON
vs
VANCOUVER, CANADA

This reminds me to tell you that the Worlds Fair that was held in Vancouver, British Columbia, Canada a few years ago prompted the people of Vancouver, Washington to erect a big four-foot tall sign at the Columbia River entrance to the city stating that they were arriving in Vancouver, Washington, U. S. A., not the Vancouver in Canada. It had become obvious that a lot of people did not know the difference or had not studied their Geography before leaving home. It must have confused a lot of people who arrived at the U. S. Vancouver expecting that they had reached their destination.

THE LIGHT BULB CHANGER

A man had to go **1768** feet up a narrow tower over the Empire State Building, with no safety lines. The email I received showed how the man climbed up to the top of the tower in order to change a light bulb. With a job like that you don't forget your tools because it's too far down to recover them if you drop them. What a view from up there. You can see for twenty-five miles to the horizon from over the Empire State Building. It makes me dizzy to even watch the view from up there even if it is seen over the computer screen and by email. I was there myself at the time the Empire State Building was the tallest building in New York and the view was terrific. I was not comfortable going up in the elevator. That is scary for some reason.

The men who build those tall buildings do a lot of climbing up to high places. It seems to me to be a very risky profession. They are much more brave than I could ever be. As I've mentioned, I am afraid of heights, but strangely enough I am not afraid in an airplane. Don't know why the difference, except maybe I feel like I have my feet on the ground in an airplane. I feel safe in the air, but do feel terror up a ladder over six feet tall.

This does remind me of the last time I was in New York, my son took me to the top of one of the *Twin Towers*, the one the airplanes hit and destroyed on September 11, 2001. Just going up in the elevator was scary enough for me. At the top you could see all over the country. It leaves a scary feeling, that great height. It was much higher than the Empire State Building from so many years before. Those elevators were more scary too.

One correspondent, wrote back to me: "Twenty years ago I was working for a steel company as an iron worker so climbing structures is not so scary. I mostly welded and the guys that went ahead to bolt the iron together were called the raisin gang and they worked mostly with no safety lines. Now this tower over the Empire State Building in the picture was real challenging. Thank God I didn't have to do this. Most of them are small skinny guys that can climb like monkeys. By the time this guy got to the top I was so very tired. No amount of money would get me even twenty feet up that tower. Anyone doing this job would have to have nerves of steel. Hope he has a large life insurance policy. That light bulb better be a long lasting one."

The man who climbs the tower above the Empire State Building sure doesn't get paid nearly enough. I wonder what they pay this guy per hour. 1768 feet straight up. It is sure incredible what people do for a living."

ANOTHER JOB UP HIGH

A little while before my husband, Tom, and I got married he had a job calling for him to climb some kind of a high tower that had to do with oil or gasoline. That was over seventy years ago so I really don't recall too much about it except it was a dangerous job.

It would sway in the wind. When he went home his clothes would smell of oil. He didn't like the job. This was just before WW2 and it was still Depression years and jobs were very hard to get so you did them anyway even if you did not like the job.. By the time we got married he was working as a carpenter.

When I look back, seventy years is really a very short time. When I was a kid a year lasted forever, but for some reason now a year is like yesterday. I wonder sometimes if I will last another eight years and reach 100. I feel quite fortunate that I am as well off as I am for I have good eyesight. I am not going to sit around and worry about anything because life is too short to waste time worrying about what might have been or what will be in the future.

MORE TRAVEL
LOS ANGELES TO VANCOUVER, B.C.

MAY 2013 Now it's time to tell you about our cruise from Los Angeles to Vancouver, British Columbia, Canada on May 8th, 2013.

My two daughters, Judi and Jackie, and I left Moreno Valley on Wednesday, May 8th for San Pedro, the Harbor in Los Angeles, to board a ship called the NCL Jewel. We stopped in San Francisco for several hours but did not get off the ship. We then proceeded on to Astoria, Oregon for another stopover. Both girls got off the ship to explore around the town of Astoria, which is located at the mouth of the Columbia River. I did start out to tour the town with my scooter, but decided it was too much for me at the time, so I turned and went back to the dock to find out about this port. I did explore around the dock for a while and met people there who could give me some information about the area.

The Columbia River is the second largest river by volume in the United States. It has one of the most treacherous river bars in the world. Many small boats and passengers have had to be rescued by the Coast Guard in this area. There are waves of twenty to thirty feet high during winter storms. Now that is tremendous. I have read about some of their rescues when written about in the news.

A group of 20 pilots makes up the Columbia River Bar Pilots that are based in Astoria.

They have the highest licensing standards for becoming a Bar Pilot in the United States.

They are chosen for the work of assisting all ships across the bar safely, day or night.

No matter what the weather, whether a small ship or a nuclear submarine or a thousand foot Panamanian cargo ship they are there to help. This bar is one of the most feared in the world. They will close the bar to shipping traffic up to ten times a year in the most severe storms. They are considered one of the best rough water piloting organizations in the word. No, we did not have to be rescued during our visit to Astoria. Fortunately, the weather was calm and smooth while we were there. There was a chilly breeze and a light mist in the air at times, but the sun was shining brightly.

From Astoria, we proceeded on to Victoria, British Columbia, then back down to Nanaimo, B. C. and finally to Vancouver, B. C., where our trip ended on May 15th. We proceeded through Customs without any trouble at all. In fact, it wasn't anything much more than to show our passports and then on we went to the bus that was taking us back to the United States and on to Seattle where relatives were meeting us.

On the way to the bus, I barely missed having an accident that probably would have been fatal if I hadn't heard someone shout at me to stop. I was way behind the rest of our group and was hurrying to catch up to them and about to cut across a yellow line thinking it was shorter. Fortunately, I stopped immediately to find that the yellow line was at the edge of a drop-off curb and I would have gone sailing over it. That curb was about six inches high, but I would have gone sailing with my scooter crashing and with the speed I was going I really believe it would have been fatal. I would have hit it at an angle so it would have thrown me further. Even when I was stopped it did not look like a drop-off line to me. It appeared to be only a yellow line guiding directions to the bus area. Lesson learned; don't get so far behind the rest of the group that you have to catch up to them.

The scenery all the way to Seattle was very interesting and beautiful. I enjoyed every minute of it. Only a few days later that we learned a bridge on Interstate 5 collapsed. Our bus was completely full and we had gone over that bridge only a couple of days before the bridge colapsed. It seems as if we had a few potentially dangerous incidents happen on this cruise. At least they were only potential, not actual.

From Seattle, our relatives took us to Port Orchard. We stayed with them for several days in their beautiful waterfront home across the water from Seattle. A cousin took Judi and Jackie on a tour of the area. I stayed with my cousin and enjoyed the scenery from her front room. The ocean view is wonderful. On Saturday, Jackie left from Seattle to return to Moreno Valley. My son and family drove over from Spokane to pick Judi and me up so we wouldn't have to fly from Seattle to Spokane. Since it is getting harder and harder for me to get around anymore, they felt it would be best for me. We planned to stay with them in Spokane for the next two months.

A BIG STORM

NOTE: This is a first hand report of a severe storm on the Eastern Coast that leveled many homes and caused the ocean tides to be fierce.

I received the following message from someone who was affected by that storm. She wrote: "*October 27, 2012 Danbury, Connecticut.* We live a couple of towns up the coast from Greenwich, Ct. shown in the photos. We evacuated 26 miles inland to a motel in Danbury, Connecticut, that would take dogs. We arrived here about 2:30 today. It's been horrendous following the weather news and preparing to leave the house. No rain or wind here now. We expect our luck has run out and we will return home to find salt water damage on our first floor. We made our evacuation plan Thursday night when they started comparing the forecast to the hurricane of 1938. Hope we are safe here and don't end up in a Danbury shelter. Darien finally issued mandatory evacuation by 7 tonight for all Darien waterfront neighborhoods. Have to include others in this email to save time."

Later, she wrote: "We came home to find a crawl space full; evidence there'd been four inches in our garage and large puddles remaining in low spots on the south end of our lot. Since then the grass has browned and the leaves have fallen off the trees, bushes and plants that stood a while in the saltwater. The roses continue to put forth buds and the flowers and the hydrangeas are getting new leaves. No wind damage and our road never lost its electricity unlike much of Darien. We moved our other car to an inland spot. We felt very lucky as we are on a low, flat, peninsula about a block from Long Island Sound on Connecticut's shore. The forecasters were warning of a repeat of the 1938 hurricane. My husband refused to move furniture to the 2nd floor; said at 70 he's too old to do that. We think about relocating for our retirement years but so many places have had devastating floods, tornadoes, fires, hurricanes, etc. it's hard to choose where to go."

Note: I heard from her later that they lost their furniture and everything on the first floor of their home. They also did not expect to be able to move back for several months. It's hard to fathom that water and wind can do so much damage! The pictures that accompanied this email showed extreme damage and deep water over a large territory.

Update—8-31-15—After recovering from the flood, they moved far south to another state and inland further.

MORE STORM NEWS
ELSEWHERE

Note: My son, David, lives in North Carolina. They had high winds but no damage from that storm.

I also heard from Oz, who lived in Pennsylvania at the time. When I asked her about how the storm affected her she wrote: "We live on a mountain, right in the middle of lots of trees, all belonging to us. Nothing happened to the house, but the insurance won't cover our trees that we lost even though they were on our property. We own over an acre of land.

We lived in Kansas for eleven years and I went through a tornado by myself. Anthony was away at the time. We had a few tornadoes there and ice storms every January. We also had a hail storm in July which ruined everyone's roofs, and all the cop cars in the city. What a mess it created. We lived in California for ten years and had only a few shakes, nothing to talk about."

I *wrote:* Sorry you lost your trees. Trees can be replaced easier than a house or lives.

They later sold their property, traveled for a while, and now live in a different state.

Four or five years ago when I was visiting my son in Acworth, Georgia, a tornado did set down there. That one did not do much damage in Acworth. I was looking out the window and I saw a tree bent over and then it went upright again (never having even a hint of being in a tornado, I just stood looking out the window. Fortunately it didn't set down near where I was at). Across the street from the house was a small forest. I was alone in the house and not at all familiar with tornadoes so I was just standing and watching it blow past.

When Larry got home, I made the remark about how fortunate he was that he had the forest to break the wind from destroying his place. Boy did I get a lesson from him. He proceeded to tell me that if the wind hit that area all that would be left showing would be matchsticks. I had absolutely no experience with tornadoes or extreme winds.

Where I lived in Washington it was common to use trees as a wind break so I had thought the same thing was true in Acworth. I had never been where the wind was so strong it would cause trees to be stripped and pulled out like a tornado does. Lesson learned.

When I was there a couple of years later, he took me around the area and showed me the results of one that had hit the area only a few months before. I could hardly believe what had happened. He had a few before and then after pictures he had taken earlier. That devastation is very hard to believe. The wind cleared the land as if a bulldozer had gone through and left the land ready to be plowed. I am more sure than ever that the earthquakes here in California are less hazardous unless they hit a large city and they surely are less frequent. That area where the tornado set down wiped out everything in its path—whether trees, homes, or animals. But people just turn around and rebuild again. The area covered several miles of devastation. I would not have known to take shelter if that tornado had come to my son's house that time I was there, so I probably would not have survived it. It was only a high wind as far as I was concerned that day—maybe ignorance is bliss sometimes. At least I wasn't frightened to death.

WE WENT IN SPITE OF THE MASSIVE FIRES

August 31, 2015—In going through this narrative again I have an addition to make. We went up to Priest Lake over the past week. We got together with several family members and rented a large house on the lake there so we could spend time with the family. My daughters, Jackie Bates and Judi Marqullan, drove up from California. Several Bergland families came up from Northern Idaho and we all had many games of pinochle..

For a while we had wondered if we would be able to go due to the possibility of dangerous conditions. We got everything ready and left early Saturday morning. The smoke here in Spokane was like looking outside in fog. It was thick and yellow. We kept checking if Priest Lake is to be evacuated. The messages said the area was in a level 1 evacuation area and asked that people not use the only road leading from Priest River to Priest Lake. The fires here are not only huge but are extensive and over a large area. The dense smoke one morning here in Spokane worried us. We kept up with the news and checked with officials daily. We seemed to be OK to go but knew the area was under Level 1 alert and that we might have to evacuate on short notice. We did go in spite of the possibility of evacuation in a hurry.

We arrived at Priest Lake and located the rental home. It was a very nice home that accommodated our large group. The whole northwest Washington and Idaho area was covered with smoke. The dense smoke did affect some of us who have a tendency towards asthma. We would have had the same conditions in Spokane. The entire state of Washington seemed to be on fire. They have had to import firefighters from other states. I thought I heard from the news report that some fire fighters were imported from Australia, the fires are that bad. Three firefighters were killed when their vehicle broke down and they were trapped. Many firefighters were injured.

My grandson, Mike, brought his boat along and launched it in the lake. Priest Lake is a fairly large lake. He took a couple out on a ride and the boat quit. Karen's sister (Karen is my daughter in law) Sherry went out and towed it in with her kayak. That made quite a picture—a little kayak pulling a big boat. The boat hadn't been used in over two years but whatever was wrong was minor and Mike fixed it. They used it again the day some of us were leaving to return to Spokane. More about that later.

Fires are terrible things. One time I was looking from the hill we lived on in Riverside California and saw the fire several miles away as it went whoosh and in less than 2 seconds it went across the hill for a distance of about a mile. No one in its path could possibly have gotten away.

I don't believe we are in any danger here in Spokane, but the rain we had last night has cleaned up the air. There is more to this story, but it is continued on another page.

SURPRISE OF SURPRISES

December 16, 2014 My email pal, OZ, called me on the phone yesterday to let me know she and her husband were coming through Yuma on Tuesday and she would like to meet me. They had sold their property in Pennsylvania and were traveling in a motor home, heading to San Diego, California to spend the winter with their son and family. They arrived this afternoon and we had a very nice visit. What A nice surprise to meet some one I had been corresponding with for several years, someone who lived clear across the whole country from me. I was not disappointed. She was a very attractive lady. We did not have a very long visit. Her husband did not stay. They had something go wrong with the tow connection to their car, which they are towing behind their motor home, so he had to go spend his time trying to fix it. I hope to see her again sometime if it can be arranged.

PREDICTIONS ABOUT 2011 MADE IN 1911

A friend sent me the following information about a prediction made *100 years ago*, in 1911, about what would be happening by the year 2011. It is amazing, but it shows what people were thinking. Wouldn't they be surprised to know how close they were to predicting what it would be like in 2011 and that those things have gone even further than they were dreaming of. I think they got their information from the computer copies of old newspapers.

I am inserting my own comments in Italics.

Predictions of

The automobile would drive out the horse except those kept by the rich for racing, hunting, and exercise. Without stables there would be no flies. (*oh yeah?*) Machinery would replace horses on the farms. (*That happened by the 1930's. It all shows what a terrific change has been made over the past hundred years. They sure were close in their predictions. Probably a lot of people did not believe them at that time.*)

Fast ships would cross the ocean in two days. Pictures sent by wire. *I have seen most of those changes during my 92 years on this planet. Airplanes have become a mode of transportation and now trains are seldom used to travel. There have been changes, changes, and more changes. Planes now cross the ocean in a matter of hours, not days.*

Some of the predictions were that there would be a huge increase in population, many other countries wanting to annex to the United States. *The immigration of people from other countries has been more than huge.* Predictions that Americans would be taller, have better health. There would be reforms in sanitation, food, and athletics. *There have been but not always for the better.* There would be an increase in life spans. Predicting that people would live in the suburbs and not in the city. *(That has come true with a bang.)*The English language would be extensively spoken and Russian would be second. There would be hot and cold air coming from spigots (*air conditioning*). There would not be smoke coming from chimneys because electricity will be everywhere for heat, light and for fuel. (*They were really right in that prediction.*) Chemicals will eliminate mosquitoes. (*Not quite*) Already cooked foods will become available and will be delivered in automobile wagons. (*We really do see that*) Photographs will be in color and sent by telegraph over long distances. (*yep!*) They predicted that trains would travel 150 mph. *(They sure hit the nail on the head that time, Japan really has them)* Air-ships would *not* successfully compete with surface cars or water vessels for passenger or freight traffic but will be used as deadly war vessels by all military nations. *(Only partly true. Airplanes have almost replaced other modes of fast travel)* Some will transport men and goods and others will be used by scientists making observations at great heights above the earth. Giant guns will shoot 25 miles or more and destroy whole cities. Such guns would be aimed by aid of compasses and telescopes from great heights. Air-ships will drop deadly thunderbolts. *They were right on the ball there (atomic bomb)* Great automobile plows will dig deep trenches as fast as soldiers can occupy them. Balloons and flying machines will carry camera attachments that will photograph within a 100 mile radius. (*True*)

Cattle and sheep will have no horns. (*They were a little off base there as there are some cattle without horns and some breeds that still have horns*) Food animals will be bred to expend practically all their life energy in producing meat, milk, wool, and other by-products.(*with chemicals*) Horns, bones, muscles, and lungs will have been neglected. (*very much so, actually*) Cameras will let men see around the world. Wireless phone and telegraph circuits will space the world. By an automatic signal they will connect with any circuit in their locality without the interventions of a "hello girl." (*phones have become automatic and now there is the cell phone*) Automatic instruments will bring the best music to the families of the untalented. (*radio, television, other new devices*)

A university education will be free to every man and woman. (*Not by a long shot, it's becoming more common, but not in the U.S.—mostly in Europe*) Poor students will be given free board, free clothing, and free books if ambitious and actually unable to meet their school and college expenses. (*Mostly not true*) The very poor will get free rides and free lunches, Etiquette and house keeping will be important studies. (*Too bad but those two studies have been sorely neglected and dropped*) Vegetables grown by electricity by putting electric wires under the soil to keep the plants warm. Large gardens under glass. Lights would be used at night to hasten growth (*Mainly for marijuana*). Refrigeration will bring fruit and vegetables from the tropics within a few days. Opposites seasons plants will be made microbe proof.(?) Flowers will grow large as cabbage heads and very colorful.

Drugs not swallowed but applied through the skin, and flesh Not only will it be possible for a physician to actually see a living heart inside the chest, but he will be able to magnify and photograph any part of it. That work will be done with rays of invisible light.(*all true in one way or another*)

THEY SOLD TRIGGER

I was a great fan of Roy Rogers, Dale Evans, and Gene Autry. I still am. I watch all the reruns I can find on TV and enjoy them as much today as I did back in the 30's when they were in the movies. In fact, I would go without my lunch in High School in order to have the admission cost to see the movie. I remember going to the Pantages Theater in Spokane to see Roy Rogers and Trigger in person.

After the show, I got an autograph signed by Roy Rogers. I kept the autograph book for several years. The personal appearance of Roy Rogers and Trigger was sometime in the 1930's when I was in High School. One time I thought it would be a nice gift for the son of the nurse who ran the maternity home where my daughters were born. All I remember now is that they lived in Tekoa, Washington. I mailed it to him and do not even know if he actually received it as I never heard. I do not know if the boy appreciated that autograph book or not, nor do I know if he even kept it, as I never heard. I only hope it meant as much to that boy as it had to me up until that time. I did enjoy meeting Roy Rogers in person, but I am not a great fan of most celebrities.

The date I sent the autograph book to the boy (I don't even remember who he was now) was sometime around 1946 or 1947, as we still lived in Idaho at that time. There was no hospital in Tekoa, Washington and I appreciated the services of the nurse. I hoped her son would appreciate the autograph.

THE END OF AN ERA: The Roy Rogers Museum in Branson, Missouri has closed its doors forever. Roy Rogers told his son, "If the museum ever operates at a loss, close it and sell the contents." The son complied. Everything sold at very high prices.

Roy bought trigger for $2500 on time payments and they made 188 movies together. The horse was special and won an Oscar in 1953. It is sad to see this era lost. These old heroes of our childhood days were Roy Rogers and Gene Autry. They showed love for their animals and we learned from that. You and I were able to grow up with these people even if we never met them. I say thanks to all those people whose lives touched ours, and made them better.

TODAY

Today the kids would rather spend their time playing video games. In this day it takes a very special pair of parents to raise their kids with the right values and morals. Our lives were drug free and we learned how to suffer through disappointment and failure and work through it.

I went to see Minnie Pearl in Portland one time. I enjoyed her performance. I would never go to another concert again. *WHY*? It isn't worth the torture of having the volume so loud it hurts your ears. The volume can cause you to have hearing loss and is not worth it.

I was in an elevator one time at Disneyland and saw a prominant "star" but decided not to bother her. I figured she might appreciate being left alone so did not disturb her.

HOW THE LANGUAGE CHANGES

AUTOMOBILE TERMS: Cars had a lot of terms that are now obsolete. I know some of you will not understand this, but I bet you know someone over 50 who might.

It was "Fender Skirts." those wheel coverings so popular at one time. Another word that has disappeared from our language was "curb feelers". Those items helped you know when you were too close to the curb.

How about "steering knobs" aka "suicide knob" or "Necker's knob"? They helped you to turn the steering wheel real fast. Never see them any more.

Very popular were the "Continental Kits" for the rear bumper extenders and spare tire covers that were supposed to make any car as cool as a Lincoln Continental. You were really something with one of those on your car.

When did we start calling the "emergency brake" a "parking brake?" When that was changed it left out the drama it inspired.

Almost all the old folks are gone who would call the accelerator the "foot feed". Do any of you know what a "clutch" is or what you did with a "dimmer switch," or what it was for, or where it was located? To explain it a bit you had to use the clutch to change gears.

The dimmer switch was located on the floor to the left of the clutch and it changed your headlights from low beam to high beam or back. You changed it with your foot.

IN THE HOME: Think of someone as you sit in your "Parlor" on your "Davenport" or maybe you call it a "sofa" or a "couch." Call it whatever you want to, just so the person listening knows what you are talking about.

Do you ever hear the phrase "store-bought" any more? Today everything is store-bought.

Once it was bragging material to have a store-bought dress or a store-bought bag of candy or a store-bought loaf of bread. Everything seems to be store-bought now.

OTHER TERMS: "In the family way" is now obsolete. "Pregnant" was once considered too graphic for polite company. It was a "visit from the stork" or simply "expecting."

There is one that should never have been changed. "*Supper*" which meant the evening meal—is now called "dinner." "*Dinner*" used to mean the noon meal, then it was changed to "lunch." If you were invited to "*supper,*" it was for the evening meal. Should still be supper in my opinion. Confusing? Dinner and supper became lunch and dinner.

I still like to eat breakfast, then dinner, then supper. It makes more sense. To have lunch should mean something you take in a lunch bucket to eat away from home and most likely it would be at noon time.

If you had lumbago then, now you would call it arthritis. A *wide spot in the road* was usualluy a gas station and possibly a house or two, or a very very small town, but usually there are no wide spot places any more as they have grown up into a big city.

Ladies wore corsets, which would lace up in the front. A proper and dignified woman wore a tightly tied lace corset as in *"straight-laced."* It must have been uncomfortable the way it squeezed them in. Nothing like that is worn today.

Ever heard of someone not *"playing with a full deck?"* Common entertainment included playing cards. A tax was applied to the cards but only applied to the Ace of Spades. People would purchase 51 cards to avoid the tax. These people were thought to be stupid or dumb because they weren't *"playing with a full deck."*

GOSSIP. With no telephones, TV's or radios, the early politicians sent their assistants to local taverns, pubs, and bars to determine what the people considered important. They were told to "go sip some ale and listen to people's conversation and political concerns".

The two words "go-sip" were eventually condensed when referring to the local opinion and thus we have the term "gossip."

MISUNDERSTANDING KIDS

Reminds me of one granddaughter who would say *"Lets gweet"* when my daughter and I got together at times. She was just barely two years old and it took a little while to figure out that she was trying to repeat what we were saying: "Let's go eat."

Another memory comes to mind: My brother was about 3 years old and was trying to sing Yankee Doodle. His version was something like this: "*Yankee Doodle went to town riding on some macaroni*" I guess kids tell it like they hear it.

THE TWO WOLVES
& OTHER WILD LIFE

This story was on the internet. Author unknown, but a good comparison in life.

A grandfather compared two wolves fighting. One represented evil, anger, greed, and resentment, lies and ego. The other wolf stands for Good. That good is peace, love, humility, kindness, empathy, generosity, truth and faith". The grandson asked him which wolf would win. The simple reply was *"The one you feed"*. So, Grandson, *"Which wolf would you feed?"*

I was reminded about wolves being shot. I thought wolves were a protected species, but maybe it has been removed from that list. I don't think people in the area go out just to destroy the wolves, but they are getting thicker now and when they go after livestock, the people go after the wolves.

One evening I looked across the road from our house in Idaho and there was a big wolf next to an old barn. At first I thought it was a German Shepherd dog. It was about 50 feet from our front door. No I didn't get my gun and shoot at it. It was fascinating and didn't bother our goats nor the neighbor's cows. If wolves in that country bring down people's livestock they pay the consequences. Too bad. Every once in a while I would hear either wolves or coyotes howl during the night. I often wished they would do it more often as I enjoyed hearing them "talk".

Among the wild animals seen in the Benewah area are wolves, coyotes, bobcats, deer, and occasionally a moose. My cousins used to stay at our house after school after someone reported seeing a couger between their house and the Benewah school. My aunt shot a bear just a few feet from their house. My cousin got a bobcat near their house. Last year (*2016*) when Tom and I went to the Benewah picnic Tom saw a cougar close to the highway on the way down the mountain. I did not see it, or I would have asked him to stop the car so I could watch it. Wild animals are in the country and can be seen if you are observant and alert.

When I was a kid I remember hearing a cougar scream and my folks saying it sounded like a woman screaming. I never did see one in the wild. I've seen coyotes several times when they ran across the road in front of our car. When we were in Yellowstone Park one time Tom's dad chased a bear away from our picnic table. Sometimes that is dangerous because they can quickly turn on you. At Yosemite Park we got up in the morning and saw the results to someone's cooler and what a bear had done to it during the night. We knew better than to leave anything outside as those bears have a good sense of smell and go after what they want. As we were cooking hotdogs, they would soon appear close by wanting to share. Park Rangers don't want people to feed them, but they do it anyway. I heard of people leaving food in a convertible car with a rag top and finding it ripped apart when they came back to it. Bears can get into almost anything. That is why you see trash containers with chains and padlocks on garbage cans in Yellowstone Park..

One time in Yellowstone we saw a guy trying to lure a bear into his car with a couple of terrified women inside. I still burn over that dangerous situation. The women were frozen with fright (with reason). Too bad that bear didn't turn on him. It would have served him right. Maybe he wanted the women to die. Tom says he remembers this event. Some people don't have the sense of a flea brain. That scene haunts me to this day. That was in 1949, the year we were in an accident on the way to the park when a girl hit our car from the front headlight to the rear fender and caused our car to roll over.

PHONE ON THE WALL—HELLO

This story reminds me of the phones we had in Benewah. They were the old fashioned kind on the wall with the crank we had to use to reach the operator. After we got the operator she would say "Number please" and then she would get the party we were trying to reach. The following story is about a young boy who was fascinated with the box on the wall that talked to him.

He lifted the receiver on that box on the wall. "Number Please" answered, he cried into the phone to her, "I hurt my finger". She told him what to do. He wanted to know how to spell fix. From then on he asked "Number Please" for everything.

PHONES AND ELECTRICITY
COME TO THE BENEWAH

The story about the "Number Please" operator reminded me about the old style telephones and triggered another memory. We moved to a rural area in Idaho in 1943, about 20 miles from town. There was no electricity, no telephones, and no paved road for a distance of twelve miles in any direction. We had a radio which ran on car batteries, and a gasoline run engine on an old square tub Maytag washing machine. When I was unable to start the balky engine I would end up washing clothes on a scrub board.

A few years later the neighbors got together and put in a telephone line. The community co-operated by furnishing and donating the timber for the poles, cut them, and delivered them to the site. While the lines were being put up, the women furnished lunches. Several of the men climbed the poles to string the wire. All labor was donated by the people who lived in this Benewah valley. The Forest Service supplied the wire; otherwise the residents supplied everything else.

We bought phones that hung on the wall and you cranked a handle to get the operator. When you lifted the ear receiver you heard the operator say "Number Please" and she would get your party for you.

This was in the mid 1940's. There were 20 parties on that one line. We got along pretty well even with that many people sharing one phone line. Our ring was probably two longs and one short ring. I do not remember that for sure, but all 20 rings were similar to that. If you needed to use the phone and someone was using it they would hear you raise the receiver and would get off the phone and let you use it. I never heard of any trouble arising over the use of the phone even though there were so many people on that one line. Today they have more than one line to the homes and phones that dial direct—no phone operator to say "Number Please". Not many people have land line phones any more unless cell phone service is not available. There are no longer any "number please" voices as everything is automatic and electronic.

Those twenty people on one phone line were cooperative and considerate of each other. It could have been like what happened to some who had party lines in the big cities. One relative tried to get the use of her phone because of an emergency and the other party would not yield it. Hers was only a two party line, but the other party could hold your phone hostage if they were the kind of persons who would do such a thing. Just having the phone off the hook neutralized the line making it useless. This never happened in the Benewah area that I ever heard of. A private line was not available at that time. We felt lucky to have a phone at all.

Right after we got the phones in, we did the same thing and cooperated to get an electric line put in. Electricity let us get a pump so we could have running water in the house as well as the other conveniences that electricity made available. I got an electric stove as well as a washing machine that turned on with a switch, not a pull cord on a gas engine that at times would not work. About the time we got all those modern conveniences we moved our family from Idaho to Spokane, Washington. That was December 1, 1951.

I have visited old friends several times in the last few years back in that Benewah, Idaho community. Many have passed away because they would be over 80 to 90 years of age by now. Now everyone out there has more modern telephones and fewer parties on the phone line, but they still do not have a paved road. There are many modern new houses in that area and hopefully will get their roads paved before another fifty years goes by.

A VISIT TO THE OLD NEIGHBORHOOD

On a visit to the Benewah Valley in 2005 to attend the annual picnic my son, Tom, took my cousin, Betty Horine Swofford, and me on a tour of the area around Benewah and Alder Creek. We noted the many changes in the past 50 years. There are a lot of new people, a few of the old-timers, new houses, and memory of the old houses that were no longer there. The house formerly occupied by the people who had originally homesteaded early in the century—the Hyde family— and later owned by the Ray Pease family, was gone. The new barn built for the Pease family no longer existed. In fact, this location of where the old post office was located on the Hyde place also shows no signs of anything ever having been at that location. The old Marquardt mill left no clue of any kind that it had ever existed.

We had a time locating where my uncle, Ray Horine, (Betty's father) had lived up the road about a mile towards Alder Creek. Everything had changed, buildings gone, trees and brush grown up, roads grown over with trees and shrubs. No sign of any kind where they had lived. The location of where my uncle Ray had his sawmill had no clue of any kind that a sawmill had ever been there. We even had a time locating the spot where the house had been, the location her mother had shot the bear, and her brother the bobcat.

There were also quite a number of changes in the Alder Creek area, just as it has been all over the Benewah area. With new people and new buildings the Benewah Valley and Alder creek are now like a whole new country. It is hard to recognize anything other than the school house that is now the community center. The past fifty years have seen so many changes that it makes me wonder what the next fifty years will be like.

Gone were all buildings and the house we had lived in on the Benewah Creek Road. Only the light pole was still standing. Even the creek was hard to locate. What had been open spaces were covered with trees. Brush had grown up in what had been our yard. The entire area looked very different. Sixty-five years really changes the looks of an area.

One of the reasons for the changes in Benewah and Alder Creek are due to the influx of all the new people moving in. One example of how this happens will follow later in the chapter called "It's a Small World". People hear about the area when it is advertised all over the country and come and buy a few acres of land and then move in. That story is an example of what can happen when the word spreads by someone advertising the property they have purchased to subdivide. What used to be many properties of a hundred sixty or more acres has been divided up into ten acre parcels. Really changes things.

TRIVIA

Put a wooden spoon across boiling pots to keep it from boiling over. (it works)

Use a staple remover to save your fingernails when adding things to your key ring.

Use bread clips to save flip-flops with split holes. It holds them together.

To put shoes in the dryer, tie the laces together then slip the laces over the door to hold them in place. They won't be making that bang noise then either.

THE 1934 MONTGOMERY WARD'S CATALOG

The catalog was sometimes called the "Wish Book." At other times it was known as MW or simply "Monkey Ward." Take your choice; we all knew what all the names meant.

When we lived in Idaho, before we got the electric line in, I had a gasoline iron like shown in the picture in the MW catalog. I was using it and it flamed up and scared me thoroughly. I threw it outside and never used it again. I reverted to putting the flatiron on the stove to heat up. When I threw the iron out the door it is a wonder it didn't start a forest fire as we lived on the edge of a forest. Fortunately it did not flame up. I don't remember whatever happened to that iron except I never tried using it again. It was a relief when the electric line was installed and I bought an electric iron.

Enjoy the browse through the catalog. Anklets 9 cents a pair, dresses for 94 cents, and a more expensive dress was $2.98. A skirt and jacket was $2.98; ladies underwear at 37 cents each (oh how bold!). Corsets cost $1.00 each. Bras for 25 cents. (don't look kids). A nice wool sweater was 94 cents. Lots of kids clothes were under $1.00. Some shoes were $1.98 and they were fashionable too. A man could get a dress shirt for 74 cents to $1.00 on sale, (it was really worth $1.29) Just look at the prices. Shoes for less than $2.00 a pair. Those silk (not nylon) stockings at 55 cents cost almost as much as a pair of kids shoes. I remember buyng enough yardage to make a dress for fifty cents (not fifty cents a yard). I believe I remember it was 19 cents a yard. I was 15 years of age at that time.

A really nice home with hardwood floors and a full basement cost the outrageous price of *THREE THOUSAND DOLLARS*. Oh how I remember. I guess it is no wonder it is still hard for me to understand the price of items to this day. Anyone who had an income equal to a week's pay of today was wealthy. One dollar an hour was good wages. Young people of today don't really realize the immensity of inflation because they never saw prices that compared to this "Monkey Ward" catalog.

For the house, an Ice Box was $8.95 and as low as $6.95. (these were those boxes that you bought ice for—before refrigerators) Flashlights with batteries were 65 cents. You could get a boiler for $1.55 with ten bars of soap included. (a boiler was that big copper container you used to heat water in). Now don't forget to get some light bulbs—they were 8 and 9 cents each. Another laundry must was a bunch of clothes pins at 40 of them for 9 cents. You used those pins to hang your clothes on the line. And don't forget that wonderful item that made ironing clothes so much easier— the gasoline iron for $2.69 (a very special value) Oh how modern it was. Remember, I threw mine out the door.

And please don't forget those darling little *DAY OLD CHICKS* so you could raise chickens for eggs or eating. You even got to choose whether they were roosters or hens. Don't know how they could tell the sex of a baby chick, but I don't know chickens unless they are fully grown up. If those baby chicks were roosters they got into the frying pan when they were a few weeks old.

They were 25 chicks for $1.90 (that was about 7 ½ cents each. They were sent postpaid by mail in a little cardboard box with breathing holes in the box so the chicks would stay alive. (They did arrive live too. I bought some that way. I remember that is the way my grandparents got them also.) And since you needed supplies for raising them you could get a 48 inch feeder for 59 cents. Yes sir, those were the days, weren't they?

OZ replied to me: "You always have an interesting story. I still have my microwave from Montgomery Ward, new in 1986. It still works but uses too much electricity. We now have one over the stove. My aunt bought me a toaster back in 1969. You just dropped the bread in and it went down by itself. I still have it, and it still works. American made. Can't beat it. Now everything is junk. That is my story. How did the gas iron work?"

In answer I wrote: It would work but I was thoroughly scared of it. It used a flame to heat the flat plate on the bottom. I was scared of using gasoline with an open flame. It probably flared up because it needed to be adjusted, but I was a scaredy cat. I was not afraid of using the gasoline lantern, but I still would not use the iron to this day. The gasoline we used was called white gas and today I don't know for sure what it is called. We bought it at a gas station. I believe it is the same as we use in our cars today.

WAGES

In 1939 my cousin worked for 25 cents an hour (no tips) at a drive-in (now called a fast food restaurant). A milkshake was ten cents. An ice cream cone was pretty expensive, because it was a nickel a scoop. You paid too much if you paid more than ten cents for a hamburger with everything on it—lettuce, tomato, onion, pickle, mayonnaise, and a generous amount of each item too. A cup of coffee was five cents or even free, and no charge for refills. There was one thing though that did cost quite a bit. Smart Alec kids would come into the restaurant and order a "pine-float." The manager finally decided to meet the kids by charging them ten cents for their pine floats—a toothpick in a glass of water. It did end their "fun" and they quit ordering a pine float. Oh yes, the waiters (not servers) seldom got a tip in those days either. They worked hard for their two dollars a day wages, and jobs were very hard to get. At the end of their shifts, the help also had to clean everything up as part of their job.

1930's INFORMATION

In those days (1930's) a high school student could ride the bus for a nickel. I still have a couple of the student bus tokens. I also have some Washington State TAX tokens—these were little aluminum tokens that were worth a fraction of a cent that paid the sales tax on a purchase. They soon quit using these tax tokens because the people found they worked quite well as washers and cost less than a washer cost at the hardware store. They were made of aluminum, were about the size of a quarter with a hole in the middle—ready made washer. At that time the tax was imposed to help pay for *"old age pensions"*—the forerunner of Social Security. The tax was a fraction of a cent but now the tax has been raised to close to nine percent of your purchase and is used for more than "old age pensions." Another token used to pay sales tax was a small red disc about the size of a dime.

Milk came in glass bottles and the bottles had a deposit of 10 cents on them. They sure did not pollute the country with bottles. That ten cents paid for a movie ticket for the kids so they sure didn't go to waste. Also the milk kept better and tasted better coming from that glass bottle. Yes, I have seen a lot in my ninety plus years. Things have really changed and I find that ninety years is really a very, very short time after all.

LEAVE IT TO KIDS TO SAY WHAT THEY THINK

My friend Oz sent me the following story: When my cousin, Raymond, age 4, went to church with our aunts and he was getting antsy during the sermon, they gave him a rosary. Bad idea. He took it and swung it around so the cross was spinning around his head. He said, "hold on Jesus, I am taking you for a ride". Of course they ushered him out of church quickly.

His sister, age 5, asked my mother why the man up there was wearing a dress. It was the priest.

Redneck tip:--Even if you're certain that you are included in the will, it is still considered tacky to drive a U-Haul to the funeral home.

SHOW YOUR IDENTIFICATION

There has been a great deal in the news about an Arizona law requiring people to prove their identity. Some people are saying people should not have to, but I will be going home in a few days after spending two months in Washington. There are those who claim no one should have to prove who they are, but here is what I have come across during my sojourn away from home.

When I boarded the ship for the cruise I took from Los Angeles to Vancouver, B. C. in Canada, I had to have a passport showing my name, address, birth date, and place of birth. Since I am a U. S. citizen why should I object to that being checked by the cruise company? Again, when I entered Canada, they wanted to know the very same information. I did not object. Why do people object to being asked about themselves unless they are not supposed to be where they are? Every other country in the world guards their borders closely, so why shouldn't we?

Why should anyone object to showing their identity when pulled over by the police?

When applying for credit or a loan, when going to the doctor, getting a drivers license, a passport, applying for insurance, college, or when ordering a boarding pass for airline or trains, they require proof. Why should anyone be exempt more so than a U. S. citizen is?

We are required to prove who we are nearly every day.

A PLANNED TRIP

Guess I have travel sickness—love to travel. When we were younger we would go places in the car, along with a tent and camping equipment. Could not do that now the way we did it, camping beside the highway on a long trip. It would be too dangerous. Times have changed, and not for the better.

On the forthcoming trip, I will be with my two daughters, Judi and Jackie, and they both have digital cameras. Both girls love to take pictures, so will probably have some this summer. We will leave the first part of June, go north to Seattle, with stops between, and head out from there to North Dakota to visit the old homesteads of our ancestors. My cousin in Port Orchard is the one we will be going with and she knows where the old homesteads are. This trip will probably take us the whole month.

I got the following letter from OZ: "It is great you have daughters that can take a whole month and just go with you. I am sure you will have lots of fun with them. I did enjoy reading about your adventures. Got your stories last night and I am now reading them. Sounds like you had a great adventurous life. Can't believe you did all that on a scooter. Did you take pictures of your European trip?"

FOLLOW UP: The trip I mentioned above about seeing the homesteads of ancestors never came about. We had hoped and planned for that trip several years ago. It would be nice if we could still take the trip but it does seem quite impossible now. I don't know what happened because we really wanted to go. It may have been because it was about that time I found I had breast cancer and ended up with emergency surgery. Or it could have been because my daughter's husband got sick and spent three months in the hospital before he died. We have never been able to go on that trip since, and now, because of health circumstances, probably never will. It was a dream never fulfilled.

MOVING PICTURES AND HAWAII

On our trip to Hawaii in 1963, I spent my time taking moving pictures and missed out by doing that instead of looking around. It taught me a lesson and I never take pictures anymore. If I want pictures, I buy them. Since they are taken by professional photographers, they are always good.

In the past I had taken moving pictures of our travels around the continental United States, Canada, and Hawaii. Those films disappeared and now the only memory I have of them is in my mind. Judi and Jackie take pictures with their digital cameras. It is a lot easier now than it used to be since you don't have to buy a lot of film and then have it developed later. Now you also get to instantly see what you have taken. That has been quite a great improvement so it's much more satisfactory.

From OZ "It is a shame about your pictures. Maybe you could write a book and call it your memories and sell it on EBay. I know someone who sold his short stories on EBay about his growing up days all the way to Nam and then some.

I have two more stories to read so I better finish up. Thanks a bunch."

I WROTE A BOOK

I did finish writing a book I started some time ago called *"Who Cares Who Milks the Cow"* and it has been published. That story is definitely not about cows. It is about what happens to a young woman after her abusive husband is killed in a mudslide and she takes on the job of finding the father of the infant whose mother was killed in the same accident and her experiences from then on. The title comes from a remark someone made about her breast feeding the baby, and has nothing to do with cows.

DON'T PUT IT OFF

Too many people put off something that brings them joy because they don't have it scheduled or haven't thought about it as long as they think they should. What about comparing the women who passed up dessert only to end up going down with the Titanic.

They might as well have enjoyed their dessert. I compare a wife who had thawed some meat and then her husband asked her out for dinner. Instead of putting the meat into the refrigerator and accompanying him, she stayed home to eat. The meat would have kept in that refrigerator. Just don't be too rigid. He might be so discouraged he would hesitate to ask her again.

Don't put off something that brings you or them some joy just because you were *too rigid or too busy.* Just be more flexible.

All this reminds me of the time we went to Tijuana, Mexico in 1946, and I saw a picture I really wanted. The cost in money wasn't much. It was probably only a dollar. My husband told me we had spent enough, so I gave up that picture.

When we got home he presented me with a pair of nylon stockings. Now this was just at the end of WW2 in 1946 and nylons had been impossible to get so were at a premium. I did not want those nylons; in fact, I hated them and felt I had no place to wear them either. I sent word out to friends that I wanted to get rid of those stockings and ended up selling them. It hurt his feelings so badly that he never bought me a gift like that again. *It_was not worth it. I should have kept them.* I guess we were both hurt over those stupid nylons. He was hurt because he thought he was getting me something special and I was hurt because I had positively wanted that picture. It was not worth it to have hurt his feelings so badly. I regret selling those nylons to this day, almost seventy years later. Again, I say it was not worth it. Things are never, ever perfect.

How about if the kids were wanting to talk to you. Were you too busy watching your favorite TV program to bother to listen when they wanted to get your attention? They will ignore you later when you want them to talk to you. It isn't worth the TV show as it will come back and bite you later.

Don't put off something that brings you or them some joy just because you were *too rigid or too busy*. Just be more flexible.

Have a nice day and go do something you want to do, not just something you think you have to do. Call a friend and go to lunch with her when she asks you to go. Don't put things off thinking you "don't have the time right now." The "right" time absolutely never comes so just do it now.

ANOTHER TRIP TO CALIFORNIA
AND LOTS OF FLAT TIRES IN ARIZONA

When we still lived in Spokane, we would usually take a trip to California every year, especially after Tom's parents moved there. We went down the first part of July 1955.

On that trip we decided to go through the Grand Canyon in Arizona on the way back home. We started home around the middle of the month. It was very hot at the time.

It was about midnight when we went through Needles California. We stopped at a station to gas up the car and the attendant told us the temperature was **119 degrees**. We continued on towards Flagstaff and about the time we were near that city, we had a tire go flat, or so we thought. It turned out the rim had split. The tire was OK. Well, we had a spare wheel with us so we put it on the car and continued on our way the next morning. My husband always seemed to have the idea that the spare was enough to have on hand and would always get us by, so we continued on our way back to Spokane with no spare wheel. I guess some people would call it a rim I call it a wheel.

We were enjoying the air-conditioned ride through the Painted Desert area. There were no houses around for as far as we could see, only desert for mile after mile. We had gone about thirty miles past the last city we had been through. We passed what looked like a gas station or store and about five hundred feet past that building my husband suddenly stopped the car and said "pile out and go back to that place." He wanted the weight off the car—another wheel rim had split and he wanted to get the car back to the building while he could still do it.

It turned out the building was a trading post. They did not have a telephone, but they did have a radio. It was the heat that had caused the rims to split. The people at the post used the radio to call back to the town. Fortunately we had a AAA card, which made someone willing to rescue us. People had been stranded out in that area before and had died from the heat. Someone from AAA came up to the trading post and insisted that everyone accompany him back to the town. He would not let any of us stay at the post. I know now it was because of the possibility we would not be able to get a rim for the car and would need to go to a motel until one could be located. The big trouble in finding anything was because it was a Sunday and everything was closed. I do not remember the name of the city, which may have been Flagstaff. The man who rescued us tried everything he could think of to locate someone to open up the wrecking yard. Finding no one, he and Tom looked around the wrecking yard themselves for a wrecked Cadillac to get a wheel replacement. No Cadillac wheels were found. They found a wheel on a Buick that looked like it would fit, so they brought that up to our car. That Buick wheel allowed us to get back on the way home. It took a while after we got back home to figure out why the brakes didn't work too well. Replacing the Buick wheel with the proper Cadillac rims for the car solved the problem with the brakes.

All of this reminded me of something about my husband, Tom, and my son, Tommy, and their habits. Tommy let his gas tank go empty and would run out of gas, then would have to walk, sometimes miles, to get gas for the car. I guess I shouldn't complain though. I ran out of gas one time. Didn't know it was low at that time. Now the tank gets filled at the half way mark. Tom, on the other hand, would have a flat tire and think he could depend on the spare. Usually he was fortunate enough to have people who were nearby enough to give assistance for a tire. One time though, he had to hitchhike twenty miles to get a new tire. He had to take a wheel so the new tire could be mounted. One tire had blown out earlier and he could have bought a tire in Bend, Oregon but thought he could wait until we got to Spokane. Ha ha ha. The second tire blew in the middle of nowhere, but fortunately the weather was not extremely hot that time. He had to go to The Dalles to buy a tire—twenty miles each way. He was fortunate enough to find someone who was traveling back towards where our car was stranded on the highway. He replaced the tire and we went on our way. That was the time Larry was driving (he was a new driver) and he was travelling quite fast when the tire blew. All I could say was, "Tom, tell him what to do". Larry evidently knew enough not to hit the brakes or we could have gone over the steep bank we were beside. Fortunately the car held steady and it just slowed down.

Tom always had the kids do plenty of driving on a trip to give them driving experience, which was a good idea. That also gets a lot of wanting to drive out of their system. That really works well. Being on a trip my husband was right there with them to supervise if needed and the kids had the "fun" of driving the family car. He did not lecture the kids, just was present if needed. I don't think any of the kids depend on the spare tire for their cars in spite of their Dad's example. I believe Tommy now doesn't let his gas tank get completely empty.

Another time we had had a flat tire earlier and on the way into Spokane the second tire went flat. We had to get our tires retreaded those days. It happened by a farmer's house. The people who lived there were very nice and loaned us a mounted wheel from their car (same kind fortunately) so we could get on into Spokane. They followed us into town to make sure all went well. That time there had been no chance at all to buy a new tire between flats. We lived about twenty miles from town. Over all, most people are very nice and I have never forgotten those people who loaned us a tire. That was about seventy years ago and I think of them every time I go past the place where they lived. Also that was during the time when new tires were impossible to get as everything was rationed. I think we ended up having a retread put on the old tire.

Speaking of flat tires. I had a flat once and a truck driver stopped and changed it for me.

Later my husband told me to never let a truck driver change a flat. I could not understand how he knew it was a truck driver, because *I had not told him who had changed it*. He informed me the wheel was put on so tight that he could hardly get it off when he went to change it later. *That was how he knew* it was a truck driver who had changed it for me.

DO YOU APPRECIATE YOUR PARENTS?

How many kids appreciate what their parents do for them, until they grow up and have a family of their own?

I look back and wonder if I ever thought anything about appreciation when I was growing up. My mother had to have had it extremely tough supporting four children alone during those depression years. I am sure I did not fully appreciate it at the time until I was grown up and on my own. Getting welfare help was not available in the early 1930's. When welfare did become available it was very strict. "Investigators" would come to your house and open up your cupboards to see if you had "too much" on hand. It is not done that way today.

I did finish high school. My sister did not get a high school diploma until several years later and after she was away from home and married. I don't know if my older brother finished high school although he ended up self-educated and was industrious enough to join the Navy and go from there. My younger brother became ill at the age of sixteen and never recovered from his illness.

I certainly could never say about my mother that she never did anything for us because she did everything for us. She did without for herself to do for us kids.

ON MY FIFTEENTH BIRTHDAY

My father came to visit us in 1937 (still Depression years) when I was fifteen years old. My mother never kept him from visiting us, but he very seldom did. This one time he came and was dressed up in a beautiful new suit. I am sure that suit was an expensive one. My father was a very good salesman who could have been successful if he had been of a mind to be decent to his family. He was a very handsome man but also a selfish man who did not support his family. His personality was such that he could make friends with strangers, but he ignored the needs of his family. Mom told me later that if he had been decent with his family, she would have put up with his abuse. When he let his children go hungry when he didn't have to, was when she left him, taking us with her even though we had nothing literal but the clothes on our backs. I remember the one dress I had would be washed at night and ironed in the morning before going to school. None of his sisters or brothers were able to understand his actions as none were like him.

On this visit, the day I was fifteen years old, he handed me some money and *asked me to count it.* All this happened in the front yard of my mother's house. I counted the money. There was two thousand dollars in that wad of money. *He also did this in front of my mother.* I don't know where the money came from, but I am sure he did not rob a bank. Well, we *walked* downtown, a distance of probably two miles and he gave me fifty cents to spend. I asked him to buy me a pair of shoes. I needed some shoes that would fit me. Want to know what he said to me? "*No, that might help your mother.*" You know, to this day I think if I heard any man say anything like that I would probably pick up a club and beat him senseless, even a stranger on the street, even if it meant I would go to jail. I don't get mad easily, but I still get upset when I think about what he said. It is a mystery how one could be so very wrong. I completely lost all respect for him after that. *I also remember the day perfectly well— because it was on my fifteenth birthday.* I could say more, but this is enough. I did not hate my father, but I sure was very disgusted with him, and he did not leave me with good memories of him. He died in 1968.

CURIOUS? WHAT ACCENT DO YOU HAVE

Do you have an accent to your speech? Someone sent me an email with an address to use to see if I had an accent in my speech. Try it sometime.

<u>http://www.lewrockwell.com/spl3/
american-accent-quiz.html</u>

I don't remember who sent it to me. It was probably OZ. I brought this up from my old files. When I tried this out, I came up with "inland north" as my accent. Since I was raised in the area of Spokane and Northern Idaho, I suppose it is pretty close to being right, although I have been away from that area for fifty years. I see that I had a different result from the first time I tried this. Interesting isn't it? Yes, everyone seems to have a different accent in one way or another. While my grandparents on my mother's side of the family came from Norway, they were quite young when they came to the U. S; but my grandmother lived in the Central states, and probably picked up an accent from that area. Grandma was about seven years old when she came here, but Grandpa was around twenty-three from what I have learned.

That is probably why they had different accents. They both read English very well, but Grandma had others write her letters for her. I never did see any of her handwriting. She was not illiterate, but may not have known how to write in English, but only in Norwegian. I don't know of anyone I could ask anymore.

My friend Oz wrote: "My grandmother came from Ireland. Her kids swear she didn't have an accent. She did. They were so used to hearing her throughout their lifetime that they no longer heard an accent. Lots of people ask me if I am from Boston or New York, because I have a South Philly accent. That was an Italian neighborhood. My dad's side is Italian, and they for sure had that Italian accent. My Grandfather and his family came from Italy and my Grandmother's parents came from Italy. All six of her siblings had the accent and then living in South Philly you just kept that accent all your life.

I don't know if I would know a Norwegian accent if I heard it".

I wrote: One test said I had a Midwest accent. Midwest could be right, as I have parents who came from the Midwest. I was told in High school that I had a slight Norwegian accent, although I don't believe it myself. My grandfather did pronounce Job as Yob (the J was pronounced as if it was Y, which is familiar in many accents from many countries). I did not notice any accent at all in my grandmother. Both maternal grandparents were born in Norway, but Grandma was only seven when she came to the U. S. from Norway. Grandpa was 23. They had to learn English after arriving here. I know they read English because I saw them reading the paper constantly.

On my father's side they were of French-German ancestry. They came over around the same time as the Mayflower, but lived in the Minnesota and Wisconsin area. I think everyone probably has an accent of some kind from the area they were raised in. I worked with a woman from Boston one time and when she got excited I could not understand a word she said. I also had a sister-in-law who said she was raised in Texas and that she would at times revert to her Texas accent. I did not ever recognize any accent.

MEMORIES RECALLED

From an email pal who reminded me that we didn't have fast food when I was growing up. At a restaurant you could get a hamburger for ten cents, but we could not afford it. Mom cooked every day. We sat down together at the dining room table, and if I didn't like what she put on my plate I was allowed to sit there, sometimes a long time, until I did like it or got really hungry. We were not allowed to complain about our food.

Here are a few other things I could have told you about my growing up years. Some parents never owned their own house. A credit card was unheard of. We walked most everywhere and seldom traveled around the country. We never owned a television until I was grown up. All pictures were black and white. The station went off the air at midnight, playing the national anthem, and recited a poem about God. TV test patterns came on at night after the last show and were there until TV shows started again in the morning. It came back on the air at about 6 a.m. featuring a locally produced news and farm show about local people. There were only three channels. Some of us could repair our own television when it went out. Usually it was a tube and you went to a store for a new tube and fixed the set yourself. No repair costs, other than the tube. The picture was quite small, compared to the sets available today.

Milk was delivered to the house in glass bottles, ready for us in the morning. It was on the front porch when we got up. Cream came to the top of the bottle. We had little coupons to pay for the milk, leaving a note to the delivery man about the amount we wanted. If we wanted cream, eggs, or butter we also left a note.

Boys who delivered newspapers six days a week started at 6 a.m. and also collected the money for the subscription. They had better not miss a house with that morning paper or they would really hear about it. The carrier paid for that paper if the subscriber refused to pay because he did not deliver. Sometimes the customer would run out on the carrier and he was stuck with the bill. That was a dirty trick on the poor kid.

Our phone was a party line and you had to listen to be sure someone else was not using it at the time you needed it. The operator would say "Number Please" and you gave her the number you wanted so she could connect you. One time my cousin needed her phone and the other person on the line deliberately kept her from using it. Yes, there were some nasty people those years also. You would ask for a number like Broadway 1234 and she would connect you to that number. Long distance was charged for separately and according to how far away it was you were charged accordingly by the minute.

Movies were made without profanity or most anything offensive and were made for everyone to enjoy viewing. That is not true today. They might even contain the foulest of language on a late night movie. Remember when Gone With the Wind had to fight to show after they included Clark Gable saying "*Damn*". That word or any similar was not allowed. That word is very mild to what you hear today. They have gone overboard now.

Growing up isn't what it used to be. We were cleaning out an old house one time and brought out an old Cola bottle. The stopper on the top had a bunch of holes in it. I knew what it was but my granddaughter had no idea. She thought they had tried to make a salt shaker out of it. It was the bottle that sat on the end of the ironing board to sprinkle clothes because we didn't have steam irons. Yes, those were the days all right.". Not much ironing is done today because material is treated to eliminate wrinkles.

MOUNT ST. HELENS

THE VOLCANO THAT EXPLODED

When Washington's *Mount St. Helens* erupted that Sunday in 1980 it left about an inch deep of white ash in Portland. Further east in Ritzville it was about a foot deep and if you can recognize it, you can still see the evidence in that area. Woodsmen in Idaho said the ash would fly up when they would fell a tree. This kept on for several years afterward.

The explosion devastated quite an area around the mountain. A very good view of the volcano was available only a block from our home, but I didn't even know about the eruption until around 8 pm that evening when I turned on the TV, so I missed it. When we left the house that morning we turned the opposite way from the direction we usually went. I am sure it must have been quite a sight as the explosion was huge. I believe it blew about a mile off the top. We were close enough that we should have heard the noise but we heard nothing, or if we did, we didn't pay any attention to the noise.

People had been warned to stay away from the area and those who did not heed that warning lost their lives that day. The elderly man, Harry Truman, got his wish and stayed. He is buried deep in the debris on his mountain that he loved.

Several months later we visited what was left of Mt. St. Helens. It is hard to describe the results. Timber stripped of all greenery was lying down as if it had been logged. Beside the road was the body of what was left of a car. Only the metal stood to remind one of the devastation of that big blowout. There was a deep crater where the top of the mountain used to be. I still don't understand why I didn't hear any noise that morning, or why I didn't know about the explosion until that evening. I may have heard the noise but did not pay attention because I was not expecting it. The noise could have gone in another direction also.

My Email pal told me: "My family and I used to go to Mt. St. Helens on camping trips and we knew Truman and his wife. When I heard that it had erupted Truman was the first person that I thought of. I knew he would never come down from the mountain. He and his wife had lived there and run the store there for many years. He had been asked to vacate but he would not. Maybe he thought it wouldn't reach him where he was located. He was wrong. That explosion covered a huge area. Truman is probably buried thirty feet deep.

When the mountain blew, I knew it had done so, unfortunately for me as I could hear it! Yes, I am telling the truth. I was working at that time as a cashier. I hadn't even turned on the radio yet and I had told my boss that Mt. St. Helens blew. He didn't believe me and we went about our business opening the store and getting ready for the day!

When he decided to turn the radio on they said that it had blown its top! That was at 8 am! I told my boss then that the volcano ash would come this way (Spokane) because that's the way of the jet stream! He didn't believe me! The boss that day was younger than I was and had no clue even as to where Mt. St. Helen's was located. They were all kidding me about it, so I bet them their pay checks! Guess who won? Yep, me! But I was nice enough not to collect on it! Anyway, that afternoon I could see the ash cloud come our way. They thought it looked like snow, except it got dark, and the street lights tried to come on. The young man that was boss that day asked me how I knew it blew, and I told him that I heard it and could feel it! Heck, my mother could hear it too. Just our hearing is really good is all.

I don't know how to explain our hearing to others. When I lived in San Jose and Gilroy, California I could hear the ground making noises all the time. Here I can't hear it as much which is good because I would have gone nuts by now.

When I lived in Gilroy I could actually hear the ground growling. It scared me because I didn't know the areas there as well as I do here. I never was able to sleep well when I lived there because of it.

Have a great evening and good night."

.*NOTE:* This email pal now lives in Spokane, which is about 300 miles east of Mt. St. Helens. People wonder all the time about animals that seem to know before an earthquake hits. Maybe a few people have the same ability as animals to hear and feel the earth moving, and Mount St. Helens was moving ahead of the blowout.

As to email pal's hearing, I might not have believed her except I personally know another friend who seems to have exceptionally sensitive hearing. I could hardly believe it when this friend would tell me she could hear a siren coming long before it came near enough for me to hear it or she would tell me there was an ambulance coming when it was still far away, but it wasn't long before the ambulance and fire truck arrived. There really are those who have super hearing abilities. It is as if she has built in hearing aids as she seems to hear so many things no one else can hear until later, and they were not her imagination. It is truly amazing to me.

TINY APARTMENTS

The email video showed the use of movable walls so a very small clever use of space could accommodate fairly comfortable living. With these apartments you sure don't want to accumulate a bunch of junk. The movable walls are quite an idea. The video looked like it could be quite comfortable if you did not accumulate a lot of extra "stuff".

I once saw in Portland who had a movable wall between their kitchen and living room. It was a great idea. The wall was on wheels so it could be moved. One direction they had a huge kitchen with lots of cabinets, then when they wanted to use the living room it was rolled back and they had a large living room. I thought it was a very clever idea. One end was on hinges, and it seemed to be very easy to move on its wheels.

If I could remember which house it was I would have gone back and studied the idea. At the time I didn't pay enough attention to the address of the house to be able to go back. I only remember the general location of the house. I think the idea was very clever and it made for extra kitchen space when needed, or extra living room space when needed there.

THE SUNSET

My cousin Elaine lives in the Puget Sound area, right on the water. She sent a picture of a beautiful sunset taken from her front porch.

This is what she can also look forward to from her living room—in the evening she can watch a beautiful sunset and at night she can see the lights from parts of Seattle. She can watch the ships in the distance as well as the ferries carrying cars and passengers going from Bremerton to Seattle. There are other ferries going across from different areas over to Seattle. In the distance she can see the cruise ships coming into Seattle, although they are not close. Using binoculars you might see more or even be able to see which line they are associated with..

One time while visiting Elaine we were sitting in her living room and when we looked up over the water we had the privilege of watching a sea lion giving birth to a pup. There have been times when you could see salmon and other fish jumping. Life is never dull when you have the privilege of such a view in front of your home.

Many times she has guests from all over the world who come to visit her and stay in the apartment she had built in the upstairs of her beautiful home. The apartment was also built so anyone staying there has the same view of the waterfront as she does in the lower part of her home. She is a very gracious hostess and has made many friends world wide that look forward to spending time with her. She is also the one I go with on the several cruises we have taken. She is fun to be with and really does enjoy having guests.

from OZ: "That sunset is beautiful to look at every day. I think living by the water is very calming. I would love to live in Myrtle Beach.

We have beautiful sunrises. You can see it out over the trees since we live on a mountain. We are high enough to enjoy it every day. When we lived in San Diego, we would go to the beach and watch the sunset there. When I lived in New Jersey, across from the ocean, I could see the sunrise. There is nothing like standing on the beaches and seeing the sunsets or sun rises. They are beautiful sights. So glad I was able to experience both. Thanks for sharing."

MINNESOTA

One cousin lives in Minnesota and she sent me some information about that state. A lot of the Norwegian people settled in the state of Minnesota and my ancestors were some of them. A little information would be interesting. Some is fact some fiction.

Author Laura Ingalls Wilder was raised at Walnut Grove, Minnesota, and was famous for writing the "Little House" series of books

Downtown Minneapolis has an enclosed skyway system covering 52 blocks. The Mall of America is famous for its huge size. The only downside to this is that a Norwegian occasionally leaves the door open. It's OK to laugh if you want to.

Minnesota gets its name from the Sioux Indian word "mah-nee-soo-tah," meaning "Lye-soaked fish people." Madison, Minnesota is known as the "lutefisk capital of the world." (Lye is used to process lutefisk) The computer says the name means "clear blue water" so the other name must be someone trying to spoof us. More laughing allowed here..

Minnesota became the 32nd state on May 11, 1858, and was originally settled by a lost tribe of Norwegians seeking refuge from the searing heat of Wisconsin's winters. (Did that say "heat"?). OK. separate fact from fiction. Date is real.

Tryng to make fun of different subjects in Minnesota comparing temperatures was one way. Cold is a relative thing, you know. At 65 degrees, Arizonians turn on the heat, but Minnesotans plant gardens. At 60 Californians shiver uncontrollably, Minnesotans sunbathe. At 40, Georgians don coats, thermal underwear, gloves, wool hats and Minnesotans throw on a flannel shirt. The story goes on and on about the difference in climate all over the country. It finally runs down to say "At 40 below, All electron motion stops. People in Minnesota ask, "Cold enough for ya?"

Yeah, yeah, yeah! I know the above could be true even though it is meant in fun. I know I have grown so used to the heat in California that I am cold in my son's house when they are sweating, literally. I have to wear a sweater. Even in Yuma I was cold while they were too warm. Oh well, their day is coming when they will feel the difference. I guess it comes with age and they are all getting there—they can't avoid it. Hard as they might try, old age creeps up on everyone whether they want it to or not.

NOW I GET TO ADD MY 2 CENTS WORTH LUTEFISK

I sure wish I knew where to buy some Lutefisk. Or a good place to get Lefse. I found the best place to cook Lutefisk is in the microwave if a person can find any Lutefisk. I used to get some in Portland, but it was very, very expensive, and since I was the only one who ate it, the rest of the family stuck their noses up in the air and tried to discourage me from buying any. Occasionally I bought it anyway. If they didn't eat any, I'd get more. For some reason they always ate some.

I also happen to like Limberger cheese. It tastes like bleu cheese. Those are the things I grew up with in my Norwegian grandmothers' house. I also find it hard to find good limburger cheese. Kraft makes a good cheese that is processed in a glass jar. The kind that comes wrapped in foil is not good. So, I like the stinky stuff. I don't eat it to smell, I like the taste. And so I am not weird—just raised like a Norwegian. Some people like goat cheese. Now, to me, that tastes terrible, the kind sold in stores. My grandmother who lived in Idaho used to make cheese from goat milk, but it did not have the strong foreign taste that is in the stores. Hers was good and did not have that awful strong "goat" flavor that I dislike. We had goats when my children were little and I found the milk had to be cared for and did not taste bad. I always figured the problem was that people did not keep their strainers and containers completely clean of old milk.

Been thinking about Lutefisk for some time now. I can make lefse myself, but not the lutefisk. Last week my son's wife, Karen, made a very nice batch of Lefsa. She is not Norwegian but someone taught her how to make it. That was probably my mother who taught her many many years ago. It was very good, and I really enjoyed it. My son and I ate most of it.

Grandma Enger used to make a cheese called Gumalost. It was not a stinky one. It seems to me I remember she boiled milk until there wasn't anything left except the solids. I don't know if she added anything else to it. Traditions die out if young ones don't follow through, then it is too late. My kids wouldn't have the least idea what gumalost is.

My husband's father (of Norwegian descent), after they moved to California, used to buy tortillas and pretend it was lefse. It looks the same but doesn't taste anything near the same. Lefse is simply made with mashed potatoes and flour. Both lefse and tortillas are what you would call a flatbread. Most people eat it with just butter on it. My husband would put jam on his. I don't like jam on mine so all I enjoy on it is butter. Tom's mother was of Irish descent and I don't believe she ever made lefse—at least I don't know if she ever did. I do not make it often, and especially since I am now alone. At times I have taken mashed potatoes and just made a patty and dipped it in flour and browned it, and that is good, but still not the same.

That brings up another memory. I was probably about fourteen at the time. I thought I'd like some lefse so I peeled a huge pan of potatoes and had them all mashed when my mother came home from work one day. I expected her to make some lefse for us. Little did I know that pan of mashed potatoes was enough to make lefse to feed several dozen people. About a quart of mashed potatoes would have been enough, but I had probably made two gallons of those potatoes ready for her. I sure don't remember her reaction, but it could not have been any too welcome coming home tired as she must have been. She made some lefse but I sure do not remember what happened to all those potatoes unless we had them warmed over for meals. For some reason I know better now than to make such a large amount of mashed potatoes. I look back now and think "My poor Mom."

While I can go ahead and make lefse, I have no idea of how much of anything to use to give anyone a recipe. The ingredients are mashed potatoes, flour, and a pinch of salt. The less liquid or milk used in the mashed potatoes the better the flavor. I would use the potatoes left over from a meal. It didn't take very much. I went by the feel of the dough to judge the amount of flour to use. It needed to be the consistency of pie dough and you roll it out just like for a pie, then "bake" it on an iron frying pan or griddle (the top of the old fashioned wood burning iron cook stove was perfect for lefse)

Cousin answered with the following: "I haven't heard of Gumalost for years! (pronounced goom a loast—rhyming with toast) I can remember my mother, Clara, either made it (I can't recall that she did) or bought it some place but the name sure is familiar.

When we moved into our second house it was big enough for the whole clan—we counted 42 at that time—I can still see my husbands' sister standing right by the big kettle of lutefisk, watching it closely for the exact moment it was ready. That's when I learned to like lutefisk. It is served with lots of melted butter.

We had lutefisk for years at Christmas dinner along with Swedish meatballs. Just three of us ate it—older daughter, Laurie, Arne, and I. Then one year Laurie said, "I don't need the smell or taste of lutefisk any more". Her husband, Denny, was not about to eat it. He said we can make our own traditions—HA! Arne is the Swede—I'm the Norwegian. And we've still made it for 62 years in October. I used to make lefse whenever I had leftover mashed potatoes.

I answered: "My aunt Mabel Horine used to make Lefse and send it to school with her sons for their lunch. Of course they loved it, but the other kids thought they had it for lunch because they were so financially hard up that it was all they could afford. The other kids thought the Lefse were pancakes of some sort. The other kids were evidently not acquainted with the Norwegians or their traditions. The boys also never set the other kids straight about the Lefse either because they didn't want to share any of it with other kids.

After the boys graduated from school they joined the Merchant Marines. This was during World War 2 so she sent them a special large package containing a special treat for them. It was a huge stack of Lefse. Of course that treat was a complete disappointment for them. Why? By the time they got it everything was moldy. They could have cried. I can just imagine how they must have felt; so far away from home and family, then to receive something they liked and looked forward to, only to have it ruined with mold.

IN MEMORY OF

IRENE ELIZABETH PETERS ENGER -- 1917--2012

"Irene Enger passed away on February 25, 2012 in Gig Harbor, Washington. A long time resident on the Burley Lagoon since 1960, Irene had turned 94 last August. She is survived by one son, Lannie Enger, of Gig Harbor, her two sisters, Elaine Smith of Port Orchard, and Helen Miller of Spokane, several grandchildren, many nieces and nephews, as well as a large number of cousins throughout the United States. She was preceded in death by her husband, Bert

Enger, and one son, Barry Enger, who was killed by a drunk driver only a mile from their home."

Irene is the one who took on the huge job of tracing the genealogy of several families. She wrote dozens of letters, and used the telephone to contact others all over this country and in Europe, then used a typewriter to print the information out. She and her husband, Bert Enger, traveled for months all over the United States and Canada gathering information, and interviewing family survivors. Irene wrote about the family genealogy the hard way, before computers. She used the typewriter extensively, and was unable to conquer the computer in the later years of her life. She was too frustrated by the computer to learn to use it at her age. It is much harder to use a typewriter than typing on a computer, especially if you need to correct errors. All of this was done with loving care. Most of us would not have tackled that job.

For months she and Bert, traveled to Canada and all over the United States to visit people who might have some information. She traced many ancestors back to Norway and other places in Europe, visited families and friends of family, and then spent many more hours typing out on a manual typewriter all the information she had gathered throughout the years.

One time when in Canada Irene decided to wander away from their motor home to look at something. Bert did not see her and assumed she was in the bathroom and drove off.

It finally dawned on Bert that she wasn't talking to him so he pulled over to check on her.

When he realized she wasn't even in the vehicle he had to drive about twenty-five miles down the road to be able to turn around on the freeway. It wasn't funny at the time but they did laugh about it later. It had been quite a shock to Bert when he realized Irene was missing. Irene in turn had to wonder how long it would take Bert to realize she was not with him. She didn't have her purse with her so she would have been stranded without any money if he didn't miss her very soon. It could have been quite bad if he thought she was taking a nap and had driven quite a longer distance before missing her.

Irene wrote a book about her memories. She lived to be just short of 95 years of age. They are worth reading if anyone ever gets a chance to get a copy. It is about several of our families, many who are mentioned in this narration of mine.

THE DAYS ARE GONE BUT THE MEMORIES LINGER ON is the title of her book of memories. She included many pages of pictures taken over the years. Along with the pictures and family histories, she included stories of interest. Using her notes Irene talked into a recorder for that book. Her niece, Cheryl, transcribed it and her sister, Elaine, wrote the book using the many notes Irene provided. The book is very interesting about her experiences throughout her long life. If it is ever available to the public, it is well worth reading and is written in a way that holds your interest. It has never been printed other than on the computer. Hopefully it can be put into a book for anyone to read. It was her sister who put it on the computer. It has not been commercially printed. So it is not available in stores. Maybe some day one of her family will get it done.

Irene struggled with a typewriter during all the years she was working at getting the information. She took advantage of not only the traveling but with the telephone and much correspondence with others in Norway and all over the United States. During the many years she gathered the family genealogy, she worked and managed a paint store, first along with Bert in a store of their own in Spokane, and then as an employee in a paint store in Tacoma, until she retired.

During her later years, after retiring, she kept busy making some very beautiful quilts. She had quite a talent for the art of handmade quilts. Many times it was a quilt that she gave as a gift. Anyone fortunate enough to receive one of her quilts treasured it. By the time she was 92 she had made over 102 of them. She finally had to give up on the quilts when her eyesight was lost. We will all miss Irene.

Irene, along with her sisters, Elaine and Helen, are the cousins I was closest to for the past seventy years, ever since they had returned from North Dakota in 1933. She was the anchor for many of the families, Enger, Horine, Bergland, Peters and many others, too numerous to mention. She was very special to my family, as her husband, Bert Enger was also my mother's brother.

I received several responses after I let people know of the passing of Irene Enger.

From JOY: "Thank you for letting me know. I did know she was in a nursing home towards the last. Irene's genealogy information is fabulous. My nephew's daughter was doing a project in college about genealogy and for two weeks we emailed back and forth and Irene's book was a terrific help—again. I called Irene and told her she got a mark of 96 out of 100!!! My nephew's daughter was quite thrilled for her A in that subject.

I found it interesting to learn Why Norwegians came to America—They were running out of land for the family members to inherit.

I would call Irene and cry on her shoulder – she'd never tell me what to do but was an understanding listener—just what I needed for a few of life's problems. And, of course, the wonderful visits we had, just to chat. We stayed with Irene in 1999 for one night when Arne had a Navy Reunion in Seattle.

I will miss her!! She was a beautiful lady. Thanks again, Peggy for letting me know.

From WALLACE W. LUNA, Jr "I remember Bert and Irene. They came down and stayed in Judy's trailer in our driveway. I remember they were worried about my dogs.

One morning when Janice came down to the shop she gave Irene the key to the gate because they had some places to go to. They went from the trailer to the house at will, no problem.

When they left and came back, Winkie would not let Irene unlock the gate. They went to a pay phone (that sounds funny nowadays with cell phones and all) and called Janice at the shop. She went to the house and opened the gate, then Winkie was fine.

If you're in the yard you are OK but if you leave you can't come back in unless we let you in. Then it was OK with Winkie.

I'm really sorry to hear of her passing. They were really nice people."

(NOTE: Their Dalmation dog, Winkie, was your best friend while you were in the yard, but if you left, you better not return without permission).

IT REALLY IS A SMALL WORLD
FROM GEORGIA TO ALDER CREEK

This story is an example that was told to me by my cousin, Irene Peters Enger. Irene was my father's niece, and she was married to my mother's brother, Bert Enger. While I am doubly related to them, they were related to each other only by marriage. Bert and Irene had an experience that we all thought would be very interesting to the people of Benewah and Alder Creek. Irene had lived in nearby Farmington for years. Having relatives who lived in the Benewah and Alder Creek areas, Irene was quite familiar with both Benewah and Alder Creek.

One of the reasons for the changes in Benewah and Alder Creek are due to the influx of all the new people. People hear about the area when it is advertised all over the country, They come and buy a few acres of land and then move in. This story is an example of what can happen when the word spreads:

The following incident happened around October of 1982 at Jekyll Island in Georgia. Now Georgia is clear across the country from Benewah and Alder Creek, *a distance of several thousand miles.* Bert and Irene had been traveling for months through Canada and throughout many areas of the United States. This is one of the experiences they had on the East Coast. Running into something familiar or that reminds you of something and someone can happen at any time or any place, even if it is three thousand miles away from where you live. The following story proves that this is really a very small world.

We had been to Florence, South Carolina. Driving further south from there into Georgia, we headed for Millionaires Island, more popularly called Jekyll Island, off the coast of Georgia. We had discovered Jeyll Island by accident a few years before and wanted to stop again. We had been very impressed the first time we were there a few uears before.. It is now a state park. It had been an island where wealthy people from New York and Miami built their summer place. These summer homes were huge! Because of fear that German submarines might try to occupy the island, all the inhabitants were ordered to evacuate during WW2. The State of Georgia purchased all of these lovely homes when the next generation lost interest in the area. The state turned this beautiful place into a state park and the homes are now museums. There is one section of new homes. Recreational homes like none other. It has a beautiful golf course with a cement pier out in the ocean for those who want to fish.

We were also interested in the great camp ground and wanted to stop again. The first time we were at the island, we camped for a week. We were pulling the trailer with the Oldsmobile this time. We wanted to see if anyone was catching anything so we decided to go to the fishing pier to see what was going on. While we were there a pickup and camper pulled in with an Ohio license plate. They got out of their truck and the lady walked over to me. She said, "I see you are from Washington. We are going to be living there soon." When I asked where, she stated "Idaho." Then I asked her where in Idaho. She told me her husband had just retired from the iron mills in Ohio and he bought 10 acres in the mountains near Coeur d'Alene, Idaho. She then wondered if I knew where that was. I told her I knew exactly where Coeur d'Alene was. She then told me it was out of Coeur d'Alene, near St. Maries. I told her I had an uncle who lived in St. Maries. She said they bought out of St. Maries, at a place called Benewah. I couldn't believe what I was hearing. Benewah is where Grandma Horine, Uncle Ray, and the Berglands lived at one time and it is back in the hills. Then she went on to say they wouldn't be at Benewah but at Alder Creek. That is at the end of the world in those mountains. Uncle Morris, Pat and Grandma Horine had lived on Alder creek and I told her I knew where Alder Creek was. She was so surprised, and called her husband who was talking to Bert. "Honey, come here: these people know where we are going." They planned to build a place and retire there. We had invited them into our trailer and talked until midnight. They were all excited about going out in those mountains. I didn't dare tell them that my dad had traded a calf for an 80 acre parcel of land in that area at one time. I didn't dare ask them what they paid for the 10 acres, but I'm sure they paid more than it was worth. We promised them that some day we would come by and see them.

The next summer while in Spokane visiting with Mom and Dad we decided to go to Benewah, and to Alder Creek, to see if we could find them! We drove, and drove, and drove. When we got to the end of the road, there was a man closing a gate to his ranch. We stopped and talked to Sam Brewer and told him who we were looking for. He said Robert and Margaret Beninger lived about a mile on down from his property. So we followed the trail and I spotted their camper. The truck was gone, but we recognized the camper. It had been taken off the truck. There was a wash basin sitting on a stump and a mirror hanging on a tree with a towel next to it. That was as much as we saw of life there. They had gone fishing. This was the end of September! They hadn't built anything yet. I said "My God, those people couldn't possibly live in that camper during the winter. That area gets snow and hard winters!" We left a note. We didn't hear from them until we received a card at Christmas time. They were in Coeur d'Alene house-sitting. That's the last we ever heard from them.

I have thought of them so many times and their big hopes. Maybe some day I'll go out there and see if they did build a house back in those hills. We live on the West Coast. We met them on an island off the East Coast separated by several thousand miles. And here we knew where they were going to live—*IT IS A SMALL WORLD!! A VERY SMALL WORLD INDEED.*

I found the names of the people among some letters. I am hoping to locate Robert and Margaret Beninger and their neighbor Sam Brewer this summer. Unless they are still in Alder Creek I may not be able to find them. If they are there this summer, I will try to look them up. Hopefully they will be at the Benewah picnic, and they will be able to tell more of this story. To see strangers three thousand miles away from your home and know where they were going to settle is amazing. It would be interesting to hear their side of the story.

P. S. SUMMER OF 2014

Bert and Irene Enger are both now deceased. Since this incident happened at least thirty two years ago, it is possible that Robert and Margaret Beninger are also gone, and even their neighbor, Sam Brewer. I thought this story was quite interesting and hope you do also. I found the names of the people among some letters I received from Irene. I was hoping to locate Robert and Margaret Beninger and their neighbor, Sam Brewer, this summer when I went to the Benewah picnic. I was unable to learn any more about them.

P. S. # 2

I was at the Benewah Valley community picnic in July 2014, but there was no word of the Beninger folks, or of Mr. Brewer. They may have moved on or may have passed away. It is hard to tell, since the above incident took place so many years ago and a lot can happen in that length of time. I had forgotten my notes before going to the picnic and tried to tell this story at the picnic without the notes. No one recognized any of the names. Evidently anything more will have to remain a mystery. It is still a very small world we live in any time you can meet people under these circumstances three thousand miles across a country. *A VERY SMALL WORLD INDEED!!!!!*

July 2017—I was at the Benewah picnic but unable to go up to Alder Creek to inquire of someone there. I emailed someone in Benewah to ask if they knew anything but got no response.

DOROTHY SCHLAGEL HOKANSON -- 1924—2009

IN MEMORY OF MY SISTER, A GREAT CAREGIVER

"Dorothy and her first husband, Lester Schlagel, became the parents of three children during the more than fifty years of their lifetime together. They were Sandra, Gary and Jim. All of them presently live in the vicinity of Tacoma, Washington. Lester preceded Dorothy in death by a few years. Both were survived by two sons, Gary and Jim, and daughter, Sandy, of Tacoma as well as grandchildren. Dorothy's sister, Peggy Bergland, and several cousins and numerous aunts, uncles and cousins, will all miss her."

Dorothy did not suffer any lingering illness before she died. Her heart just quit and she died peacefully. She spent her final couple of years in a private care home. Dorothy seemed to be happy there. She was 85 years of age at the time of her passing away.

I will always remember Dorothy for the very wonderful care she gave to our mother for the last ten years of her life. Our mother lived to be past 93 and had become both deaf and blind in her last few years, so she needed intensive care.

When I notified people of Dorothy's passing, I got to thinking about the fact that Dorothy had a problem with a form of illness that was mental. I know some others may have friends or relatives with the same problem and I hope this may be a little encouragement to those who do. Some people with a mental problem just cannot cope with life's every day problems in some way.

My sister had the problem of not making friends with her neighbors. She mostly ignored them. Dorothy had that problem most of her adult life and because she could get quarrelsome with neighbors and others, they left her alone. She did improve in her later years, and did finally make friends with one of her next-door neighbors. Her problem seemed to be that she would verbally accuse someone with something ridiculous, taking the person by surprise, not knowing what she was talking about. If she took a notion she didn't like someone—imagining things about them— she would, on the basis of her flimsy thoughts, verbally attack them. She didn't go out looking for trouble, but she might make disparaging remarks to anyone if they tried to get acquainted with her. This discouraged anyone from seeking her friendship. She did improve greatly in her last few years. I don't know why she was able to do so well as a caregiver, but not as a friend to anyone otherwise. Maybe it was fulfilling to her to be a caregiver. Dorothy was neat and clean and a good housekeeper. She was an excellent seamstress. She was really a great artist with her sewing machine and had made many beautiful quilts. That kept her busy most of the time and it was a rewarding accomplishment.

Dorothy was a wonderful caregiver for our mother, and also for the man she took in and cared for for several years after her husband, Lester, died. Harry Hokanson was the paternal grandfather of Dorothy's grandson. She took Harry Hokanson in when his own family didn't treat him right. His health was not good. He had been an officer in the military and was retired with failing health. He was diabetic and required special help. I think Harry Hokanson recognized that caregiver quality in her and when he treated her so very well, she really responded. Their getting together was a blessing for both of them in their old ages. She was afraid to offend him in any way because she was afraid if she offended him he might leave so she made a real effort to be kind to him. Harry was outstanding in the way he treated my sister. The entire family was so very thankful for the man's kindness to her and he was rewarded with great care in his last years.

Harry told me one time, "She is a little cracked (I think that was the word he used), but she takes wonderful care of me." He treated her really well. He would take her out to dinner, bring her flowers, supply some groceries, take her on trips, and treated her adult children as if they were his own. What more could anyone ask? She responded very well to him. It really worked out well for both of them. Dorothy cared for Harry for several years. They were married about a year before Harry died. She really grieved over his death. She lost her very best friend and grieved so very much when he died.

One day something happened that she had to go to a neighbor for help. The police were called to assist her. This brought on the State taking over and putting her under conservatorship. No one informed me of what was going on and I was surprised to learn the State had taken over. By the time I learned about this it was too late for me to do anything for her or about her. The state took over and cancelled everyone else's rights.

Everything had been kept from me. For some reason they thought it would be too much for me because of my age and because I lived so far away in Southern California. I may have been in my 80's and two years older than Dorothy but I would have been able to care for her. Younger people seem to think being older makes a person somewhat "helpless." They have to get older to find out for themselves that is not true.

When I did find out she was in trouble, I acted. Dorothy had been placed in a large facility for assisted living. When I visited her I was really appalled at the place. Her room was clean but too small and cramped to be comfortable. There were hundreds of residents in that facility, which were too many for her mental condition. When I left, she became very frustrated. Because she hadn't wanted me to leave she acted up after I left and bumped a walker into another patient. She was removed from that facility and placed temporarily elsewhere until a more satisfactory place could be found..

I tried to fix things so she could come live with me. That is when I found out all that had been going on. It was when I was going to insist on helping her that I was informed that the judge had cancelled all Power of Attorneys for her, which included mine. I would have had to go to court to enforce my PA and it would have taken a long time to overcome the process of what had been done. It was about that time that she was placed with a nurse in a private home with a total of four people there. That seemed to be working out quite well. She was happy at that home and was there for about two years until she passed away.

Yes, I will always remember my sister, especially for the wonderful care she gave to our mother, and to Harry Hokanson in the last years of their lives (Our mother lived to be past 93 and had become both deaf and blind in her last years, so she needed intensive care.). I am also thankful to the man who was himself a wonderful person. He treated my sister the way any woman should be treated and the result was good for both of them. Harry must have realized that. They both ended their lives in a much happier environment because of each other. Their getting together was a blessing for both of them in their old ages.

In going over this story I got to thinking about what those with a mental problem might be capable of in spite of their illness. Some people may have friends or relatives in the same position and I hope this may be a little encouragement to them who do. Many people with a mental problem may not be able to cope with everyday problems. After all, the mind can get sick as well as the rest of the body, and we all have to cope with any kind of illness no matter whether it is located in the body or the mind.

1935-1939 – HARDSCRABBLE TIMES

Email friend—February 13, 2012: "You are fortunate to have such a good memory.

My parents didn't have money, and neither did my grandparents. We made do with what we had and were thankful for it all. We never said "We don't like" or disrespected our elders in any way shape or form. We would catch heck for that if we did and we would get spanked for it as well. If we swore we would get our mouths washed out with soap! Not anything like the kids are today that's for sure.

My great aunt and uncle owned a farm in Auburn which used to be Green River at one time. My mother's side of the family came to Washington in 1880. At the time they <u>bought their farm with a down payment of five cents.</u> My great great grandparents are buried on the south knoll of that farm.

They found an ad in the newspaper for the property in Green River, hooked up a wagon and their team of oxen, drove their herd of Norman War horses from California to Washington. Then they settled there for the rest of their lives.

Zerah had gone back to Michigan to talk to an Arborist about planting apple trees on the farm. Those apple trees were still there in 1975 when my great uncle died. The saplings had been shipped when snow had covered the track so deeply that the train couldn't move. There was no heat on the trains back then either. So Zerah got off and followed the tracks to where he could go for help. He knew trains well as he used to help lay the bed and tracks for them. Anyway, Zerah made it, whereas most of those people who were on that train died from the cold.

I know how badly it hurts to lose your grandfather. I was the one that my grandfather wanted next to him when he passed away. I don't know why either except that I had spent most of my life with him and my grandmother, not only in their care of me but my taking care of them as well. That's when I first found out that I wanted to be a nurse (which never happened because I messed up my back pretty badly back in 1981).

By the way, I love your stories and I hope that you are not only writing them on here but down so that your kids can read them too! I wish I had better memories to share, but I don't. Yes, I remember some good things like my mother teaching me how to crochet and do other crafts. My mother had a beautiful smile.

My grandfather used to tell us that we weren't poor, and that the state of mind of being poor was just that "a state of mind". If you believe that you are, then you are, but if you believe that you are not poor, then you aren't, so to speak. They had food, shelter, clothing and everything that the Lord promised us. And that's all he promised. The rest, well, that's sort of a different story. We had gardens, (veggies, fruit, etc.) The men in the family went deer hunting, fishing, etc. for the meat. My grandfather was a commercial fisherman at one time so they had all the fish that they could eat, too.

Anyway, that's enough of my story. Have a great day! Your friend

More Email: I had written the following message to my email pal who told me she had several relatives who had emigrated to Palouse, Washington:

What you wrote me was very interesting. I had relatives who moved to Idaho and to Palouse, Washington, which makes me wonder if there could possibly be any connection. It's a small world and it is always possible, We don't know why family left the Central states and moved to Palouse and to Spokane. Do you know why your relatives left the eastern states and moved to Palouse? I have a brother buried in the cemetery there. He died as an infant. My grandparents are buried in that cemetery in Palouse also. Please let me know whatever you might know or remember. I listed several names and ask if any of them mean anything to you. Thanks, Peggy

*Her answer follows:*FAMILY HISTORY –– July 13, 2011: My family moved from Missouri sometime between 1900 and 1902. My great great grandfather died in 1894. I haven't been able to find his wife (the mother Talitha (Tabitha?) of my Stephen) either by his grave or in the same area as he is. So I don't have a clue as to where she is buried at! So the 1900 census has her at about 75 years of age, widowed and living with her son Stephen and daughter-in-law Isabelle. It has always been my understanding that Stephen (my great grandfather) was a lumber grader for the Potlatch Co. but the 1900 census has him as a farmer. This is possibly because he took over the farm where his father and mother were living. However, I have no proof of land ownership records and I find James Ackles passing away in Marion, Grundy County, MO. instead of in Galt or Trenton, Grundy County, MO. They had a daughter together also, her name was Lydia and she married a man by the name of Philpot (surname). They lived in KS, but I find no records of their mother ever living with her either. Strange to say the least about all of this but that's what I have right now. I haven't been able to go to MO to find out anything. My understanding is that they don't care about the cemeteries (the older ones) and so they are unkempt and vandalized badly. So it wouldn't do me any good to even attempt that, and the states did not put out death certificates until 1907. So, I guess that one just has to sit the way that it is, unfortunately. The family Bibles were burned by a great aunt on my grandfather's side, just because she wouldn't send it to her brother (the only one living by that time), who was my grandfather.

My grandfather Estus Bruce Ackles was born November 2, 1902 in Lapwai, Idaho, then the brother that follows him was born in 1904 in Weipe, Idaho. There were a couple (I think) born and died in Palouse, Washington between 1910-1912 and buried at the only cemetery that is there, a child by the name of Helen Marie b. 1912, died Nov 2012, and then Marie Lucille b. 1909 d. 1993 in Texas. By the 1920 census they are here in Spokane. My grandfather stated that he was here when the Division Street Bridge fell in to the river with the Trolley car on it between 1911and 1915? I would have to go look that up I guess.

Peggy, there wasn't much in Palouse, Washington at the time that we are speaking of, just the Potlatch Company, a tavern and a few other stores like a mercantile type store. The only other profession is farming. If Elaine is looking for census records on the Palouse, Whitman County Washington maybe I can help her a little bit. Another thing she can try (free) is the Washington State Digital Archives and of course the family search.org site. Let me know OK? None of those particular names you sent ring any bells for me. But that doesn't mean that they weren't all there at one time.

To answer your question as to why they came west is really unknown to me or the reasoning for it. I know that Missouri farming is a very hard life (so my cousin tells me). I also know that there was a lot of persecution back then about religious beliefs. I also know that Mormons were run out of MO and so it might be true about other religions as well including Jewish people which my gr-grandfather was, a Rabi. So, I am sure they had their reasons for coming west. Do you know the reason why yours did?

On February 15, 2012 I wrote: I will be 90 in three months and I do remember things like this. Many streets and highways were not paved. My grandparents lived on a farm in Idaho so we had food and shelter, but I do remember one family lived in the woods where they used tree limbs and brush to build a shelter. They had children, some were my age. I was so impressed that I even remember their family name, it was Stone. I know my grandparents shared food with them.

Besides milk and meat they raised a garden. My grandparents raised chickens, turkeys, and had cows for milk. They had very little cash money. I especially remember Grandma had canned Bing cherries and I loved cherries and thick cream. I helped Grandma churn the cream into butter in an old barrel shaped churn. I think they sold cream to the creamery and also eggs from their large flock of White Leghorn chickens. The big roosters would attack you if you did not watch out for them.

My grandfather died in 1931 from Cancer. I turned nine two weeks after he died. I think he suffered quite a bit from that cancer as there wasn't much that could be done for him at that time.

FROM OTHER PEOPLE

A WONDERFUL STORY

Whose memories are stirred by my memories: February 21, 2012—*Julian Apodaca* sent me the following memory of his after he received the above email from me.

Hi Peggy: I really enjoyed reading this email. It made me think back to my childhood and how much the world has changed. I was born in Albuquerque, N.M. in August 1950 so I am almost 30 years your junior. Still, I too have vivid memories of my own childhood.

I remember living in a square house with four big rooms with an attic and a screened porch in front. It was made out of adobe brick so it was warm in the winter and cool in the summer. We had electricity but no running water. Water was at the pump in the back yard. Stove and heat were wood and coal fueled. I was raised by my mother and Great Grandmother (my Grandmother died of cancer 2 months before I was born) and never knew my dad. We lived in that house until I was in the middle of second grade.

I remember having an icebox before we had a refrigerator. I remember chopping wood for heating and cooking, or heating water to bathe. We did have a black and white TV but we didn't own a car. I remember my great granny growing a garden and drying and canning for winter. Amazing, because all of this was before I was the age of seven and a half, at which time we moved. I think back now and realize my Great Grandmother was quite old at the time. She died at the age of 97 when I was 25, so you do the math.

She would chop wood and cook and bake, not to mention washing clothes. Both she and my mom used an old, (new at the time), wringer washing machine. None of the modern conveniences, yet we were always clean and our meals were so delicious. Imagine that, baking in a wood stove. Well, like I always say, "pigs don't know pigs stink," when you don't know any better.

My Great Grandmother was born in New Mexico before it was a state (statehood 1913). She didn't care much for Mexicans, remarkable because she didn't speak much English, but she was extremely proud of her Spanish ancestry. Her Great Grandparents had settled in New Mexico when it was a Spanish territory. Consequently I grew up bi-lingual. My mother believed in a good education and struggled to send me to Catholic school, something I will always be eternally grateful for.

Do you know which state has the oldest capital city in the U. S.? Give it a guess, come on, just guess. Give up? It's Santa Fe, N. M. founded in 1610. Think about that. Long before the Pilgrims arrived the western United States had already been settled. I didn't learn this in school. The nuns that taught me told me that the country started with the pilgrims.

In my 30's I went to N. M. with some friends to go skiing in Taos. We were catching a flight in Albuquerque and decided to have dinner in "old town." The restaurant had post cards near the cash register and I happened to pick one up and read it. It asked "which is the oldest capital city in the U. S.? If not for this I never could have known that bit of trivia about the state I was born in…so there you have it, now you know the rest of the story. I hope my memories bring back fond memories for you as yours have for me - *Julian Apodaca* (Julian Apodaca lived in Moreno Valley at the time he wrote this note.)

PS from Peggy—I really treasure this story and appreciate Julian sending it to me.

I have read from several books that there were Spanish people who came to the western part of this country very early. They left many signs that they were here long before the early Pilgrims settled the Eastern coast of the U. S.

EARTHQUAKES DO HAPPEN IN CALIFORNIA

I wrote on *5/12/12* the following about *email and Earthquakes*: We had a small earthquake here this morning. It was a 3.8 shaker around 8 a.m. It was just a good hard jolt of about one-half second long, nothing more all day. Some people were standing in front of my place and I went out and asked them if they felt the quake. Their answer was, "What Quake?" The epicenter was north of San Bernardino. I suppose that some day we may have a big quake, but those small ones are sometimes never even felt or even noticed.

That minor earthquake did frighten my friend, Maryland Nygren, enough that she jumped up and started to run for the door, ended up tripping and falling and breaking her hip.

California is not the only state that has earthquakes. They have happened all over the United States, but not much is ever written about them. Concentration on earthquakes seems to come from California for some reason. Maybe that is because of the 1906 big quake and damage to San

Francisco, which was the basis for stories and plays for many years.

In 1811 to 1812 a monstrous earthquake called the New Madrid earthquake was felt over at least two million square miles. It was felt from Canada to New Orleans and in Boston and Washington, D.C. If it happened today there would be few buildings left in that area. The possibility of damage to parts of Illinois from earthquakes originating outside the state is dominated by the threat of a repeat of that New Madrid earthquake.

I was writing to a friend and after almost a full page of typing it suddenly disappeared. I had almost finished this email and it was suddenly gone and I could not get it back. That has happened before. Maybe that wasn't a real earthquake this morning after all, it might have been me. I am upset about what is happening with my computer so maybe I was mad enough at the computer to shake up the whole county.

I am trying to "clean house" but it sure is a chore. The cleaning part is trying to get rid of the excess stuff I have accumulated over the years. I sold two cabinets and two really nice chairs that I no longer was using. Feel it is time to rid out all excess stuff. Of course it is only the good stuff anyone else wants and I have lots of small stuff that no one wants so I am giving it to anyone who will take it.

Well, I am tired tonight, so see you all later.

Cousin **wrote back:** I clean out and do such a terrific job and it seems in a very short time—where did all that stuff come from? We'll just have to keep working at it. I feel if I get some of this stuff done now it's less for the kids to have to do later..

I started a "Survivor folder" a few years ago—I started out giving it the name of "Funeral folder" but a survivor kit is what they'll have to do. It took me two days to get items together and I knew where everything was filed, like copies of credit cards, and bank pawords. Got daughter, Laurie, who lives two miles from us, to co-sign on checks and safety deposit box. I listed what is in the safety deposit box such as Abstract of Title, etc., and Arne's discharge papers from the Navy, I saw this article on what to start putting together, and hope I got it all done right.

Yes, I feel sometimes I spend much too much time on the computer working out the kinks. They just pop up for no reason—oh, well, I really do love the contact of emails so will have to suffer through the rest. Joy.

MEMORIES OF SEVERAL TRIPS AROUND THE COUNTRY

OUR 1966 TRIP TO CANADA

It was in June of 1966 that we left Riverside, California for a trip into Canada to visit the area where my husband had been born and lived until he was eight years old.

At the time we left Riverside the weather was very cold. We had purchased an old school bus that had been converted into a motor home. It was a bit primitive, but we were comfortable for the most part. It was a good way to travel.

To be sure we would have no troubles on the trip, Tom had installed a rebuilt motor into that bus before leaving home.

We headed out towards Utah over a nice highway. Then we came along to a steep grade. That is when we encountered engine trouble. We headed off the road into Zion, Utah and stopped at a garage. The mechanic had us park the vehicle where he would be able to work on it and yet let us occupy it while we were there. We ended up having to get another rebuilt engine for that bus. The motor had to be ordered from Salt Lake City and with the time that took and the time to install it we spent a few days there. We were able to use the bus facilities during our stay without any problems. It was equipped with a toilet and with cooking equipment so we were fully self-contained. After the new motor was installed we went on our way. We had no further engine troubles. Evidently the first rebuilt motor was not a good one.

We continued on our way towards Yellowstone Park, then on north into Canada. We went through Banff, Alberta and enjoyed the scenery. We did not see the elk in the city or in the populated areas at that time, but there were "farms" where there were big herds of elk behind fences. We found them quite interesting to watch. The people who approach these elk in the cities are quite foolish as they can attack people and sometimes really do so without warning. At one city we visited a zoo and enjoyed the entire day. Of special interest was a pair of small bear cubs and their antics. We spent a lot of time watching those little babies. The whole park was especially beautiful with well kept grounds. The shrubbery was trimmed into clever sculptures like elephants, bears, and other wildlife. We enjoyed the entire time we spent there.

The weather at times was quite cold as it was early June and there was still some snow on the ground in places. In fact it was the first two weeks in June and it was really cold here in California when we left Riverside. That converted bus made for a wonderful trip. We had a propane heater in the bus for heat and it was very welcome. Yellowstone Park had snow piled as high as the top of the bus alongside the roads.

We were cozy and warm until we got into Canada. The second day there our propane heater leaked propane and caught fire. My son was standing in the doorway and had presence of mind to grab the fire extinguisher and put out the fire. That fire could have spread very fast and trapped us inside the bus. David was only eleven years old at the time, but he knew enough to grab that nearby extinguisher and use it. From then on we had no heat. We dressed as warm as we could. I used the stove to heat water hoping to warm things up and also used a rock that I heated up on top of the stove. Looking back that was also dangerous to do as the rock could have exploded and caused damages that way.

The weather was beginning to get seasonally warmer and we were comfortable most of the time after the early morning passed. By the middle of June, the weather had warmed up so it was quite comfortable all the time. We continued on North to where my husband was born and lived until he was eight or nine years old. Crop failure after crop failure caused the family to move back to the States. Mostly the crops froze out.

While in Canada we visited people who Tom remembered, and amazingly several remembered Tom and his parents even after such a long time. We got to see the old school house where my husband started school—a one room school house. In those days there were a lot of one room schoolhouses throughout both the U. S. and Canada. We were offered a chance to buy the building, now abandoned, for $300. It was in nice condition but what could we do with it? It was in Northern Saskatchewan and we lived in Riverside, California. It would be a long way to move it. We met people my husband remembered from childhood and they remembered him. Everyone treated us royally and we had a nice visit with all we met.

One family who lived in town took us to visit another family Tom had known as a child. All had been students in the one room school house at the same time. The second family lived on a lake. While at the lake, we were given a nice boat ride after they had provided a big picnic lunch. Both families remembered that Tom's father, Edisto Bergland, had run a bus service while they lived in the town called Paddockwood. I am sorry I don't remember the names of the families, only remembering how gracious all of them were to us and how very friendly and welcoming they were.

We parked our bus by one of the many lakes in the area and thought we would be eaten up by the thousands of mosquitoes that evening. When we looked up the very elderly people living on the lake they turned out to be the ones who had been very close friends to Tom's parents. They owned all the property surrounding the lake. They informed us they had made arrangements that the land could never be subdivided because they felt it should always be open forever.

We had a wonderful visit throughout the part of Canada that we toured. The trip was well worthwhile. We felt very welcomed by our Canadian neighbors to the North.

When we left Canada we spent a few days in Seattle and vicinity. We then continued South on Highway 101, along the coastline, enjoying every minute of it. Because we were not in a big hurry, we visited many places we would have ordinarily missed in a rushed trip. By the time we returned home to Riverside, we had been gone a month. It was a trip we won't forget.

FROM OZ: "As usual you make me wish I was young again. So many times we wanted to travel to Europe but something was always coming up. Maybe I am not meant to leave the U. S.

Have been to the east side of Canada where we spent six months. Loved every minute of it. Been to Mexico but was not impressed. We went there only because we lived in San Diego. We flew from Pennsylvania to San Francisco, spent a few days and then headed down the coastline highway. We stayed near Big Sur after spending some time there. Then we went down to 7 mile (?) whatever, then to Disneyland, and then on to San Diego. We spent 10 days vacationing and then moved there for ten years.

From San Diego we moved to Kansas. We spent six months in Canada—Quebec, Ottawa, and a lot of other places on the east coast.—Toronto and some ski resort. It was a fun time. My husband was sent there to work for his company and go to school there. Gary and his family came for a few days. We love traveling, when we go to Ohio to see his family, we do the 5 hour drive. When we go to Myrtle Beach we do the ten hour drive. We even traveled back and forth from San Diego to Pennsylvania for the ten years we lived in San Diego. Always by car, oh I think we flew 2 times. This time when we go to San Diego we will fly.

You were so lucky to have been able to travel when you did. I guess that was a lot of money at the time but the wonderful memories you have. Can't put a price tag on those memories. Thanks once again for sharing.

Oh, by the way, I shared your story with a few friends. I just thought it was a remarkable one. Hope you don't mind. I did remove your email address but left your first name.

Congratulations on your new book and hope it makes the New York best seller list.

MORE TRAVEL NEWS

About three years ago my cousin called me about a cruise she wanted to take and also wanted me to go with her. The cruise was from Vancouver, B. C. to Japan, Korea and to China. I wanted to go, but the cost is something I had to think about. It was a bargain at $1700, but I didn't have the courage to spend that kind of money when I don't have a job or something to fall back on. My daughters thought I should go, and since I had a roommate the $300 a month she pays me would make a big difference. My roommate, Georgie, is very pleasant to have around.

I ended up NOT going on that cruise. I guess I really should have gone and do regret that I didn't spend the money.

Elaine got someone else to go and it turned out to be a very pleasant trip. Hindsight is always better than foresight. I really should have gone. I wasn't as crippled up in my legs at that time as I am now and I know I would have enjoyed the cruise.

What OZ wrote to me after I told her about the cruise offer (before I turned it down.):

"I have one word for you....GO!!!! Do not pass up an opportunity like that. You'll be in your 90's looking back and regretting it. My husband had a chance to go to Ireland with his grandmother. That was before we were married. He didn't want to leave me. Love is blind. Ha. He regrets it to this day.

Never pass up the chance to just go. I lived in New Jersey and it was ok but missed my family in Philadelphia, Pennsylvania—Philly. I was a teenager when we moved there and I was in school. I didn't want to make friends, so I didn't.

When we finally moved back to Philly, I hated the neighborhood.

So again, I didn't want to make friends, so again, I didn't.

When I married we lived in Philly and I got to see my family. (When I say family I mean grandparents, aunts, uncles, etc). Then we moved to San Diego, I hated it. I was homesick. We moved back to the Philly area, I loved it.

My husband couldn't find a good job, so back to San Diego we went. It was worse the second time around. I made two good friends in San Diego and we are still friends. Then we moved to Kansas and lived there 11 years. Made email friends. Big deal. I didn't even talk to my neighbors in KS or CA. We were in a store checking out and my husband started calling to someone. I asked him who he was. He looked at me like I was an alien. Here it was our neighbor across the street. How bad is that???

I am glad that when we moved that my grandparents had been dead by then. Otherwise I think I wouldn't have moved at all. I asked him to come back every year so I could visit my family. Driving from San Diego to Philly at Christmas every year was, sometimes, an ordeal. Now that we are back in Pa, we are still far from Philly. Not many family members are left. (Family being aunts and uncles).

Two years ago I got in touch with some cousins and we met for the first time. Some have kids as old as me or younger. Now we meet every year at my son's house. Again we are having a reunion. This time I am hoping there will be more cousins. Well, I rattled on long enough about my boring life. Yours is more adventurous. OZ.

A VISIT TO KANSAS

May 2009: Jackie and I went on a three week trip. We left on U. S. Air and went through security without any trouble in Ontario, California. I took my scooter and made do with my suitcase as a carry-on. Jackie checked hers and had to pay $15 for checking it. I figured the airfare was enough without paying anything more for baggage. I had learned to pack lightly and not to take too much.

We landed for a short stopover in Phoenix. We were met by nephew Bob Bergland in Kansas City. It was a three-hour ride to Fort Scott from the Kansas airport.

Bob had bought an older home that had been thoroughly remodeled. It was beautiful. They had two bedrooms and two bathrooms downstairs. Upstairs they have three bedrooms and another full bathroom. Jackie had a room and they had two air mattresses for me in one of the upstairs bedrooms. Well, one of the mattresses leaked air and I ended up having to get up during the night. All I could do was scoot over to the stairway and manage to stand up that way (I have trouble standing up even from a chair any more). The bed on the air mattresses was really comfortable but it got lowered when the air went out of the top one. I can't even crawl on my hands and knees any more, so I just found a comfortable chair and sat in it the rest of the night. I do this all the time at home anyway. I sleep about four hours and am wide awake from then on. After that night I slept on their davenport downstairs. The bed Jackie slept on was so high I couldn't climb into it. The mattresses and box springs are now made so thick that the finished result is height. I ran into this one time at a motel. The motel bed was so high I could not get into it.

Kansas is flat as far as you can see. Not even a hill in the distance, at least where we were visiting. They had a lot of rain so there were dozens of shallow lakes all over, and lots of trees that had new leaves on them. While there, we went over to Branson, Missouri. The country around Branson was hilly, not flat like Kansas. We got into Branson late in the afternoon and that evening saw one show. It was good and very entertaining, but that was all we got to see that evening.

The next day we saw a little bit of the town. Jackie went to a shopping mall that looked interesting but since I have trouble walking, I went with Bob and Anneta to a car show. I sat in the car by choice and tried to rest. They were gone less than an hour, then we went looking for Jackie. Bob went into the mall and couldn't find her. I needed to go to the bathroom so I finally went inside and then found Jackie, only to learn they had scooters to loan out. If I had known about the scooters I'd have gone with her. The mall was very interesting, with many kinds of merchandise.

We started for home after eating lunch. Bob is very busy and could not take any more time away. I am glad he was able to spend two days with us. They live about three hours driving time from Branson. While I am glad we were able to visit there, it is not a place where I would want to spend much time unless we had a motor home and could take the time to leisurely go around the place. You have to pay to see each show so it can also get expensive.

From Kansas City we proceeded on to visit Larry and Robin in Acworth, Georgia.

FROM KANSAS TO GEORGIA

We left Kansas on Tuesday. When we went through security at the airport, I had very little trouble, but Jackie had one bad time with security there. They wanted to throw all her medicine away because it wasn't in quart size baggies. She had to argue with them to keep them from throwing her prescriptions away. She had ordered wheelchair assistance and none showed up to begin with. She was told she had to go "home" and get baggies. She told them to get her a wheelchair then, and they said they couldn't, it wasn't their job, etc. She did have her stuff in a plastic bag. She had stuff in small bottles because we are told they don't want large bottles. Anyway, in Kansas City they were not very nice. I think someone went and got some kind of a bag to satisfy them. Maybe they were just showing their "authority." I have been through quite a few airports and never ran across anyone as rude as that bunch were. We had exactly the same stuff in our luggage in Kansas City as we had left with in Ontario, California, and had no trouble in Ontario.

We finally boarded our plane, went on to Charlotte, N. C., and had a stopover there of about an hour. We stayed on the plane. I guess the stopover was delayed from leaving because of tornadoes in the Atlanta area. We had a nice visit with the crew on board.

The flight on into Atlanta was good. Larry met us at the baggage area. In Atlanta, you have to take a train from the plane to the baggage pickup sight. Since I had my scooter and two bags to handle, I had to really scramble to make it onto the train in such a way to be able to get off again towing two bags. I am allowed two bags because one carries my CPAP machine and the other is my "carry-on" bag. Medical equipment is not "baggage" that is counted. My scooter is considered a wheelchair. When I arrive at my destination they bring it up to the door of the plane again. By the time we got down to baggage, we didn't have to wait long for

Jackie's bag. By this time she had paid $30 for her checked bag, then another $15 again to go home. I have learned to take less stuff—still didn't use all that was packed in one bag.

Jackie and I accompanied Larry on his job around Acworth. This way we got to see the country and visit with him while he was driving. We made arrangements for Larry and Robin to take us up to North Carolina to visit with Sue after returning from a trip to Pigeon Forge and the Dollywood theme park with my two grandsons, Alex and Kyle.

Alex and Kyle drove us up to Dollywood to spend the day there. We had rain all the way up and I mean it really poured a huge amount all the way. I thought it might ruin the trip if it was raining all the time. Just about the time we arrived in Pigeon Forge, the rain stopped and the sun came out. We went to the theme park when we found out if you arrived after 3 pm your ticket was still good for the next day. We spent the rest of that day at the park and really enjoyed it.

We found that by buying a season pass you got in free the rest of the year and didn't have to pay for parking, plus you even got a twenty-percent discount on anything you bought in the park, including food. I bought Alex a season ticket and the next day we didn't have to pay for parking. The next day I also bought a season pass for Kyle. His cost less as all he needed was to have entry, not the discount or parking. They were delighted and said they would use the passes. Larry's boys are now just under 16 and 19 years old as of this writing (time flies). Once you entered the park there was no further charge for the shows. We saw everything clear up until closing time at 8 pm. We let the boys go on the rides that interested them, but they kept hunting us up and checking on us. We all had a very good time the rest of that day. The next day we went as early as the park opened and spent the entire day there, busy every moment. Larry had borrowed a scooter for Jackie and I had mine, so we had a great time.

Jackie and I got to see Dolly Parton in person. She just happened to be there that day. We also toured her bus. It had cost $750,000 and had 750,000 miles on it. She now has a new one. They told us that when they leave Tennessee they drive straight through to Los Angeles without stopping. She has two full-time drivers plus a lady companion. Talk about luxury. The bus even has a dishwasher and two bathrooms.

A few days later Larry, Jackie, and I went up to North Carolina to visit my daughter-in-law, Sue. We didn't get to see granddaughter, Shannon. The first thing I asked Myrtle, Sue's mother who now lives with them, how many bedrooms the house had. She smiled and said "four." One bedroom is downstairs, and then she smiled again and said "guess who gets the downstairs one." It was very noticeable that she was as happy as a lark there.. They have been working hard on the yard. It is really beautiful, becoming like a park. The house is very nice; the kitchen has lots of beautiful oak cabinets. The front porch has a wraparound porch across the front and down one side. The house has hardwood floors throughout. It is an older home, but well built. The town is a small town, but I liked it and felt "at home" there.

CELL PHONES

Maybe this will help explain why I hate cell phones for the most part. They are so invasive that it is like someone is standing over your shoulder twenty-four hours a day.

When I am in an automobile with friends and the cell phone rings and another passenger answers it, I really resent the thing unless it is an emergency. It has the same affect on me as all the advertising calls that come on my phone at home. It is also the same as if they were in the middle of the night waking me up from a sound sleep.

LATER—Since I wrote that email above, I have purchased a cell phone. It is friendlier than the first phone I had and so far I am not getting unwanted calls. Evidently no one has had my phone number before as I am not getting soliciting calls. It has features that are easy to use. I can easily find out how many minutes I have used. It has a speaker phone feature that is very helpful as the higher volume helps my hearing. Instead of having to guess on some things it has plain yes and no buttons hich eliminate a lot of confusion. I sold my mobilehome so the cell phone is my only phone.

From Oz: "I don't like cell phones either. In California you are not allowed to be on your phone in restaurants unless it is a WIFI restaurant. I don't use mine at all, ever!!!

My son and his wife don't have a house phone, useless waste of money to pay for two phone companies. The cell is the only thing they use.

I have known people who sit across the table from each other and text. What a waste of money. I mean really!

If you want to get right down to it, emails today take the place of writing a letter. No one seems to do that any more either. I write my friends and aunt because they don't have a computer and it is nice anticipation waiting for that letter to arrive in the mail. Gives one a sense of closeness to those who are so far away. I guess we are just old school. *OZ."*

MANY USES FOR W-D 40

As presented from my computer friends: WD-40 was created in 1953 by three Technicians at the San Diego Rocket Chemical Company. Its name comes from the project that was to find a **W**ater **D**isplacement compound. They were successful with the *fortieth* formulation. Thus "WD-40." The Corvair Company bought it in bulk to protect their atlas missile parts. It is made from oil.

Vandals sprayed red paint all over a neighbor's brand new pickup. One neighbor went to get his WD-40 to clean the red paint off with it. It cleaned up without harming the original paint. Spray WD- 40 on the distributor cap of your car; it displaces the moisture and allows the car to start. Remove bug guts with WD-40 so they can't eat the finish off your car. Removes road tar and grime from cars.

If you've washed and dried a tube of lipstick with a load of laundry, saturate the lipstick spots with WD-40 and presto— lipstick is gone. Removes tomato stains from clothing. It will clean your shower door. It also works on glass, on your stove top, and removes dirt and grime from barbeque grills. WD-40 is also good for untangling jewelry chains. Keeps scissors working smoothly; lubricates noisy door hinges on vehicles and doors in homes. It removes black scuff marks from the kitchen floor. Keeps rust from forming on saws, and saw blades, and other tools. Keeps bathroom mirrors from fogging. Keeps pigeons off the balcony (they hate the smell).

WD-40 attracts fish. Spray a little on live bait and lures and you will be catching that big one in no time. It takes the sting away from ant bites immediately and stops the itch. It is great for removing crayon marks from walls. WD-40 removes all traces of duct tape.

Some Folks have even sprayed it on their arms, hands, and knees to relieve arthritis pain.

MY SPOKANE VISIT
SEPTEMBER 2009

We found it was about $150 cheaper to fly to Spokane out of Los Angeles instead of Ontario. So on the day of departure we headed for the Los Angeles airport.

As it was in the middle of the afternoon, the traffic wasn't too bad. Of course we missed the right turnoff to make a smooth arrival at LAX so we got a chance to see some of the city of Los Angeles as we tried to find our way back to the terminal. The exit into the airport is not marked very clear so if you are not in the right lane of traffic at the right time you get a chance to try to find your way around. If you are not familiar with that area, you get to hope you hit the correct street to arrive at your destination. We went around a few blocks before we found the right street into the terminal.

After we found the correct street to alight from our vehicle, we found someone to help unload my scooter. As we had printed out our boarding pass before leaving home I had a smooth ride to the elevator and then on through security. The security people were very nice to me here (not like the ones a couple of months earlier in Kansas City—didn't like them at all) I got to ride my scooter right up to the door of the airplane and the attendants took it someplace and loaded it on the plane, ready to ride right along with me to my destination. When I got off the plane it was right there very conveniently waiting for me..

The timing of our arrival at the airport was pretty good as I didn't have to wait very long for the plane to arrive at the gate. After a short ride the plane landed in Sacramento and when everyone whose destination was Sacramento had departed from the plane there was about ½ an hour before the plane was again reloaded to proceed on to Portland. I was invited to visit the cockpit and talk to the pilot. I asked him how he could handle all the instruments (there seemed to be hundreds of them) and he told me that was why there were two pilots flying the planes. Well, I was so interested in visiting with the pilot, that I didn't notice all the people boarding and walking behind me to their seats. This airline is Southwest and they don't assign seats—you pick your own. Your choice of seats is governed by the time you arrive at the gate and get in line after the priority boarding arrangements of people with children and the disabled. I nearly lost my seat. But one of the other nice passengers who was alert chased everyone away who would have taken my seat. I had chosen the bulkhead as it gave me more leg room. I really appreciated the concern of the other passenger as my legs cramp up to the point of not being able to stand on them if they are cramped. When we landed in Portland the layover was not very long and I stayed in my seat. The arrival in Spokane was very smooth and by the time I was ready to depart the plane, my scooter was waiting for me at the door. I got my baggage and my son and daughter-in-law headed for their home.

A few days after arriving in Spokane, my son took us to a dinner show located at the state line called "The Rocking B Ranch". It is held in a large barn, which I imagine may have been a dairy barn. Old farming machinery was throughout the building and tools hung on the walls. All was authentic old machinery now replaced with power instead of horses and cattle. The minute you arrived you were invited to have all the coffee, water, and lemonade you wanted. The price of admission covered everything, including entertainment and food also.

Very interesting and it all brought back childhood memories of my Grandparents and their farm in Idaho. The entertainment started out with a family group playing country music. Two of their youngsters played all the instruments of their band. I had a chance later to talk to the younger ones and asked them their ages. The two boys were eleven and thirteen. You should have heard how talented these kids were on all the instruments, but I was really most impressed at how they played the fiddle. I really envy their ability. While the fiddle was especially good, they were efficient on the guitar and mandolin also. I had a chance to compliment them on their performance, which I really enjoyed.

After the family group had played for about an hour, it was announced there was a show performing at the outdoor theater. All were invited to go outside to that show. It was a slapstick play about a great shoot-out. After the villain was slain it was announced that the dinner was ready to be served, buffet style. It consisted of roast beef, barbequed ribs, apple sauce, beans, salad, baked potatoes, greens, and desert.

The food was good and then after dinner another group of entertainers came on stage. They were great and again they all performed with guitars, fiddles, base fiddle, and all the other instruments of a country band. The lady who played the fiddle was a fifth place fiddle champion of the United States. In my opinion she might as well have been a first place winner. She could really make that fiddle sing. One performance she did was to make the music sound like a bird—identifying which species it was. To say the least, the evening was one to remember. I enjoyed it immensely. This was real country music, not rock and roll that is now called country music that really isn't country music. One act consisted of the employees of the restaurant crew coming on stage and doing a lively square dance. Oh what the people of today are missing when they don't have the old barn dances and the great square dances and the very friendly get-togethers.

All of this brought back more memories of my uncle and his family who would play for our Benewah, Idaho community barn dances. My two cousins could pick up any stringed instrument and play it immediately, even if they had never seen it before. In addition to good music there was always the potluck dinner. Sometimes there would be an auction of something like a pie and the person winning the auction would get to eat with the one who had made the pie. I miss this kind of good entertainment. It is rare any more.

The old barn dances were fun, but for some reason you don't hear of them any more. People nowadays really don't know what they are missing. Sure is too bad. All this good entertainment was free too. People were glad to volunteer their talents and didn't expect to be paid for it either. The potluck dinners that accompanied the music showed off the ability of the cooks, who brought special dishes for everyone to enjoy. These are the kind of the "Good old Days" I would like to see returned. We may not have had the convenience of electricity or even running water, but we had good neighbors and many good times. I miss them.

I grew up in Spokane and it hasn't changed too much since I left here, except like most of the country, the population increase caused everything to spread out clear out to the Idaho state line. I remember when I was a teen-ager going "out to the country" to pick strawberries. Now all I can say is "where is the country. There is no more country." It is now all mostly city to the Idaho state line.

All this brings back memories of what happened at the strawberry patch. My aunt would pick a few berries in one row and then when it looked like the next row was better she would move there. Well, the owner, who was an older Italian man, told her "You Picka da here, picka da dere and picka all over the patch". Guess it impressed me at the time because I never forgot his telling her that she couldn't picka like that.

It was in the winter of 2009 that my daughter, Jackie, decided to visit family in Spokane. Jackie lives in Moreno Valley, and has lived there since she was 14 years old so she was thoroughly used to warm weather and it was never very cold in the winter time compared to the climate in Spokane. She was about ready to return back to California when there was a big snow storm and she was stranded in Spokane for a while. She decided then that she was not a fan of snow and cold weather and glad to get back to the warm California climate.

BREAKFAST IN TEXAS

Bears in the Parks. The email showed several deer eating at a table with a couple. Have you ever invited such guests to breakfast? Wonder what he was giving them. Were they eating the same as the couple? What was in the big bowl? Interesting—The deer seem at home with this couple. The deer in the background are watching and don't seem to know what to make of all this.

Reminds me of the time we were in Yellowstone Park and had an uninvited guest try to join us. It was a bear. My father-in-law chased it away. Fortunately it did not turn on him. Bears can be very dangerous. It was that very same trip that we saw a man try to entice a bear into his car with two very terrified women in it. Someone should have shot that darned fool. (I mean the fool, not the bear) It looked to me as if he was trying to get them killed. He was laughing all the time he was trying to entice the bear to get inside that car with the two elderly ladies. Those bears in Yellowstone Park are not tame and they can be very very dangerous. But there are always fools who won't listen or pay attention. GRRRR

Come to think of it, that was in the summer of 1964. I remember because that was the year I got a bunch of silver half dollars that were not "sandwich" coins. Those coins slowly disappeared over the years since then. Someone was helping themselves to them.

Another time we went to Yosemite Park in California. We camped over night but in the morning our neighbors were a bit upset. They had left their ice chest outside and inside was food. One of the resident bears had torn the ice chest apart to get to the food inside.

Bears are extremely strong so you should not assume they don't know how to open up any food container you might present to them. They have been known to rip apart a convertible car with a canvas top when food or even garbage was left inside.

Email pal wrote: "That is interesting. Last time I was through Yellowstone was in 1961 on the way back from a national convention with my parents and my son. We went to Deerfield Beach Florida for that and on the way back we went through Yellowstone.

When I was in Alaska we had a moose that used to visit us every morning. I have never seen deer being served breakfast before, but have heard of it. It was probably deer pellets of some sort is all, and it was probably in the bowl too.

I can understand that one. We have been to Yellowstone also, but when I was in Alaska the bears were mean! But my problem is that humans leave their garbage in a burn barrel out there where they live and the bears come around because they smell it. Well, they get shot for that! Sure made me mad! I was always told to make a whole lot of noise when a bear comes around so I used a pot and a lid and clanged them together to get rid of her. However, all she did was go to the next property and cause problems so the game warden shot her. Later I was talking with the game warden and he said they will use her meat to feed people. I told him that this should have never happened, if the garbage had been properly taken care of.

However, winter is hard up there and their winters start at the end of September. The bears are still actually feeding and not hibernating yet. The only problem with this bear actually getting killed is that she had a cub down by the creek waiting for her! So the game warden and his friend had to go get the cub, bring him with them, and then ship that cub somewhere for fostering. What a mess if you ask me! They should have trapped her and gotten her and the cub together and set them free somewhere else. It was definitely not the fault of the bear, but humans instead.

ROAD RAGE

An email about road rage reminded me of a time about 40 years ago. I had a situation when a bully was holding up traffic by driving about 20 MPH in the inside lane and would not move over from that lane. The traffic was very heavy and everyone had to pass him on the right. It was on a holiday weekend going north. The highway was four lanes wide divided by a grass strip. Traffic had piled up for at least a mile behind him. I thought I had a solution. I signaled for a right turn and someone in the right lane let me in as soon as it became safe. I got over into that right hand lane then I immediately turned on my left turn signal. I got in front of that bully, which wasn't very hard as no one was close in front of him. I slowed down slowly to about 10 or 15 MPH, and he finally got the hint and moved over. Then I resumed my speed as soon as he moved over. Others honked their approval. On the way home, I saw the same driver but he was in the right hand lane and not holding up the traffic. I assume he got the point I was making. He was not stuck in that inside lane. He was either being very thoughtless or just plain dumb-bunny dumb and stupid. He should have observed that traffic was fast stacking up behind him causing a dangerous situation.

My daughter pointed out to me that sometimes this solution could lead to more trouble. The guy at fault might have a gun and the results might not be as expected. You never know how others will react. It did solve the problem for a lot of drivers that day.

NOTICE FROM POLICE

We had two neighbors who were police officers. This was sent to me by one of them.. To be forewarned is to be forearmed.

Beware of paper on the back window of your vehicle—it's another way to do carjacking. When you get into your car you look into the rear view mirror and see a paper stuck to the middle of the rear window. Don't get out of your car to remove that paper or whatever it is. If you get out, when you reach the back of your car, that is when the carjackers appear out of nowhere, jump into your car and take off. They practically mow you down as they speed off in your car. Your keys are handy in the ignition, ready for them to leave in a hurry.

I bet your purse is still in the car. Now the carjacker has your car, your home address, your money, and your keys. Your home and your whole identity are now compromised.

Don't fall for this scheme. Leave the paper on the car until you get home or to a well lighted place. Don't be curious about that piece of paper on your back window. Caution is always needed, but with the unemployment situation as it is now, we need to be more cautious than ever

TODDLER'S PUBLIC POTTY BREAK

The news told about a woman who got a ticket when her three-year-old son relieved himself on their two-and-a-half acre property. The police officer had been parked at the end of their cul-de-sac. He approached and ordered the child's mother to go inside and get her photo ID, then issued her a $2500 ticket. He had observed the child pull down his pants to relieve himself.

When the mother and daughter protested that he was only a toddler and that he was on their own property where they had lived for more than eight years, the officer responded that it didn't matter because it happened in public view. The parent was shocked that she was given a ticket and that the ticket was for such a large amount..

The story was picked up by national news where it sparked outrage.

Later the Police Chief stopped by and said they were dropping the charges.

"We told him we appreciated him coming and for all his help. He didn't have to come by the house. That was nice of him to do that," said the family.

LOST KID PLUS POTTY BREAK

What this kid did is the same as a whole lot of little kids have done over the centuries. I was in downtown Spokane one time when one of my sons—the one who was three years old at the time—stepped over to the curb and relieved himself. He just unzipped his pants and I doubt if many people actually saw him do it. He did not pull his pants down and made no fuss about having to go. It was all over by the time I saw him.

At that same time my six year old daughter disappeared. This was too much for me to handle. I looked all around the area, went back inside the store where I had been shopping and started to panic. The police station was just around the corner, so I headed there, expecting to get help in searching for her, not knowing if she was lost or had been kidnapped. They had her there. I collected her and headed for home immediately.

I still don't know how she ended up at the police station, but it sure was a relief that she was there and not a victim of a kidnapper. She had not been gone but a few minutes. Between the two kids that day I had had all the excitement I cared for.

Thankfully the one who stood at the curb did not cause any disturbance. No tickets that day. I don't believe little kids were ever cited for anything in those days, and especially not little ones who were just being kids. None were even criticized for showing some affections for their little friends by hugging or kissing their five-year-old friend like the one cited a couple of years ago. It was so stupid it made national headlines in the papers.

Sometimes people do not use the sense that they were born with. Both incidents in Spokane were embarrassing, but neither one was fatal and we all lived through it. I won't say now which boy it was and the daughter is deceased, so I suppose I might be the only one who remembers the incident. I guess I am just thankful all my kids are grown up now.

From OZ: "That was the dumbest ticket ever written. Trust me when I say your son wasn't the only one. I have seen boys do it, but never girls. I think the cop was nuts."

MORE ABOUT PEOPLE
AND THE BENEWAH VALLEY

July 13, 2008--The Marquardt Saw Mill employed quite a number of people in this area. There had been several saw mills around the vicinity at one time, but they are all gone now and there is no evidence that they ever existed. My husband hauled many truck loads of lumber from the Marquardt Mill to Spokane and Moses Lake, lumber that was used to build many of the homes in both cities.

I would walk past the Hans Sether place along with Alta Fletcher, on our way to and from school. Alta was the daughter of Georgia and Bill Fletcher, Esta's sister. Mrs. Sether would give me cookies and a glass of milk. I loved that kindness on her part and never forgot it. That was around 1928 when I was six years old.

Mr. and Mrs. Sether raised two boys, Archie and Frank Miller, but I do not remember their going to school when I did. They may have been considerably older than me. One time, in 1938, on a visit to my uncle in Alder Creek I met Tom Bergland. It was two years later that Frank Miller came to visit our family in Spokane. Frank invited my mother and me to go with him to visit the Berglands who had moved up to Spokane and were running a garage and gas station in Hillyard. Well, I had liked that good looking fellow named Tom Bergland so when he called me for a date to go down to Benewah for a dance being held in the schoolhouse, of course I accepted. A year later we were married and that marriage lasted sixty years until Tom had a fatal fall and passed away.

About an incident with Hans Sether: When we lived in Benewah, Hans was walking past our house as we were sitting down to lunch. Tom invited him to have lunch with us. Well, Tom's uncle Otto had just been there and he was very deaf so I was used to talking quite loud. We ran out of some dish I had made and Tom asked me if we had more. Not remembering that Hans was not deaf but having been used to talking very loud for the benefit of Otto I whispered to Tom that we were out of the item. I remembered quite some time later that I had thought Hans could not hear me. I was not embarrassed at the time because I was not thinking of the hearing difference of the two men. It wasn't until later I got to thinking about what had happened and realized what did happen. Can you imagine being in someone's house and having lunch with them and then hearing them whisper quietly they were out of something. I'm still embarrassed now, even if I wasn't at that time. Being 20 miles from town we didn't always have supplies on hand.

My son and I fully enjoyed both visiting with the old timers and the newcomers to the Benewah valley who were at the picnic. As they advertise the annual get-together around the country, I recommend that everyone who wants to have a nice time should attend one of these annual picnics. These old fashioned kinds of get-togethers are fast disappearing so if you don't want to miss out on a fun way to spend a day, go next year. It is usually held the next Sunday after the fourth of July. All it costs you is to bring a covered dish to share with the others who come. A good time is guaranteed.

THIRTEEN HOURS AROUND LOS ANGELES

June 23, 2010—My daughter, Jackie, along with my youngest son, Larry, his wife, Robin, and their two sons, Alex and Kyle, stopped by early (8am) to pick up daughter Judi, and me for an all day trip to Los Angeles. Larry and his family were visiting from their home in Georgia. The first thing was breakfast at a restaurant before leaving Moreno Valley, then to the freeway heading west. Since we could not eat all our breakfast, we each took our muffin along to eat later.

Traffic really was not bad so the ride was quite smooth all the way there. Using a GPS we found our way to our first stop, which was the UCLA thrift store. Of course, that went smoothly too, as someone pulled out of a parking space just as we got there. That thrift store must be well known, as everyone seemed to know about it (except me). My son and his family live just north of Atlanta, Georgia and they knew about such a place. Of course, the girls seem to be much interested in "vintage" clothing. Styles you and I wore when we were much younger. Even the boys found things they bought. After a bit of sightseeing at different locations, what did they find but another "vintage" market. We didn't stay long in any of the places. More sight-seeing. Some of the areas were clean around the stores and the streets were reasonably clean of trash, but a few places were trashy and

I wondered why the merchants didn't at least sweep the sidewalks in front of their businesses. Things sure are not the same as when I was young, when the merchants took pride in having the sidewalk in front of their business swept up every morning. When I was young some even hosed the sidewalk down too. Thankfully the stores were reasonably clean inside and the merchandise well-arranged.

Traffic was not bad during our whole day. Not often you can say that. We even had the fortune to find a place to park whenever we needed it. In the meantime, we ate our "snack", the left-over muffins from breakfast. This held us over until mid-afternoon when we located another "known" place. The place was a very small restaurant where you parked in back and there they had outside tables with umbrellas for shade. The name was "Pink." The block wall had a very pretty mural painted on it and there were lots of tropical plants around. The place looked very clean. You placed an order out front—standing on the sidewalk in quite a long line; then you brought your order through to the back yard. It was quite interesting and the food was excellent. I guess you would call it "fast food" but was different from anything we have around here. I never found out why the name was called Pink. I was amazed that someone who resided all their life in the Eastern part of the States, like my son's wife, would know so much about places in Los Angeles.

With our GPS we located other sightseeing areas. What an invention that thing is. We went directly to where we wanted to go without getting lost or unnecessary driving. We were really "lookey loos" around town this day. Of course we headed for the "Avenue of the Stars," Hollywood Boulevard, and spent a lot of time. Then up and down we went to read the names on the stars. (I recognized many of the old-timers, but not some of the newer names, although the rest of the family knew most of the newer and not the older ones—guess you'd call that a fair exchange). We went on both sides of the street and into a few buildings. There in one of the buildings was a coffee shop where we could each get the kind of drink we wanted. We were still too full from lunch at Pink to eat anything more. Sitting in this little café let us rest and plan the rest of the afternoon.

For some reason, people don't seem to be able to see scooters and will actually run into one. We do not seem to have the same trouble with cars. Maybe the drivers are more observant of pedestrians. I found that to be true in Europe also. Only once when we crossed a street and came to a corner did the crowd bunch up together so I could not get back onto the sidewalk. When I attracted their attention by blowing my whistle, everyone moved aside so I could get back onto the sidewalk. They did it smiling too, so it all turned out OK. That was the only time I've ever used that whistle, although at times I've sure been tempted.

After spending a couple of hours in the area of the walk of the Hollywood stars, we headed for the big Hollywood sign. We knew the direction of the sign, but not how to get there, so again we used the GPS to guide us. Leaving the downtown area, we went into an area of big houses and started up the hill. We went around and around and around on narrow roads that required pulling over to let oncoming cars pass.

It seemed that houses were stacked one on top of the other. Some houses also appeared to be small, although they may have reached towards the back of the lot and been long and narrow. Land must be terribly expensive there, as everything was crowded tightly together.

After it seemed like it took forever misunderstanding the GPS directions at times, and backing up a time or two, we finally got to an area where several of our group could take a hike, which some did. Some hikers were coming up the hill so we asked them how to get up to the big Hollywood sign from where we were at. With their directions, about half an hour later, we continued up and around some more and got to the top of the access. At the top of the road was a gate and a sign that no hiking was allowed beyond that point, but we got a good look from there. It is too bad some people are destructive so landmarks have to be isolated in order to preserve them. After we were satisfied that we had seen enough we started for home.

The whole day had been very interesting to all of us. Although it was almost 8 pm. the traffic on the way home was a bit heavy, but went smoothly all the way back to Moreno Valley. It was barely turning dark and we all got home around nine o'clock. A good day that had gone well, everyone tired, but glad to be home. Thirteen hours well spent doing something different and not expensive.

TIME MOVES FAST

You wonder where all the years have gone—they simply disappeared into nowhere. We try to remember all the hopes and dreams we had. Some dreams were fulfilled and others just went somewhere else when we had to give them up for one reason or another. Our kids grew up. Just yesterday it seems they were babies. Today they are Senior Citizens.

Now my friends are retired; they move slower than they used to and their age is showing. We are now all like the ones we used to see and thought they were so old. We never dreamed that one day we would be old just like them. When I was twenty, I thought thirty-five was really old. Yes, our lives are approaching Winter in spite of us. There is nothing we can do about it except to accept it. I doubt if we would go back even if we could and we really wouldn't want to. Things would not be the same.

Barring illness, our minds stay almost the same as they were when we were twenty years of age. We are seldom prepared for the aches and pains and loss of strength that goes with aging. There are some things I wish I hadn't done, some I should have done, and many things I did do. All this goes in a lifetime. Don't put off too long the things you would like to accomplish. Life goes by too quick. Tell your loved ones about the things that you want them to remember. Hope that they appreciate and love you for all the things that you have done for them. Hopefully they will remember that you loved them in all the past years. Where have all the years gone? They have passed like a jet plane was tugging then.

AIR TRAVELS--HAWAII—YES, I HAVE BEEN THERE

A story about airplanes reminds me of our flight to Hawaii in 1963 and our experience with a troubled plane. Our flight from Los Angeles to Hawaii was smooth. It was on the return home that we began to have troubles. That was the time 165 of us chartered a plane with the charter company called *THE FLYING TIGERS*. This was a group of aviators who had formed a company after the end of WW2.

On the way into the airport, driving into Los Angeles from Riverside, we stopped at a restaurant to have lunch. As we were not at all familiar with any of the restaurants we just picked out a very nice-looking one. Our car group consisted of a neighbor couple, my husband and me, and two of our children. We sat down in a booth and a waitress came over. She was about six feet tall and had very long hair. I thought she was quite pretty, but thought nothing further about it. She didn't stay long and another older server came to our table and took our order. We ate our lunch and proceeded on to the airport to board our plane. We parked our car in a long term parking lot and along with everyone else boarded our plane.

It wasn't until quite a long time later that I got "educated" and when I look back I now realize that tall six-foot waitress was not a woman. Seems we had stumbled into a "gay" establishment and they quickly recognized that we did not know anything about their place. This was the reason they switched servers on us. We enjoyed our lunch and look back at the occasion as an adventure.

The whole trip was eventful from beginning to end and we all thoroughly enjoyed it. All went smooth all the way to our destination. There was no turbulence on the flight over. Upon arrival all 165 people were greeted with leis and each group went their own way.

Our own group of ten was met at the plane by the Hawaiian friends who had made arrangements to take us around the island. In that tour, they pointed out the many features of the area. It was so very much more than we would have had from a commercial tour or than we could have done on our own. We saw the cemetery of the soldiers who died in the Pearl Harbor bombing raid in 1941. We saw all the unusual places along the shore. I don't think they left anything out. We visited farms growing pineapples and went through the canning factory. We got to taste fresh pineapple and drink lots of fresh juice.

These kind people became our hosts and went all out to see that we were well taken care of. There were two cars in our party of ten. The hosts' brother, the driver of our car group, had taken a day off work just to do this for all of us. Around noon we were feeling hungry so my husband offered to buy lunch for the two groups. We stopped at a restaurant buffet and everyone ate. After we had all eaten, Tom went up to the cashier to pay the bill, only to be told it had been taken care of. We found out that we were guests and were not to pay for the meal that day. After the tour of the island was over, we were taken to their home. They had an apartment seven of us shared. They had kept that unit vacant knowing we were coming. After depositing our luggage in the apartment we joined the rest of the group in their home. We went inside and visited for a while, then returned to the apartment for the night. The next morning we found a note on the door for everyone to remove their shoes before entering. It was later in the day that we noticed stairways leading up into all houses that had shoes lined up on every stair going up. We found out they consider it a sanitary measure, which it surely is. Being ignorant of this custom, we had entered their home with our shoes on.

Not wanting to be a burden to our hosts, Tom later went out to rent a car, which was his custom. It wasn't until much later that we found out this was also an insult to our host. She had made arrangements to take all of us out to a Hawaiian luau and now had hurt feelings. These kinds of problems come from not knowing the customs of other cultures. In return, they didn't know about the culture my husband was raised in. He didn't want to be a burden on anyone and especially on anyone as kind as these folks were being. By this time, the lady gave up on taking us to a luau and as a consequence we never did get to one. To further add insult to injury, the day we were to leave, we stripped the beds and took the sheets to a Laundromat and had them washed. We felt this was only common courtesy. Were we ever wrong!!! It was the final straw. We just did not know that if you are the guest of a Hawaiian native, you are one of the family and they supply everything. We had no intention of insulting or causing hard feelings, but we did, all by accident. The lady had planned everything for us to have a wonderful time in Hawaii and, through ignorance, we ruined it for her and it also made us the losers. We didn't know this until after we got home in California. I did thoroughly enjoy the trip though ignorant.

That was 50 years ago, so I imagine everything has changed greatly since then just like all over the rest of the world. What an experience that was. I do know now that we need to learn what some of the customs of other people are before going to their area.

It was on the return home that we began to have troubles. We reported to the airport at the scheduled time then had to wait for the plane to arrive. We waited for several hours before word came that the plane was in. After that long wait we finally boarded the plane and after another half-hour were told to go back into the airport, but not to leave the area beyond where we could be reached easily. The weather was warm and everyone decided they were thirsty so all 165 of us descended on the restaurant fountain. The poor waitress worked as fast as she could when, just as some of the drinks arrived, it was announced that we needed to board the plane immediately. We boarded just as had been instructed. We sat waiting in the plane for about a half-hour before the plane started to move out. At last we were ready to go.

The plane started down the runway. Oh boy! We were off!!! Finally. The plane was really picking up speed and about to lift off into the air when we felt the pilot using the brakes. We knew the flight was being aborted. Next, the plane was being turned around. As it was taxiing back to the boarding gates, the flight attendant announced, "Ladies and gentlemen, we just had a tire blow out." A few seconds later she said, "We didn't have just one tire blow out, there were two of them." When we arrived at the boarding gate it was announced, "You may go inside the terminal and order a meal at our expense."

It took a while for the restaurant to prepare so many meals at one time, but it worked out to take up some time that was more pleasant than standing around and waiting. As if that wasn't enough and after we had waited for a long time to get the tires replaced, we learned the wait would be even longer. It turned out the plane had engine troubles. We had to wait the rest of the night for the plane to be repaired. I don't know if there was any connection between the engines and the tires, but whatever it was it was taken care of. We got home without any further trouble.

Engine trouble, late arrival, lunch and thirst, two tires that blew out on take-off, return to the boarding gate, twelve hour wait in the airport while all the troubles were being taken care of, etc. We finally did get started. After several hours in the air I noticed we were flying along the coastline of California for a long time instead of coming straight into the airport in Los Angeles. This seemed strange but later found out the pilot had changed course because of stormy weather. He said we had all been through enough trouble at the airport without having to suffer a bouncing plane in turbulent skies. He took a roundabout way home instead of flying straight into the airport. All the passengers clapped their hands to let the pilot know we appreciated his flying skill that got us all home in one piece, safe and sound.

Other than the plane being in trouble, our trip to Hawaii was very memorable. While the troubles with the plane were not pleasant at the time, I can look back on it and it really gives me "something to talk about."

THE OUTHOUSE

Those of us who have lived where we had to use an outhouse will appreciate this story. We know just what an "outhouse" is, and are glad when we no longer have to use one. I don't know who wrote this story, but it strikes home. I condensed the story, but of course it also triggered my memory.

A little boy lived in the country where the family had to use an outhouse. The boy hated the outhouse because it was hot in the summer and freezing cold in the winter and the stink was bad all the time. The outhouse was sitting on the bank of a creek and the boy was determined he would push that outhouse into the creek if he ever got a chance. After a big spring rain one day he thought it was a good time to accomplish what he wanted to do. He found a pole and started pushing at that old outhouse. It finally tumbled into the water and floated down the creek.

That night his father asked him to accompany him to the woodshed. It was inevitable that he meant a spanking and the boy asked his father, "Why?" Dad replied that "someone had pushed the outhouse into the creek" and asked him if he did it. The boy admitted it, but also added that George Washington didn't get into trouble when he told the truth. His Dad replied, "Well, son, George Washington's father wasn't in the cherry tree."(anonymous)

One memory I have isn't from very long ago. Going from Riverside, California to Yuma, Arizona we needed a rest stop before we got into Yuma. The only one available turned out to be between El Centro and Yuma and it was just one of those portable toilets, which is pretty stinky in that hot climate. Since that time a building has been put in the area and the grounds have been fixed up to be presentable. No more "outhouse", but it has now been abused and is almost worse than those portable toilets. People have messed it up so we will not stop there unless it is an emergency. I sure do not understand when the state tries to make it nice for people, someone has to come along and destroy it. Water had been supplied so there were flush toilets, but people have dirtied it up so it isn't very nice.

OUR OUTHOUSE

Almost three years ago I received a poem about "The House Behind the House" which brought up what happened to ours one time. The house behind was an outhouse.

This happened during the seven years we lived in the Idaho community called Benewah. We had no electricity, or running water. We carried our water from a small creek.

One of the kids tried to light the toilet paper in the outhouse—not the roll of paper but the used paper in the bottom of the pit. If it had caught on fire it undoubtedly would have burned the outhouse, the woodshed, and root cellar, plus the house we lived in. The possibility of it also starting a Forest fire was great because we lived right on the edge of the forest about fifty feet from the house.

I was never completely sure which of the kids did this, as they all denied it. It wasn't until a few years ago that one confessed, sheepishly, that he did it. My son who was 8 or 9 years old at that time finally owned up to the deed. I don't remember if there ever was any punishment other than a good lecture. By the time he finally told us he was the one, he had been an adult for many years. All the kids got a very good lecture at the time about how serious it was. (I had suspected who it was as it didn't seem likely it would be one of the girls). It never occurred again.

COEUR d'ALENE

I sent pictures of Coeur d'Alene to my correspondents and received an answer from some asking if we ever went back there. I explained to them that the pictures I had sent were old ones, but it would give them an idea of what the country looked like. Some people claim that anyone with lakefront property felt they had been practically taxed out of their property. Coeur d'Alene is where I was married seventy years ago. It used to be a nice ride "out in the country" from Spokane. It is heavily filled in from East of Spokane to West of Coeur d'Alene. Now you won't see very much open country like shown in those pictures. There are freeways through and it is shortly past the city of Coeur d'Alene that the main highway goes east to Montana. I remember when the highway that is now a four-lane freeway over the mountains had been a two-lane road known as the "Camel's Hump." I doubt if anyone ever calls it that now. It is not steep and winding as before. The grade was so steep the car would boil on the way up. There had to be water tanks beside the highway for people to use to cool down the overheated car. When it rained the highway became muddy and was hard to navigate with automobiles that did not have the horsepower that the present automobiles have today. When it rained the roads became muddy and many times a car had to have help to navigate up the road. At times, someone had to get behind the car and help push it over.

My correspondents wanted to know how far Coeur d'Alene is from Moreno Valley, where we live now. I would say Spokane and Coeur d'Alene are about 1500 miles from Moreno Valley. When we go up there any more we go by air. When we used to drive it was mostly on I-5 along the coast. Since everyone also wanted to know more I wrote:

Coeur d'Alene is about 25 miles from Spokane, Washington. My oldest son lives in Spokane Valley, which was actually a part of Spokane that used to be referred to as "the Valley" until it was voted into a separate city. Like here in California you go from one city to the next but you don't know when you change cities because they run together.

OUR TRIP THROUGH NEVADA
IN WINTER AND SNOW

This was in January of 1955. I am not completely certain about the year but it was definitely in January. It was Winter when we went down through Idaho and into Nevada. It was cold and snowing. The highway in Nevada had been closed before we got down to Ely. The snow plows had been through and the Highway Patrol had just reopened the highway going South. They should not have let us go on and we didn't know the difference. They did let us go and we went on our way. They must not have realized how far we were going or may have assumed we were stopping at a motel in that city, because it was late afternoon and starting to turn dark and becoming much colder. By that time of year the days are short and darkness starts about 4 pm. We felt it was too early to stop. The distance between Ely and Tonopah is 127 miles with nothing in between them.

Later, blinding snow started coming down and by then we did not dare to stop—there was no place to stop or to turn around. We ended up following the highway by seeing fence posts in places above the snow, as well as the piled snow berm left at the side of the road by the earlier snowplows. We had to stop every once in awhile to clear the packed snow from under the fenders. We also had to hope the fence posts that we saw at times did not depart away from the highway or we might have ended up over a bank into a ditch. After midnight, we got to Tonopah and found a hotel. By the time we got there, the snow was about a foot deep on the highway. It's a wonder we made it. That was a dangerous trip.

Never want to go through anything like that again.

Fortunately my husband and his brother were both experienced drivers in snow or we would not have made it. Also, the car was in good shape and had enough gas. If we had stalled, we probably would have frozen to death.

There was no way anyone could walk in that deep snow to get help if we had stalled. We were not dressed for weather outside the car. It is a miracle that the car was able to go through snow that was about a foot deep. Although the road had been plowed of snow earlier in the day, more had fallen since the plow went through. It was the new snow we were fighting with. Of course, there was no other traffic on the highway so we had no other tracks to help guide us. How we stayed on the road is a mystery. Some towns through that area are also up to 100 miles apart. The old hotel we found in Tonopah looked mighty good to us when we got there. Our eyes were hurting from the glare of the snow. We were all exhausted and even though the hotel was old, it was as welcome as a luxurious castle.

KITCHEN SUGGESTIONS

To add humor to your day, post this sign in your kitchen:
**THIS KITCHEN CLOSED DUE TO ILLNESS,
I'M SICK OF COOKING.**

When my granddaughter, Jessica, was a little girl, she made a plaque with that saying for me. I kept it in my kitchen for many years. Now it is in Yuma on the wall there.

REGARDING HOUSEHOLD TOOLS: One of the best household funnels I have is one I purchased in the car accessories department of a store. It was made to funnel oil into the engine of a car and the opening was just a perfect size for use in the kitchen. It fits a medium-size bottle top. Didn't cost much either and I use it constantly.

Use a small funnel for separating egg whites from yolks. Crack the egg over the funnel. The whites will run through, and the yolk will remain.

To remove marks made by permanent markers on appliances and counter tops, use rubbing alcohol on a paper towel.

Blood stains on clothes? Pour a little hydrogen peroxide on stain. May need to repeat.

Use ¼ cup of peroxide in the wash instead of bleach to whiten clothes. It's color-safe too.

Peroxide mixed with water is great for washing mirrors and windows and will not streak.

To easily remove burned-on food from your skillet, simply add a drop or two of dish soap and enough water to cover the bottom of the pan, and bring to a boil on the stove top. (I use some dishwasher soap for that purpose, it works wonders as Dishwasher soap is stronger.

To get rid of itch from mosquito bites, apply soap on the area and get instant relief.

Get rid of ants by drawing a chalk line on the floor or wherever ants tend to march.

Use air freshener to clean mirrors. It does a good job and leaves a lovely smell as well as the shine.

For splinters, simply cover the splinter with scotch tape and then pull it off. It removes most splinters painlessly and easily.

To remove stains from the bottom of a glass vase or cruet, fill with water and drop in two Alka Seltzer tablets.

Vinegar will also remove calcium and stains from bottom of glass or vase. Put enough in bottom to cover stain and leave over night.

A muffin tin is a handy holder for carrying hot baked potatoes.

Quick frosting idea: place a solid milk chocolate-mint wafer on top of each cupcake after removing from the oven. After it has softened, spread wafer over the top or leave as it is.

ANOTHER VISIT TO SPOKANE

June 26, 2013 On this visit to Spokane, I contacted my cousin, Betty Swofford, and she reminded me of the times she and her sister, Vera Mae, would come to my house after school to wait for their father to come pick them up. Their father was my uncle, my father's brother. This is the uncle I was visiting at the time I met my future husband.

A cougar had been sighted in the road between their house and the Benewah school, so it was a safety measure for them not to walk that couple of miles by themselves. There were other wild animals in the area also, such as bears and bobcats. My aunt Mabel, their mother, had shot a bear right near their house one time, and one of their brothers had killed a bobcat earlier. The area they lived in was about two miles up the road from the Benewah road crossing towards Alder Creek, and the schoolhouse.

When the girls became of high school age, my uncle moved his family into St. Maries so the girls could go to school without having to ride a bus during the winter seasons.

A year or two later--on one of these trips to the Benewah picnic, my son saw a cougar beside the road on our way down the mountain. There are still wild animals to be seen there, like bear, bobcats, and lots of deer.

STILL ANOTHER TRIP TO SPOKANE

This was written for the residents of the mobile home park where I lived.

September 2007—Well, your traveling neighbor is back again, with no plans for another trip in the very near future, but as I said before, I will go at the drop of a hat. I have just returned from visitins my family in Spokane, Washington. It was a very busy month for me.

I called several relatives I wanted to visit with and to invite them to go with me to the annual Benewah Valley picnic. All of us had lived in this Idaho community for several years. I was sorry to find out one cousin was quite ill, another was helping her daughter relocate after her husband had died. This was very disappointing, but that is the way things turn out at times. It ended up that just my son and I went.

The picnic is held annually in the old one-room schoolhouse which has been turned into a community center. I went there some eighty years ago for a few months in the first grade although I had started school in another one room school near Viola, Idaho. This same school is where all three of my older children started school before we moved back to Spokane. One woman, Mickie Walker was going to be 100 years old the following October. She remembered me from when we had lived in this community although we moved away fifty-six years ago. I missed seeing the ones who could no longer attend the picnic. When we had lived in this community, named Benewah, water had to be carried from a well into the school house. They had now discovered an artesian well nearby. With that convenience, as well as electricity becoming available, an indoor restroom had been installed. No more outhouse.

When we moved to this Benewah, Idaho area in 1943, there was no electricity and no telephones available. While we lived there the neighborhood residents got together and put in a telephone line We also got electricity into our homes. Because we had to have a certain number of houses for the power company to install the lines, we were short one house, and the people who lived in that one house said they had never had electricity before and could do without it now. In order to get the line in for everyone else the neighborhood group told the man they would wire his house for free and pay the basic electric bill for a year. We got our power. He got his house wired and electric lights. Everyone ended up happy. The basic electric cost was $3.00 a month. The wiring cost was only the materials.

My other daughter and her husband arrived from Moreno Valley by the middle of July to visit in Spokane. This started the pinochle players to playing almost every evening. All being avid pinochle players, we lost a few games, also won a few.

Of course, visits to a few garage sales were in order. We found a few things to buy, but I had to be careful as my suitcases were already full. By the first of September I was back home in Moreno Valley. I enjoyed my visit to Spokane and the picnic in the Benewah Valley but of course it is always good to come home again. Now I can look forward to another visit next year.

HELPFUL SUGGESTIONS

Self-defense experts have a tip that could save your life. Get a can of *WASP SPRAY.* It is inexpensive and more effective than mace or pepper spray. The cans typically shoot 20 to 30 feet, so if someone tries to break into your home, spray the culprit in the eyes. That will give you a chance to call the police or to get out. With Mace you have to get close.

Did you hear about the little boy who told his grandmother that fireflies were just mosquitos that followed you inside and needed a flashlight so they could see.

POEMS, RECIPES, STORIES
AND OTHER STUFF

The following are copies of articles I wrote for the news letter of the Il Sorrento Mobile Home Park I have lived in for eleven years. Many items were news of what has happened to the residents who were my neighbors. Some articles were written for friends and for special occasions. Some very special people died and should be remembered for making life more pleasant for all of us. They did not expect to be paid for their many hours of work. Many are still alive and spend many hours on our behalf. We really appreciate them and they need to be remembered also. Other things were what I was doing around the park. Some stories are rhymes and some are about my travels. I also include a few good recipes tried out on occasions when we had large dinners

THEY GRADUATED FROM
COLLEGE OR HIGH SCHOOL

Since I had several nieces and nephews graduating
from high school or college I wanted to write a few
words of encouragement to them. I wrote the following
lines and now I change a word or a name here and
there to fit the occasion as each one graduates.

Alicia Crowell went to school
"Because," she said. "I am no fool.
I'll get an education that is first rate
Qualify for a job that is better than great."
So she struggled and studied night after night
Decided procrastination was not very bright.
Studying hard without much sleep

Hit the books for a better job to seek.
Now that long-sought day has finally come
She's graduating because she's not so dumb.
An educated gal she turned out to be
Says "A better job is now waiting for me."
Some smart employer is out there someplace
Hiring someone to enter the rat race
Alicia Crowell is bound to be
The one chosen now; she's the best you see.
She didn't give up and drop out like a fool
Used her head and stayed in school.
She got that education after studying so hard.
Now I say to Alicia, "Go get it, Pard".

IN HONOR OF THOSE WHO GENEROUSLY VOLUNTEER

The Obstacles in Our Path and the Purse Under the Boulder

An Important Lesson about the way people act.

A large boulder was placed in the middle of the highway to see if anyone would remove it. Many simply walked around it, complaining. Finally a peasant came along, quit what he had been doing, then pushing and straining, he moved the stone to the side of the road, where he found a purse containing a note granting the contents to the person who removed the boulder.

(The author of that condensed story is unknown to me—but the *volunteers* who help out so very unselfishly are really the ones granting the rewarding "Purse under the Boulder")

How many appreciate all the volunteers who work so hard to make things pleasant for all of us? Without them it would be pretty dull and this would then be just an uninteresting place to sit and do nothing.

Thank you, one and all, who donate your time, without pay, to help make things brighter for all of us. We, the residents, are the ones reaping the pay for all the hard work the voluteers keep doing. *We are the ones receiving the "purse under the boulder."*

The story inspired me to write the following rhyme. I sent a copy to the local food bank.

VOLUNTEERS AT THE FOOD BANK

All you volunteers at the Food Bank
Are the nicest people I would like to thank
The crew works hard to distribute those boxes of food
Even if the people who get them are sometimes rude.
The hundreds of people who come through the line
May not appreciate your help all of the time
Some gripe and complain while waiting for their box
But others are quiet just like a sly old fox.
Quiet and thankful but waiting to pounce
For the contents in the box is what really counts.
Clients take a number to wait their turn
Want to sit down so their feet won't burn
From standing in line for such a long time
The numbers really help shorten that line
Waiting in line after getting that number
Keeps them awake, there's no time to slumber.
Then they get inside and what do you know

More people are there to run the show
Keep order in the line all the way back
Record the paperwork needed to keep track.
Who gets what and the amount of the prize
Depends on the number in the family size
Then month after month they keep coming back
To see those volunteers helping keep track
So thank all you folks who volunteer
To do all the work and still show such cheer
By doing so with a great big smile
You have really gone that extra mile
We really appreciate what you do
Thanks to you, and all your crew.

Thank you one and all for jobs well done. Hope you're not offended by my rhyming pun.

IN APPRECIATION FOR THOSE PERSONS WHO VOLUNTEERED

They spent many hours helping in one way or another to make life better for all of us living in this park that we call our home. They were very special people.

The following verse about Melba Allen comes after she suddenly passed away. Melba was known as "The Sunshine Lady." She was the one who kept everyone notified of those living in our park who were sick or needed some special help. Because our park streets are a puzzle to navigate at times, she was always available to direct people.

IN MEMORY OF MELBA ALLEN

We've lost our Sunshine Lady, it's sad to say
We would see her greeting us day after day,

Smiling and waving from her porch on space nine.
A friendly face we could see all of the time.
She helped direct people who got lost in the park
For to find a way out may be like being in the dark
So smiling at them she'd tell them where to go
To find the gate out or to the clubhouse you know.
Melba kept track of those in the park who were sick
To comfort them she was really so quick
Don't know if there is anyone her shoes we can fill
Did not give us much time to learn she herself was ill.
She'd greet everyone entering or leaving.
Which has left us now in a state of grieving.
Now, who will show strangers the best way out?
We will miss you Melba, there is no doubt.

Another resident who was such a great help to everyone living in the IL Sorrento Mobile Home Park was Al Jones. He picked up the monthly news letter and used his own vehicle to deliver it into our mailboxes at the end of every month. We always looked forward to receiving the news letter and there it was, without fail, right in our mailboxes.

IN MEMORY OF AL JONES

We lost another resident from our park,
Leaving space 106 in the dark
He helped deliver our Park News Letter
And no one could do it any better.
Right on time it always came
Now it will never be the same
Replacing someone like Al Jones
Is like trying to do without telephones.
Now how will we get our park news letter
It will be hard to find another go-getter

Like Al Jones our friend and neighbor
Who helped us all with his kind labor.
It cannot be done we all agree
Everyone will miss you, not only me.
We will remember you Al at month's end
When the news isn't delivered by our kind friend.

+

The following memorial is written with a sad heart. For several years, ever since Maryland and Dick moved into our Park they never failed to appear at the club house to prepare our donuts and coffee. Maryland was never seen without a happy smile on her face, serving the donuts and laughing with all of us. It was a sad thing when she fell and injured her hip, but she was back the minute she was able to walk, even with the broken hip and then the hip replacement. We will miss her for a long time.

IN MEMORY OF MARYLAND NYGREN

Maryland hosted our Wednesday morning get-together
For the past few years, no matter the weather.
Rain or shine she was always there
Now we are sorry to have an empty chair.
Smiling and happy she would always appear
Rewarding us with her smiling good cheer.
She and Dick would have the coffee ready
You could depend on them to be so steady.
She broke her hip a few months ago
After an earthquake frightened her so.
She jumped up and ran, a fatal mistake
It caused her to fall and her hip it did break.
She still came to the clubhouse to let us all know

It is a good time to gather together to show
How friends can enjoy visiting with each other
And learn to know our neighbor is not a bother.
Maryland came to help us every week
Friendly gatherings she always did seek
So enjoy your coffee and doughnuts my friend
Our grief at her passing will not soon end.

Maryland Nygren was always cheerful and never missed a Wednesday meeting with those of us who came to the clubhouse to enjoy her company while we ate donuts and drank coffee. She will be missed for a very long time.

Since I live in a mobile home park I enjoy the many features we have available. Among the beauty here are the flocks of ducks of many varieties. These are wild migrating birds but at times you would not know it. They have become so used to seeing so many people around who do not molest them that at times they are so tame that cars have to stop to keep from running over them. They are a delight to watch. They are rewarded with a serving of grain every afternoon. I think they can also tell time because if the grain is not out at a certain time they head for the house where the man lives who delivers the grain to them. It is really fun to watch their reaction.

FISH AND DUCKS IN OUR PARK

The ducks and fish in our park are there for us to enjoy
The ducks swim in the pond with the fishes, and, oh boy,
To see the ducks come running for grain is a sight.
They are so tame they seldom ever take flight.
The ducks fly around and seem to be at ease,

We sure enjoy seeing them as us they really please
So graceful and beautiful we see them each day
Although once in a while they do fly away.
Come back again later still lovely and pretty
We love to have them visit our private little city.
Fish in the pond some catch and don't eat
But say they are fun and a great sporting treat.
The fish eat the mosquitoes which helps very much
The mosquitoes we hate because when they touch
The bite itches like mad, we hate to report
Those darned mosquitoes must think it great sport.
Be glad we have fish in the ponds in the park
Enjoy them always from dawn until dark.
We can sit on the bench and watch them at play
Glad they are there to enjoy every day.
So with the ducks and fish we love to live here.
Maybe the only thing lacking would be a small deer.
Since we don't have one of those cute little things..
We'll settle for fishes and the birds that have wings.

SOME PEOPLE WERE UNFORTUNATE WITH A NASTY FALL

Like my friend Patsy Helms

Last August in the year 2008,
Patsy Helms broke her arm it is sad to relate.
Patsy Helms went to a garage sale
So goes this very very sad tale.
Stubbed her toe and down she went
Broke her arm and so was sent
To get it fixed lickety split.
Did not enjoy it one tiny bit.
Doc put her arm into a cast

Sent her home to recover fast.
It wasn't so fast by any means
One cast after another, or so it seems.
Now it's slowly healing bit by bit
So hopefully she is now feeling fit.
She's getting around we're glad to say
We got to see her at the meeting on Sunday.
Since she has her arm in cast and sling
A bouquet of flowers would be the thing
It might cheer her up this very day
And never happen again, we sure do pray.

THE BANK AND THE SURVIVORS PROBLEMS

The email told about someone who had passed away and the survivors tried to let the bank know she had died. The account had a zero balance, but they kept adding a service fee, late fees, and interest on those late charges. The family notifying the bank that the woman was dead and the bank paying no attention or refusing to remove the charges.

Collections wanted to see the woman to talk to her. The family invited the bank to send the Collector to the house, and when he came they invited him in and asked him to sit down and wait for the woman, who was deceased. After quite a long time the collector became disturbed and demanded to see the woman. They told him he was seeing the woman—her ashes were on the mantel right in front of him.

I emailed that anonymous story to several people as it was interesting and somewhat funny. Then I commented that this account probably isn't true but it sure makes an interesting story.

The following was one answer.

I remember when my brother in law died, my sister called the phone company to discontinue the service. Because her name was not on the contract they would not cancel it. She told them he had died, so they sent her a bill for the next month. She calls again, same thing, he is dead but he was cremated. She told them to come and get their phone and they can converse with his urn.

Another time, years ago, a woman in our neighborhood lost her husband, she had him cremated and his cremations sat on the mantel in an urn. When the bill collector came, he demanded to speak to her husband, so she invited him in and told him to take a seat facing the mantel. He does, and she leaves the room. The collector soon starts yelling, "Where's your husband?" She said, "You are looking at him, so start talking."

So do I believe your story? It is quite possible that it is true. You can't fix stupid, even with duct tape."

OUR TRIP TO CALIFORNIA IN 1946

That was the year we went down to California to visit relatives who had moved there. It was our first trip to Southern California. The trip ended up being quite an adventure. We left our residence in Idaho early in the morning and drove over to the Coast southwest of Portland. That evening we started hunting for a motel room. Rooms were at a very big premium in 1946. The war years had demanded all the housing available and there had been no time to recover any housing at the time. We tried a number of motels with the same answer—"no vacancies." Tom's elderly parents were exhausted and needed to have a bed by then. We found a motel and Tom made sure all windows and doors were thoroughly locked. I wondered about that at the time as we were used to trusting everyone up until then. It was a case of take that room or sleep in the car. We had ended up in a motel that had had a murder committed in the room a day or two before we arrived.

I don't know how Tom slept that night, but the rest of us did well. We had no worries about the room because we did not know about what had gone on before. My husband did not tell me about the room until many months later. Never told his parents at all.

MCDONALDS IN 1946

Macdonalds—the early days: Someone sent me a picture of the McDonalds Hamburger Stand from before 1946. This brought back more memories. I found the picture quite interesting. I remember going to McDonalds in 1946 in San Bernardino. *They were selling a lot of hamburgers for fifteen cents.* This was before they became a franchise. The building was not much to speak of, and certainly had no resemblance to the present day Mcdonalds.

They were becoming well known by 1946 and were quite busy. They had started out selling barbeque meals, but began to notice they were selling more hamburgers than anything else. I guess I can say *"I knew them when"* before they became BIG.

It was on this trip that we first tasted tacos and burritos. This was something different to us. We found out that we liked them and never miss a chance to buy or make them since that time. We got tacos for 23 cents at that time. Now they are somewhere around $1.00.

ON THE WAY HOME 1946

On our way home, we rode down the *"Grapevine"* at a fast pace. This was before it became a freeway (Interstate 5) and it twisted and turned like a grapevine. Again, it was a case of wondering why we were going so fast—the reason was that our brakes had failed and we were "riding it out." On top of the brake failure, the car had started to smell like burning oil. About the time we got to Willows, California, we looked up some friends that would let us stay at their place because we had to overhaul the car to get home. It was our in-laws automobile. This was immediately after the war and all cars were old and well-worn by that time.

That trip was full of excitement when we look back on it. At home, we had left our two daughters with my husband's sister and left our car for her to use. Well, as if our troubles were not enough, she had something go wrong with our car and barely escaped going over into the river with her family and our girls. Whatever it was that went wrong caused something to prevent the car from being steered and fortunately the brakes held. I believe it was a tie rod that jammed.

Is that enough to go wrong? Of course not. On the trip we had taken our four-year-old son Tommy with us and he became feverish and didn't seem very well. The reason was that he was coming down with the Whooping Cough. Before we had left to head to California, we had stopped at my mother's house in Spokane and my young brother was coughing lightly. He didn't seem sick and my mother had taken him to the doctor, so we thought nothing of it until about the time we returned home from the trip and our son "Whooped". Yes, it had been Whooping Cough that my brother had been coming down with. Believe me, Whooping Cough is no fun. My youngest daughter, Jackie, was only a year old at the time and she had it the worst of all. There were a lot of children who came down with it that year.

The trip home from Metaline Falls, a city north of Spokane, was uneventful and we got home to Idaho without further troubles except the Whooping Cough which never seemed to end. Oh yes, I had it myself when I was a kid, but I got a light case of it along with the kids. Evidently you can get it more than once, or at least I did. It was no fun with three kids down with that cough all at the same time. It is a miserable disease.

A FIRE IN NEW YORK

An experience in New York

As written home. February 30, 1980 "We've had some excitement around here for the past couple of weeks. The Margaret Hotel—unoccupied and being renovated. It was next door to where I am living. The building caught on fire 2-1-80. When I first looked out my window at 4 AM I thought it was building 107. I came out my door at the same time another brother did and we ran down to the 107 office and he had his wife and me moving cabinet files away from the window just in case it spread over. The fire broke out on the top (12th) floor and had been blazing for about half an hour when someone finally authorized for the building 107 to be evacuated. At that time I had been working like an Alaskan Malamute to get all the equipment away from the windows and to prepare for the worst. The other brother was in the safe getting all the valuable documents and etc. out.

At one point I peeked through the curtain to look at the fire and watched a fireman at the control panel on his hook and ladder truck. At that point I looked 12 stories up at the roaring blaze and it was so intense that 2 and 3 stories down it was blowing out windows and raining glass. All of a sudden I saw it blow up up there and the whole middle section of the top 2 stories came down like a meteor shower. I watched a 10 food steel beam land right on the truck where the fireman had just been standing. He was hurt but is still alive. It hurt 6 firemen all together and did one hundred thousand dollars of damage to that one fire truck.

Everyone in the 107 building had to stay out for 3 or 4 days because of the hazards of the hotel wall caving in and falling on the 107 building. The brothers and sisters were called "*The boat people*" because they had nowhere to go. Some of them were in their pajamas until Saturday or Sunday. We all put them up in our rooms.

We let the firemen use the 107 building roof and terraces to spray water and gave them all the facilities they needed. We were the only building close enough and high enough so they could use their hoses. Their hook and ladders were only about 8 stories high, and that is not nearly high enough. Also, it was freezing the water as soon as it landed on anything and that included them. *The temperature was 10 below* zero. We gave the firemen sandwiches and coffee. They really enjoyed themselves!(?) For about 6 days they used the 124 building lobby and so did the police, because, since the entire 12 stories were all new hard oak flooring that burned intensely hot, all it left was a weak, tottering shell that was too dangerous to leave be. The contractor had just done 5 million dollars renovation work and was selling units at 85 to 90 thousand dollars each. Since many were in the framing stage it burned like a torch! Now they have cranes over there to tear down the gutted mess. All is safe for our 107 building now. It's amazing.

LOOKING BACK OVER THE YEARS

December 21, 2017 I look back over the years and realize that while I might be past the age of 95, as I write about my lifetime experiences, time has really passed very fast. No one can really say that time lags, because it does not. It starts out slow like the small airplanes started out a century ago and then speeds forward like the jet airplanes do today that can go faster than the speed of sound. Our lives are like those airplanes.

I know more has happened in my lifetime than I have written about, but there is no space large enough to tell it all. Memories from eighteen months to ninety-five years may seem a long time, but it really is not long at all.

Life is really squeezed into a tiny space. Enjoy it while you can, and contact those older relatives and friends of yours to get them to tell you about their own experiences, don't delay and wish you hadn't. Their "little stories" can end up being "big stories" in the end as I wind this story down I am survived by five of my six children, eleven grandchildren, and eight great grandchildren. I still plan on reaching my goal of at least one hundred years of age. See all of you then. Those years will fly by just like the jet planes do—faster and faster and faster.

. As I go back over this material I will update a few things. That is why some dates may seem mixed up, due to my updating material.

THE LAKE VACATION

We got back from a week vacation to Priest Lake. We had rented a large house so we could gather together with several family members who had come up from Southern California and some from Idaho.

Some of the group went out in Mike Bergland's boat after he got it running. It quit on him a little way out from shore and Karen's sister went out in her kayak to rescue them. Sherry wrapped a rope around her waist and paddled it back, towing him in. It was quite a sight to see as Mike's boat wasn't exactly a very small one. Mike's boat had not been running for a couple of years but the problem was simple to fix.

We were restricted as to what we could plan to do because the area was under level 2 restrictions due to the massive fires in Washington State and northern Idaho. Level 2 meant to be ready to evacuate. Level 3 meant to get out immediately. The whole northern Washington and Idaho areas were covered with dense smoke. We still enjoyed our visit anyway in spite of the smoke and ash rain.

Saturday morning Mike took several out on the lake again with his boat. They later told us the wind came up after they had been out a short while and the water became quite rough so they turned around and pulled the boat out, gathered all their belongings, then started back to Spokane. Judi took pictures of the high waves. The wind was blowing quite strong which riled the lake. It had been smooth when they left shore.

On Saturday we had all packed up our belongings and Karen's sister, Sherry, and I started for home. On the way out we met several patrol cars with lights flashing and sirens going, so figure we left at the right time, and that level 3 had been declared. We all got home safe and sound. The smoke was so thick we could only see about equal to a city block in the distance. Several people were wearing masks to filter their breathing, which was especially hard on those subject to asthma. Mike had taken his boat out on the lake but did not go far before the lake started getting real rough so he turned around and they all started for Spokane.

Spokane was covered with smoke. It rained during the night so today is quite clear. Haven't heard yet what conditions the fires are in around the state but hope it rained enough to at least slow them down and to cut the awful heat a bit for the firefighters.

I started my memories with a fire, guess I will have to end it with another one. None of our family was injured in either one. I am leaving you with my memories, some good and some bad.

SUMMARY AND AFTERTHOUGHT

September 18, 2016. I have been thinking about the years of my life. When I was very young we lived during the depression years under low income conditions. We did not have much in the way of material goods like the kind which is available today. I never had a bicycle, my mother never had a car, nor a TV, but we had a radio and a roof over our heads once my mother left my father.

I look back to the years when I grew up where the family earned a living during the depression years using so many ways to get by. They would cut cord wood and haul it out to the farms to sell to the farmers who used it for their kitchen stoves or heating their houses. The same farmers would buy fence posts cut from trees felled from local forests, using the posts to fence in their fields to either keep their cattle out or to keep them in where they belonged. A few times they bought a gallon or two of home produced whisky which was delivered to the farming community—unavailable in stores due to prohibition laws. Because of the prohibition laws it was unlawful and those selling or delivering it risked being arrested. No large amount of whisky was made or sold, but it did happen. The price was about three dollars a gallon. Not a large amount of money but $3.00 would buy more than a week's worth of groceries in those days. Prohibition and home made whisky sales ended in 1933.

Of the four children in our family, none of the others completed high school. I graduated from North Central High

School in Spokane. I did like school and the subjects I was taught in my classes at NCHS have been used throughout my life. My sister got a high school diploma many years after she was married. My brother joined the Navy and I do not know if he got any high school certificate. My youngest brother became ill and did not finish high school.

I married right after graduation from high school, raised six children until the youngest one was nearly six years old and my oldest son was eighteen before I went to work outside my home. My first job was in California at a fruit and vegetable stand. It was seasonal work and when that job ended I went to the state employment office and they sent me to a lumber wholesaler who operated from his office in an older downtown house. Some people were afraid of going to work for a man alone in an old house office. Conditions like that could possibly be dangerous. I did take the job, and it turned out that he was the most considerate employer a person could have. He paid me well, and told me that if I ever needed time off for anything for my family to let him know. He said family was important. There were a couple of times when my husband, who was in Real Estate, called and asked if I could go with him to San Diego. All I was asked to do was to be sure the bank deposit was made for the day and I was able to leave.

When I had applied for this job, it required shorthand as I was to be a secretary and the office manager. I had had neither a refresher course in shorthand since high school, nor had I had experience in office work. Well, it had been 20 years since I had gradated from North Central High School. Happy to say, I remembered my shorthand and he dictated slow enough that I was able to take it down. Only once did

I write a letter where I could not make out a single one word of my shorthand as dictated. By the time I typed the letter he was way off in Reno for a business meeting. When he came back to the office, he had to fill in that one word. He did not fire me over the error, but I never forgot this mistake.

This was before cell phones so I could not phone him for that word I could not figure out.

I worked for this man until he moved his office from Riverside to Palm Desert, and that ended my job with him. He called me one time and asked me to come over to Palm Desert to straighten out the books for him, as the woman he had working for him had messed them up somehow. I went over to Palm Desert, straightened out his books, stayed over night at his home with his wife, started back to Riverside, got only a couple of miles out of town and the car quit on me. It was out of gas. The freeway was crowded with fast traffic. Very fortunately a woman stopped and took me back to a gas station where I got enough gas to get home. No cell phones those days. I have never run out of gas again. It was mighty scary. Now when my gas tank gets below the half way mark I get it filled full.

My next job was with the State of California as a registration clerk. I worked there at the Department of Motor Vehicles for seven years. We moved to Portland in 1974 and had been there a while when I studied to become a tax preparer, and worked for H&R Block for six years. When my husband died in 2001 from a fatal fall, I returned to California.

I retired several years ago. When my legs gave out on me so it was difficult to get around I decided it was time to give up living alone. A couple of years ago I moved in with my son and his wife. Together we live in Spokane during the summer months, then for the winter months we live in the warmer climate of Yuma, Arizona. At the age of 95 I am very fortunate to have reasonably good health and a pleasant home and surroundings in which to spend my days. Believe it or not, at 95 I am not old. Those are just calander numbers that keep on getting larger each year.

PRESIDENTS AND KINGS

I have lived during the time of several different presidents being elected in the United States. The first one I remember was Franklin Delano Roosevelt who was very popular. He is the only one ever elected to a fourth term of office. He was president from 1932 until his death on April 22, 1945, during his fourth term in office. After he died during that fourth term, a law was passed that two terms was all that would be allowed in the future. At the death of Roosevelt the vice president, then automatically became the new president. I do not remember the presidents before Roosevelt, probably because of my age at the time. Roosevelt was constantly in the news headlines when I was around ten, an age a child is more apt to pay attention to what is going on world wide.

One president, John F Kennedy, was assassinated while visiting in Texas. Later, an unsucessful attempt was made on the life of Ronald Reagan. President Reagan survived to complete his term in office.

At the time I was born England was ruled, not by a president, but by a King, George V.

I mention England because the United States has strong ties to that country which affects us, seemingly more so than any other country. King **George V** of England had a long rule and died in 1936. When he died the Prince of Wales became the new monarch. The prince became kING George known as **Edward VIII** but he abdicated the same year in December of 1936 to marry the woman he loved. This put **George VI** next in line as King of England. King George VI ruled from 1936 until he died in 1952. At the death of King George VI there were no male heirs in line for the throne so his daughter, **Elizabeth II,** then became the Queen of that country. In this year of 2017 in her nineties *she is still the reigning monarch* and going strong. The next in line for England is a male descendant, one of her sons. Her oldest son was married to princess Diana who became very popular world wide. Unfortunately Diana was killed in an automobile accident, leaving two sons who are now grown up, the older one in direct line to eventually inherit the throne of England, possibly instead of his father, who is next in line.

TO SUM IT UP

I will be 96 in a few weeks, and I have lived before television, antibiotics, credit cards, ballpoint pens, nylons (but we did have silk stockings), and rabbits were not Volkswagons. We made our own diapers and never heard of disposable diapers. We had five and dime stores where you could buy things for five and ten cents, a coke was a soft drink for a nickel. You could mail a letter for three cents, a penny postcard came with a stamp printed on it and cost a penny. You shifted your cars gears because it was not automatic, you could buy a new car for $700, the streetcar or city bus ride was five or ten cents, and gas was eleven cents a gallon. But who could afford those things. My mother worked for 25 cents an hour for work that today pays $15 an hour. Yes, times have changed.

When my daughters started to school, little girls wore dresses, slacks were unheard of on girls. In fact, they were warmer in winter with slacks, so I sent them to school with slacks. This was in a rural country school. I discussed it with the teacher and she agreed with me that in many ways it was a better idea. It was about this same time that it was raising a big fuss over the dress code all over the country. Now it is a common thing for girls to come to school in slacks winter and summer. Times really do change.

PS. I do want to make a request from my family or anyone else reading this narrative, please write down the things you remember that this has triggered in your memory. It would make a nice story for your family

PS #2

I would love to hear from anyone reading my story.

bergland86@hotmail.com

Peggy M. Bergland
14813 E. Rich Avenue
Spokane Valley, WA 99216

I wish to thank the many friends and relatives who contributed to my story by sending me emails or wrote notes that added to the story. Thank you, OZ, Melody, Joy, Elaine, and even the unknown authors whose work helped me to refresh my memory.

Printed in the United States
By Bookmasters